Vanessa Martin is Emeritus Professor of Middle Eastern History at Royal Holloway, University of London. *She is the author of Creating an Islamic State* and *Islam and Modernism* (both I.B.Tauris).

'A very good book.'
— Nikki Keddie, Professor Emerita of History,
University of California, Los Angeles

'An interesting book that is the first to examine history from the bottom up for the Qajar period in Iranian history.'
— Rudi Matthee, University of Delaware

THE QAJAR PACT
BARGAINING, PROTEST AND THE STATE IN NINETEENTH-CENTURY PERSIA

Vanessa Martin

Paperback edition published in 2018 by
I.B.Tauris & Co. Ltd
London · New York
www.ibtauris.com

Hardback edition first published in 2005 by
I.B.Tauris & Co. Ltd

Copyright © 2005 Vanessa Martin

The right of Vanessa Martin to be identified as the author of this work has been asserted by the author in accordance with the Copyright, Designs and Patents Act 1988.

All rights reserved. Except for brief quotations in a review, this book, or any part thereof, may not be reproduced, stored in or introduced into a retrieval system, or transmitted, in any form or by any means, electronic, mechanical, photocopying, recording or otherwise, without the prior written permission of the publisher.

Every attempt has been made to gain permission for the use of the images in this book. Any omissions will be rectified in future editions.

References to websites were correct at the time of writing.

ISBN: 978 1 78831 115 1
eISBN: 978 1 78672 969 9
ePDF: 978 0 85771 598 2

A full CIP record for this book is available from the British Library
A full CIP record is available from the Library of Congress

Library of Congress Catalog Card Number: available

To Javad, Lili and Neda

CONTENTS

Abbreviations viii

Transliteration ix

Acknowledgements xi

Introduction 1

1 Background: Religion, Society, Politics and Trade 8

2 The People, the State and the British in Bushire and Kharg Island 1836-1850 29

3 Shiraz: Urban Protest and the Balance of Power in Fars 48

4 Isfahan: Popular Protest, Social Control and the Emergence of Collaboration 74

5 Popular Demonstrations by Women in Nineteenth Century Iran 95

6 The *Lutis*, the Turbulent Urban Poor 113

7 *Sarbaz* – the Unruly Soldiery 133

8 Slavery and Black Slaves in Iran in the Nineteenth Century 150

9 Slaves II: Haji Bashir Khan – Love in a Complicated Climate 170

Conclusion 183

Glossary 192

Bibliography 194

Index 210

ABBREVIATIONS

IO	India Office, British Library
FO	Foreign Office, National Archives, London, Britain
MAE	Ministere des Affaires Étrangères, Nantes, France
MFA	Ministry of Foreign Affairs Archive, Tehran, Iran
MTM	Mo'asseseh-e Motale'at-e Tarikh-e Mo'aser-e Iran (Institute for the Study of Iranian Contemporary History) Tehran, Iran
PRO	Public Record Office (now National Archives), London, Britain
SAM	Sazman-e Asnad-e Melli-ye Iran (Iranian National Archives), Tehran, Iran
ZDMG	Zeitschrift der Deutschen Morgenlandischen Gesellschaft

TRANSLITERATION

The transliteration system is that of the *Cambridge History of Islam* with its Persian additional and variant forms, and without diacritics. Where proper names of authors or institutions have an established spelling in English language texts, that has been preferred to the transliterated version. Certain Persian words frequently used in the text have been rendered in normal font on the grounds of familiarity.

ACKNOWLEDGEMENTS

I would like to thank the Central Research Fund of the University of London, the British Institute of Persian Studies and the Royal Asiatic Society for their invaluable contributions to my programme of research. Whilst on sabbatical in Iran in the autumn of 2002, I was able to study new material in the archive of the Ministry of Foreign Affairs Centre for Documents and Diplomatic History, which would not have been possible without the support of Dr R. Nazarahari, and the assistance of Mr Mulla-Qasemi and his staff. The Iranian National Archives (Sazman-e Asnad-e Melli-ye Iran) proved a very fruitful source for documents on the Qajar period, and I am grateful to Dr S.H. Shahrestani, and members of the archive staff, for ensuring my work was so productive. Mrs Asili found unpublished manuscripts relevant to my work at Tehran University Library, and Mr Vahid was most helpful in guiding me on the newspaper collection of the Majlis Library. I am grateful to Dr M. Haqani, Director of the Institute for the Study of Iranian Contemporary History (Mo'asseseh-e Motale'at-e Tarikh-e Mo'aser-e Iran), for sifting out relevant correspondence from the vast collection of the papers of Zill al-Sultan. Dr S. Sajjadi's permission for me to use the library of the Great Islamic Encyclopaedia (Da'erat al-Ma'aref-e Bozorg-e Islami) for long hours was invaluable, as was his guidance over sources and illustrations. I also greatly appreciate the interest and support of Mr A. Mir Ansari of the Islamic Encylopaedia Foundation (Bonyad-e Da'erat al-Ma'aref-e Islami) kindly permitted me the use of their library, and I am particularly grateful to Mrs A. Monfared and Mr M. Afshari. The Department of History at Isfahan University were most generous in having me as a guest for a week, for which I am especially obliged to Dr A. Montazerolghaem. Dr M. Nouraei was kind enough to locate sources in Isfahan and to introduce me to the libraries there. Dr G.R. Vatandoust made me welcome in Shiraz and involved me in scholarly activities at Shiraz University. I am also grateful to Dr K. Kamali Sarvestani and the staff of the Fars Encyclopaedia (Daneshnameh-e Fars) for the use of their library. Professor A.R. Sheikholeslami was kind enough to introduce me to the local historians of Bushire, and I wish to express my thanks to Mr A.K. Mashayekhi, and the staff of the Bonyad-e Bushehr Shenasi (Centre for the Study of Bushire), Mr S.Q. Ya Hosseini, Mr H Zanganeh,

Mr M. Hajipour and Mrs M. Mansourizadeh for making my visit to Bushire so fruitful and illuminating. My thanks go especially to Mr R. Salami for his invaluable assistance with the reading of hand written documents in Tehran. Mme M. Mustiere provided most useful information on the material in the Centre des Archives Diplomatiques de Nantes. I would like to express my appreciation to Professor F.C.R. Robinson and Professor M.E. Yapp for their support, and to Dr M.A. Kazembeyki for his advice on sources in Tehran. Dr A. Bulookbashi, Dr M. Sefatgol, Dr S. Ansari, Dr S. Cronin, Dr Z. Mir Hosseini, Professor R. Tapper, Professor W. Clarence-Smith, and Dr. I. Schneider have been kind enough to make suggestions about my subject. The interest of Dr K. Bayat, Mr H. Moghaddam, Dr J Gurney, Dr E. Bahari, Mr M. Tafreshi and Miss Mariam Emami has also been most helpful. I am above all most grateful to my husband for his support throughout the writing of the book.

INTRODUCTION

A Historian's View

The origins of this book lie in two questions – one of greater and one of lesser consideration – each related to the other. The main question is, how did a country the size of Iran contrive to retain its independence and to keep foreign control at bay for over a hundred years, in the nineteenth century and beyond? To some extent the answer lies in the ability of Iran to balance the rivalries and interests of the British and Russians in its role as a buffer state. From the early nineteenth century, Iranian rulers and governments became adept at playing one power off against the other. However, such a strategy would not have been effective in a power vacuum. Iran was also able to resist foreign conquest because it devised methods of bargaining to keep external powers at bay. More particularly to the study of this book, Iran also derived the power to endure, from internal political cohesion created by an intricate system of negotiation and consensus. That in turn compensated for a minimal army, and limited central government revenues.

Here it is argued that Qajar government depended not only on the use of force for control of its subjects, but just as much, or rather more, on a consensus understood in deed rather than word. Such a consensus was itself shaped from a complex system of checks and balances. These in turn depended on people at all levels negotiating politically, and bargaining with the state and with one another. Thus Qajar government was not just based on force, it was based on negotiation, through a series of manoeuvres that drew in the poor as well as the rich and powerful. The role of the elite in politics has to some extent been examined on the one hand by S. Bakhash in *Monarchy, Bureaucracy and Reform under the Qajars: 1858–1896* (1978), a discussion of the political factions of the court and bureaucracy, and in Algar, *Religion and State in Iran 1785–1909* (1969), a consideration of the relationship of the clergy and the state, as well as in A. Amanat, *Pivot of the Universe Nasir al-Din Shah Qajar and the Iranian Monarchy 1831–1896* (1997). My purpose is to look at how people below elite level were involved in the political process, and what influence they were able to exert, as well as to illustrate the ways in which they were organised so as to alter government policy.

Further, people at the popular level not only negotiated, they could also be assertive in the way they dealt with the state. Thus the segments of society studied here are found to have been demanding of their rights, not trampled underfoot and resigned. There follows the question of the basis on which they challenged the state, in a society before the arrival of modern ideas. My view follows Lambton's in *Qajar Persia* (1987) that the conceptual framework within which they worked emphasised the notion of justice, but I consider their conception of justice to have been as much Islamic as Shi'i. Further, I attempt to trace the debate between state and society on what was just and what was not just, on the rights of the state and of the community and of the individual, in the practical context of the nineteenth century. I look at how it worked out, and how it was argued in routine situations rather than great rebellions. Indeed, in this perspective, rebellion is not so much the breakdown of a bargaining process as its continuation by other means. This is another way of saying that rebellions need to be studied in the context of ongoing struggles and negotiations, rather than simply events in themselves. Inevitably, in a society so poor, where there was such pressure on resources, the essence of the struggle or rebellion was nearly always financial, relating to taxes, the rise in the price of essential goods, or manipulation of the currency.

The inspiration for this perspective comes from two main views. The sources for the first are the work of two scholars in particular. One is M. Moslem, in 'The Making of a Weak State', *CSD Perspectives*, Research Paper No. 6, University of Westminster (1995). He argues that the Constitutional Revolution was overwhelmingly shaped by the characteristics of existing society, in which the notion of the state, in his view, barely existed. The other source of inspiration has been H. Katouzian's 'Liberty and Licence in the Constitutional Revolution of Iran' in *Iranian History and Politics* (2003). Katouzian sets the Revolution in the context of state–society relations in the past, and demonstrates the value system which shaped the movement for *mashruta* (in this context conditioned constitutionalism). Moslem and Katouzian both drew pessimistic conclusions from their studies, whereas my concern is not so much to evaluate the subject in terms of what it produced, but to understand it further from the perspective of a section of the participants.

The second main view is one with a wider perspective, E. Burke's *Struggle and Survival in the Middle East* (1993). This is the first major study in modern Middle Eastern history to attempt to consider historical events from the popular perspective, and to consider the role that they had, by interpretation through individual case histories. Such an evaluation is all the more important because sources of all kinds are mainly focused on the elite, as a result of which much is missing from the historical accounts. The origin of the sources on elite and middle class views have obfuscated the willingness to resist and manipulate at the lower levels of society. To some extent also historical accounts have been won over by what Marcus, in his study of Aleppo, identified as 'the passive flocks representing an official ideal more than a political reality'.[1] With regard to individual case studies, the material we currently have on the Qajar period does not permit a series of studies of ordinary people such as Burke provides. However, where possible, attention is drawn to the contribution of individuals, and in one case, that of the black slave, Haji Bashir Khan, there is sufficient documentation for a fuller study.

The second and (for this work) lesser question, concerns the origins of the Iranian Constitutional Revolution of 1906. The Revolution has been explored from a number of perspectives. Browne, for example, in *The Persian Revolution of 1909* (1910), stressed its progressive nature; M. Ettehadieh, in *The Origins and Development of Political Parties in Persia* (1980), looked at political development, and most particularly the emergence of the social democrats; M. Bayat, in *Iran's First Revolution*, (1991) made a study of the influence of the heterodox radicals, and their calls for social, cultural and political change; and my own work examined the conservative 'ulama (clergy) in *Islam and Modernism the Iranian Revolution of 1906* (1989). The most recent major work in English, J. Afary's *The Iranian Constitutional Revolution 1906–11* (1996) focused on the lower levels of society as well as modernist views. It covers the role of women, and of the peasantry, in addition to that of poorer groups within the towns, but from the time of the Revolution itself. Otherwise the vast literature of articles and chapters in foreign languages, and much of the texts in Persian, has concentrated on the role of the secularising intelligentsia in the Revolution, and on its subsequent influence. It has looked at the introduction of western institutions and law, and the advocating of ideas such as freedom of expression. This work, however, arises very much from a historian's question, which is – how did the mass of contemporaries, those who participated in events, who had little or no contact with western ideas, see the revolution, and what did they want from it? Therefore, my preoccupation is with the continuing ideals and goals in Qajar society, and how the west was being interpreted at less educated social levels in the latter part of the nineteenth century.

Further, in a country so large and diverse, with different ethnic and social groups, it is not possible to say in one work, what the case was for everyone. Therefore, I have chosen, as far as the sources permit, to concentrate on the popular level in the urban areas in the south of Iran. I have done so in the firm belief that many more different kinds of studies are needed for us to evaluate the Constitutional Revolution, particularly from the point of view of different regions and their specific politics. I have also done so in the belief that, with the centenary of that event, such studies will appear. In addition, as a result of a desire to enlarge our knowledge of Iran in the nineteenth century, I have focused on the period 1834–1896, not just to show the political problems of lower social groups in a largely premodern period, but also to provide background to the understanding of the Constitutional Revolution by tracing the progress of change in the period before it. The 1830s saw the passing of Fath 'Ali Shah in 1834, and with him some of the older values of Iranian rule, which had inhibited the reforms of his son, 'Abbas Mirza. Muhammad Shah, his grandson and successor, was a ruler in a different style, not least because he had to face modernity in the form of increasing trade and gathering pressure from the imperial powers, Britain and Russia. The book ends in 1896 with the death of Nasir al-Din Shah and, the beginning of a new chapter in Iranian history, with the coming of the Constitutional Revolution. Examination of the years from the late 1880s onwards in particular shows how change gathered pace, and many of the features of the Constitutional Revolution were beginning to appear alongside older values. In this respect the study is able to resume and develop Keddie's detailed discussion of the protest over the tobacco concession of 1890–91 in *Religion and Rebellion in Iran* (1966).

Finally, since this book seeks to examine the political activity of people from the lower social groups, it would be useful to offer a definition of the term. The term 'ordinary people' is normally used for such groups, and I wish it might be so for this book. Unfortunately, even for urban areas, the material on the political activities of people at this kind of level is slight, although their views may be detected in the choice they make of a more influential and well-placed representative, usually a member of the 'ulama (clergy) and the way in which that person seeks to keep their support by representing their views. Therefore lower social groups is preferred to ordinary people, and it relies heavily on the Persian distinction of *daulat* (government) and *ru'aya* (subjects), that is to say the elite who were the court officials, the state bureaucrats and great landowners and the tribal khans, and the mass of the subjects. In Qajar Iran the powerful were really those who were possessed of might, that is to say an armed support base, amounting to the groups just mentioned, who also intermarried. The 'ulama, especially the prestigious *mujtahids* (leading clergy), wielded great influence and were considered to be intermediaries between people and state, but in this work they will appear in effect as the leaders of the people. Such an interpretation of their position follows the view I presented in Chapter II of my first work, *Islam and Modernism: the Iranian revolution of 1906* (1989), where I demonstrated that the 'ulama were not financially independent of the laity, and, in particular for the purposes of this book, had to rely for funding on the pious contributions of their religious following. This following in turn expected support for their own political causes, and were furthermore liable to give their canonical contributions to those of the senior clergy (*mujtahids*) who showed themselves most amenable to their own views. Thus the clergy in many ways represented not only their own interests but those of the laity.

Another very influential group was that of the more wealthy merchants, who did not belong to the ruling stratum and were regarded as subjects (therefore non-elite) in Qajar times by the state and tribal chiefs. Of course, the wealth of major merchants meant they had the means to manipulate both state and society, from bringing pressure on officials and landowners who were indebted to them to purchasing mass support among the poor of the bazaar. As far as possible, they have been distinguished from lesser merchants and other lower social groups, but urban politics was a skein, as will be described in Chapter I, and it was simply not always possible, given the source material, to unravel all the individual strands.

Thus the lower social groups in this context include some who were, in terms of education and life style, well above most in their standard of living. The point is that, although they could exert great influence, in the case of the merchants through their wealth, and in the case of the 'ulama through their religious calling, they had neither power nor the right to govern and rule. Inevitably, members of the elite enter the story, but in my efforts to concentrate on those whom history forgot, I have distilled their presence as far as is possible, to compensate for the fact that so much remains in writing about the elite, and so little about other groups in society.

The book is divided into three case studies, Bushire, Shiraz and Isfahan, and four thematic chapters, with one individual study. The case studies attempt as far as possible to show how a variety of groups at the popular level challenged those in power in specific political contexts. The case studies also provide an opportunity to demonstrate continuity and change. The four thematic chapters concentrate on some of the less advantaged members of society, namely women, soldiers, the turbulent urban poor, and slaves, bringing out their culture and their particular problems. As might be expected, this material has been dictated by the nature of the source material available. Chapter 2 on Bushire focuses on continuity and change in demonstrating the popular role in the trend towards centralisation and the elimination of local powers. A foreign power, the British, became involved in the local processes of bargaining, and in the incident involving the expulsion of the admiral from Bushire, the people wrote a history of their own. This chapter also shows, early in the nineteenth century, the importance of popular assembly and consultation in shaping the development of a community. The story of Shiraz in Chapter 3 recounts the popular role in the interaction of town, state and tribe, and how the struggles to control the city influenced tribal configuration. The impact of the international economy and of modern technology initiated new forms of popular organisation towards the end of the period. The study of Isfahan in Chapter 4 addresses the question of social control from the government perspective, and shows how the powerful and the powerless managed each other. By the latter part of the century a new vocabulary, influenced by the foreign based press and new ideas from the west, was beginning to produce a new language in the politics of the city.

The first of the thematic chapters, number 5, looks at the political role of Iranian women at the popular level, a subject much under-researched for Iran in the nineteenth century. It emphasises the strength of their involvement as part of the community in political battles. The organisation of women's demonstrations could be sophisticated, even choreographed, showing that there are older roots to the role of women in politics than had previously been thought. By the later nineteenth century women seem to have been slightly better off and better educated, and seeking a more prominent role, as is demonstrated by the subjects of the *ta'ziyya* (religious) plays. The culture of the turbulent urban poor, the *lutis*, is explored in Chapter 6, looking at the problems of defining this group. They derived peculiarly Iranian characteristics from the influence of the culture of literary epics, as well as from Twelver Shi'ism, particularly the cult of Imam Husain. Although to some extent lawless, they had a role in ensuring social justice and defending the community against oppression. The lives of soldiers, studied in Chapter 7, and a very poor group in society, demonstrate the problems of lack of pay, of random justice, and of the absence of institutional support. The chapter studies the ways that the powerless could negotiate for a modicum of improvement in the quality of their lives. It also suggests that the army was dangerously weakened as compared to urban society by the end of the century. The final topic of the book is slaves, with one individual example. By contrast with the Americas, the Islamic framework and economic factors combined to ensure that slaves were well treated in Iran, being mainly in the service sector. Even in the agricultural sector in the south east their lot does not seem to have been appreciably harder than that of other Iranians.

The primary sources for the book present a problem because, even over such a long period, they do not say much about the level of society under study. As Hambly has observed, 'Documentation which served as the starting point for the research into medieval and early modern France of the Annales School is almost wholly lacking for nineteenth century Iran.'[2] State correspondence tended to remain in the hands of senior officials, and there is nothing like the sources of the poor relief system, and the court and parish records, which so inform the social history of England in the eighteenth century. About three quarters of the material I found dates from the years 1889 to 1896, but, given our need to know more about the earlier decades of the century, I have, as far as possible, used what material there is to highlight events further back in time. It is hoped that more may eventually come to light, perhaps from theological libraries, from family papers mentioning particular retainers, or from royal rescripts (*farmans*). Until such a time, the most valuable material has come, not unexpectedly, from the consular records in the British National Archives, and from the works of the many travellers of various nationalities who passed through Iran in the nineteenth century (quite a number of which have been translated into Persian). Some useful material was found in the papers of the India Office, now in the British Library, though it does not vary much in type and content from that in the National Archives. In the same manner, the French National Archives in Nantes provided additional information, particularly from the 1850s and 1860s, as well as over the tobacco concession, some of it deriving from a more relaxed and less mistrustful attitude on the part of the Iranian government.

There are abundant sources in the archives in Iran, though the great majority are in Tehran. In particular, the National Archives (Sazman-e Asnad-e Melli-ye Iran), have many and varied documents, including rescripts, telegrams, tax demands, and petitions, all of which throw light both on popular protest and how the government handled it. The diplomatic correspondence in the Ministry of Foreign Affairs Archives illuminates the Iranian government's policy on the slave trade, and the measures it took to reduce it. These archives are also useful for the crises which erupted over the tobacco trade and the Imperial Bank in the 1890s.

From the point of view of the sources of Isfahan province, the Institute for the Study of Iranian Contemporary History ((Mo'asseseh-e Motale'at-e Tarikh-e Mo'aser-e Iran) houses the papers of Zill al-Sultan, who, as governor of Isfahan province in the latter part of the nineteenth century, in effect ran a state within a state. The collection yielded a most useful correspondence between the principal cleric of the city, Aqa Najafi, and Zill al-Sultan. Copies of the newspapers *Akhtar* and *Habl al-Matin* in the Majlis Library provided a different dimension: the views of reformist intellectuals, journalists and traders. Finally a variety of libraries, including that of Tehran University, have unpublished manuscripts, such as Sa'adat's *History of Bushire* (1921–2). Published document collections, such as those of Afshar and Safa'i, give invaluable additional texts, and there are detailed chronicles and local histories, such as Tahvildar's *Socio-geographical History of Isfahan* (1877).

Notes

1   A. Marcus, *The Middle East on the Eve of Modernity*, New York 1989, p. 120.
2   G. Hambly, 'The Traditional Iranian City in the Qajar Period', in *Cambridge History of Iran*, Cambridge 1991, VII, p. 542.

1

BACKGROUND: RELIGION, SOCIETY, POLITICS AND TRADE

The Islamic Background

Iranian society, and particularly at the levels with which this work is concerned, was shaped by the Islamic law, the shari'a.[1] From the point of view of the people, though the shah claimed legitimacy on the basis of hereditary right, and implied it through divine guidance in titles such as Zill Allah (Shadow of God), or played upon the concept of *farr-i izadi* (divine grace), what mattered was that he should conform to the shari'a. Ultimately the authority of his regime depended on the fact that he be understood to be doing so. If the shah was abiding by the shari'a, he was exercising the kind of rule prescribed by God through the Prophet, as manifested in the Qur'an. Through the Qur'an and its exegesis, God's will for human kind had found a more tangible shape in the shari'a, and the shari'a being divine in origin provided for all contingencies at all times. Therefore the shari'a formed a rightful way forward and complete order for a whole society, anticipating all its needs and its expectations. Most particularly the shari'a provided for justice ('*adl*), a concept which, under a number of terms, is reiterated many times in the Qur'an, and is associated with purity, piety, fair conduct, temperance and welfare. Its root means to set straight, or to equalise or to balance. In the practice of alms giving (*zakat*), the idea of justice provides a means of distributing wealth and ensuring a measure of social justice, as well as fairness in conduct towards others. Justice is both implicit and explicit in the shari'a, which seeks to shape the believer into one who engages in acts that are of benefit to the community, and avoids those which may harm it.

The specific association of justice with balance in Islam is expressed in another term *al-mizan* (the balance) which is seen at the heart of all things. It is equated with the golden mean, to which all believers are called (Give just weight and full measure; we never charge a soul with more than it can bear, Qur'an VI, 152). Therefore justice in Islamic society carries the implication of creating a series of checks and balances so as to accrue maximum benefit for the community. The relationships between the various individuals and groups of a society must be regulated in such a way that they are balanced, that they are based on a mutual sense of obligations, and that they involve reciprocation, thereby avoiding the chaos and disorder with which Islam is threatened, because good Muslims cannot follow their true path.

To ensure a balance is maintained the state must seek to understand the context within which each problem emerges, and the ways in which the most significant factors may be balanced against one another. Such a judgement also involves weighing changes and their effects, deciding what reciprocation can be successfully encouraged, and dealing appropriately with the forces of disturbance and disruption. The state may be guided by implicit understanding on the part of society and its individuals of the rights and duties of the state itself, of the religious community, of the groups within it and of individual believers. It is the duty of the state to ensure just rule, which in turn delivers stability, and of the subject to be busy with his affairs, pious and obedient. It is the right of the state to expect such obedience, to reward it and to punish transgression, and to receive its due taxes. It is the right (*haq*, pl. *huquq*) of the individual to seek redress for his grievances, and to demand justice in the form of equitable and balanced treatment. If that balance is not achieved, then justice becomes injustice (*zulm*), a term implying that limits and boundaries have been exceeded, that moral anarchy prevails and that right has become wrong.

Further, the appearance of *zulm* (oppression) has economic implications, for without justice and well-being, there can be no good trade, and without trade there can be no loyal subjects, and without subjects, there can be no state. Put another way, the ruler has to insure an equitable balance of resources and so good order not only in his manner of government, but also in his personal munificence. The gifts he bestows should go to each in a proportionate share, so as to avoid the disorder and anarchy which may arise if certain of his subjects feel that they are in a state of injustice. He must also be sure to share his bounty with those who have been most loyal to him. Finally, he must devise policies to provide in economic and financial terms an equitable balance between the different components of society, and further to ensure that the mean struck is sufficiently flexible and adaptable to absorb change.

The concepts of justice implicit in the Qur'an and the shari'a are not found only in the law itself. The custom and culture of the Muslim country reflect the principles of its religion, so that they are implicit in local practice, even though they may not be referred to explicitly. In other words Islamic values are understood by both state and society in their relationship with each other, and in the means by which they negotiate to resolve disputes. Thus customary life and practice of long standing can be understood to be part of the shari'a, for if the shari'a has permitted it, then it cannot be a violation of the precepts of Islam, particularly given the Qur'anic principle that what God has not forbidden, He has permitted.

The people of society understand that they and the state are part of the same value system, known to both of them, and are perfectly capable of asserting their rights on that basis, most notably in a process of bargaining with the state. They are also aware that the greater the wealth they have, the stronger their bargaining position will be. Conversely, they realise that if they possess neither wealth, nor prestige nor power, they cannot in reality depend on moral obligation alone to secure their rights. Therefore they must depend on numbers, and unite in an implied threat to the stability of the state, thereby advising the ruler, that if he does not reform his ways, he will no longer have prosperous subjects, indeed, he will have no subjects at all. The people thus have ways to shape state policy using the value system of Islam, and their powers to organise, so they may influence the course of events and initiate change.

The process of achieving unity depends on the successful deployment of the particular networks of any individual or group, in such a way as to enhance their position and power to negotiate. Thus clan, employment, and district connections can be brought into play in a process of negotiating and bargaining in which Islamic values provide the justification for the positions adopted. Such connections also provide, in the form of evidence of support, a validation of the demand for rights in which the individual or group is engaged. Conversely, one who lacks the necessary networks to support a claim is left dependent on the principle that it is an obligation on society to ensure that the burden of poverty does not fall too hard upon one person.

Since this understanding is broadly Islamic, it is inherent in Shi'ism. Justice played an important part in the political thinking of the Shi'a, certainly from medieval times onwards. In the Twelver Shi'ism established in Iran in the sixteenth century under the Safavid dynasty, a broad consensus emerged on the duties of kings and subjects to each other, and the concept of justice was implicit in these relations. It is encapsulated most clearly in the writings of Muhammad Baqir Majlisi (d.1699), who wrote:

> Know that the justice ('adl) of kings and amirs is one of the greatest things conducive to the well-being of men. The justice and righteousness of kings and amirs is the cause of the righteousness of all the people and bring about the well-being of the regions, while their disobedience and wickedness bring disorder into the affairs of most of the people of the world and make most men inclined to become like them.[2]

Thus the ability to be fair, to balance, to ensure that grievances are redressed is vital to the benefit of state and society, and its absence creates the turbulence and insurrection and anarchy which are the attributes of oppression. Majlisi further argued that the possession of authority by kings put upon them certain obligations, which their subjects had the right to expect that they honour. These included that the ruler should treat the subjects justly, and with kindness, especially as they were weak and powerless, and that the king should exercise mercy, and not punish in haste. Majlisi goes on to say that all holders of authority, of whatever kind, have a duty both towards God and towards those who are subordinate to him. Thus:

> Each person, according to the extent of the dominion granted to him, has been given some favour, and according to the extent of that favour, thanks are demanded of him; gratitude for every favour is the cause of increase and abundance. And in the case of each person gratitude consists in conducting oneself towards others as God commanded, and in observing the rights (*huquq*) which God established for them . . . Thus if kings, in their power and their dominance, show gratitude and pay attention to the condition of their subjects and give them what is their due (*huquq-i ishan bikhanand*), their kingdom will remain, otherwise it will quickly disappear.[3]

On the question of rights and duties of kings and subjects, Majlisi was specific. He stated that kings had claims upon their subjects, who, in return for their protection and the defence of their religion, lives, wealth and honour, must pray for them and recognise their rights, especially when they have behaved justly. The diligence of kings in attending to the interests of their subjects, also means that those subjects will be economically productive, a matter that is of benefit both to themselves and to the state. Conversely, a country in a condition of oppressive anarchy cannot be economically productive, and therefore cannot yield the taxation needed by the state.

In the Qajar period the influence of this theory of kingship may be discerned in a letter from Nasr al-Din Shah to his son Zill al-Sultan, demanding to know why there was a disturbance in Isfahan:

> You, 'ulama and people, must know that in the issue of the interests of the subjects, the shah is kinder than all others, and must seek their well-being. And they should know that if there is a threat to the country and its independence, and to the shari'a, the first to prevent it is the state. Therefore, whatever policy it carries out should be perceived as being for the benefit of people and state, and none should ask why or wherefore.[4]

The shah is not only stating his concern for his people, he is implying that he knows best, and that the reason that he knows best is that he is just. He is also intimating that he is carrying out his obligations to his subjects by being humane and by helping them in their need. This view applies not only to himself but to his government, that is to say to those whom he has appointed. Although the views of the 'ulama on the royal authority varied, in practice they tended to accept its validity as long as the shah maintained and equilibrium and protected Islam.[5] An approximate consensus on the relations of religion and state was reflected in the correspondence and official documents of the time. The well-being of the community, the government, the monarchy and the country were seen as interconnected.[6] In correspondence the leading 'ulama referred to the shah as 'Defender of Muslims' and of the religion and the shari'a.

The performance of his duties according to Islamic principles legitimised the shah's rule, and he had to be seen to be performing them. The shari'a and its interpretation were restraints upon him, and the decisions implemented in his courts, whilst not a literal application of the shari'a (which was in any case not specific on many matters) nevertheless had to conform to its values. For this reason conflicts between shari'a and *'urf* (customary) practice, generally ended in favour of the shari'a. That said, the administration of justice was less than perfect, and though the shah might grant petitioners' requests, his commands were not executed, or if they were, the implementation was allowed to lapse, and matters became as before.[7] In reality the shah had to arbitrate in such a way as to ensure the shari'a was respected (though not uniformly literally observed), the revenue was collected, robbery was repressed, foreign threats were kept at bay, the assertion of royal power was not too rigorously interpreted, and some grievances redressed. If he succeeded, his subjects were acquiescent; it was when any of these matters came out of balance, that his problems began.

The shah, however, did not base his claims to legitimacy solely on the application of the shari'a and the defence of Islam. The coronation ceremonies of the Qajars demonstrate a claim to legitimacy by virtue of their descent from kings, and the power which that conferred.[8] In the title Zill Allah, the shah claimed to rule by authority delegated to him from God, as the one most suited to protect the shari'a, and also to rule justly (which is to say, in essence, that his authority came from God through God's law). Another source of legitimacy was the ancient Persian belief that the possession of *farr-i izadi* (divine grace) conferred on a ruler the right to succeed to the throne, and to be regarded as legitimate, and to rule by divine will. This theory is manifested in the shah's claim to be the Qutb (Pivot of the Universe), a role that was evident in prestigious ceremonies and grandiose titles.

It has been decided, however, not to explore these other bases of legitimacy here, for as will become clear in the succeeding chapters, when the shah's urban subjects (and perhaps others too) were displeased with him, they cared not for divine grace, hereditary right, nor the epithet of Pivot, but for his duties as an Islamic ruler, to regulate, equalise and maintain the balance. It was useless for him to claim he had authority from God if he did not exercise God's law, and it was also useless his styling himself Zill Allah, if he did not enforce and protect the shari'a. They would withdraw their loyalty and fidelity if his reign was not associated with justice, and they would find means to withhold their taxes if their grievances were not redressed. They would not respect his commands and those of his subordinates if he failed to reciprocate with due attention to their welfare.

The real basis of the shah's rule was power, seized by his ancestors from others before them, and both disguised and buttressed by the dynasty's various claims to legitimacy. Power, particularly coercive power, and the justification that the shah brought through his veils of legitimacy for his policies, meant that he could act in a way that was absolutist. He was in theory answerable to no precepts or conditions, and could act according to his own will, rather than to the counsels of reason – but it did not usually profit him to do so. True, power conferred on him much personal authority, and a strong sense of justification in any course of action he took, but the mutual interests of state and subject meant that he was bound by society: by the possible detrimental effects of any policy on the prosperity of his realm. Therefore his subjects not only bargained with him, they did not always acknowledge his commands.

Power and Society

Power in Iran resided in a shah who was mighty in a state that was paradoxically weak. The shah was powerful because general recognition of his authority enabled him, albeit by cumbersome means, to command the greatest body of force. Power was conceived of in terms of the ability to keep general order and to protect the country against external enemies. The wielding of power and the control of society was carried out by a number of means, which involved both force and cajolery. In legal terms, the shah was the ultimate court of appeal by virtue of his royal prerogative, which he exercised through the *'urf* (customary law), (by contrast with shari'a, or religious, law administered by the 'ulama). The *'urf* law covered criminal cases and administrative matters, on which the shari'a had little to say, and was administered by any official of rank, who had the power, deriving from the shah, to enforce the execution of his judgement. On the one hand the shah used intimidation, military repression, summary executions and a variety of brutal punishments, the purpose of which was *'ibrat* (chastisement as example). Inducements, on the other hand, involved the conferral of offices, tax farms, titles, awards, exemptions and monopolies, all of which were used to manipulate supporters and potential trouble-makers alike.

Power also did not mean commanding the commerce, education, health and welfare of society, matters that were regulated in communities themselves, whilst religion was left to the clergy, unless it was a threat to order. In a country where communications were weak, and bureaucracy minimal, power was also devolved, and the shah depended on the co-operation of many tribal, ethnic, religious, local, bureaucratic and commercial figures and groups. In particular, power was devolved to the provincial governors, appointed from outside the province but usually with some local connections and knowledge. More often than not, as the century progressed, the governors were also members of the Qajar ruling family. Like the shah their preoccupation was with law and order, in addition to which they raised taxes, both for the centre and for local needs. One significant outcome of the system was that taxes, especially the land tax on which the state depended most, were remitted irregularly, in varying amounts, and sometimes not at all.

Another attribute of the local governors was that they had their own militia, with which they were supposed to crush opposition and lawlessness in the provinces. The recruitment of a force of their own meant that they were determined to protect their own vested interest and power base. Correspondingly, the shah had only a small military force, as little as a few thousand, at his immediate beck and call at any one time. As will be discussed, this force was also irregularly clothed, paid and armed. The shah was therefore much dependent on his punishments and inducements, as well as co-operation with the multiplicity of groups that he ruled, and with their influential leaders. The country, as a result, was backward in terms of development in terms of communications, economically, and in its administrative and legal systems, and it survived on a minimal revenue.

On this point, it is worth briefly contrasting the resources of the government of Iran with those elsewhere in the Middle East, most notably Egypt, and the Ottoman Empire. In Egypt, for example, the growth of the cotton economy from the early nineteenth century initiated a range of development in other areas, especially finance investment. This in turn led to much improved communications, most notably the construction of the Suez Canal, which assisted Egypt's advance economically, in education and administration. The Ottoman government, on the other hand, embarked on reform of the army, which in turn produced a whole range of reforms in other areas, especially the law, the administration, and secularised education. All Middle Eastern governments were weakened by corruption and embezzlement, especially in the gathering of taxation, but in terms of inspection and monitoring the Ottoman government, for example, had procedures for inspection, investigation and recovery which were to some degree systematic by contrast with Iran.[9]

In addition to the internal powers mentioned earlier, there were also external ones, namely Britain and Russia. Iran's geographic location and mountainous terrain led to its becoming a buffer state in the imperial ambitions of these two countries. Britain and Russia both drew Iran's borders, suppressed Turkoman incursions in the north-east, protected trade along the southern coast, and interfered constantly in the politics of the country, notably Russia in the north and Britain in the south. The interests of the powers, as well as their rivalry with each other, had to be taken into account in Iranian government policies, and they too became drawn into the processes of bargaining. Until the late nineteenth century, the ambitions of the British in the south, which occasionally appear in this work, were reasonably controlled by the Iranian government. By the 1890s, however, the link between imperialism and commercial development meant Britain was adopting a much more overbearing attitude to involvement in Iran.

Nevertheless, foreign involvement in Iran – commercial, political and ideological – forced change and subtle shifts in power between both the government and people and the different sections of society. In particular those engaged in the introduction of world economy, and of cash crops, including merchants as traders and agents and the towns as centres of commerce, grew in affluence and influence as compared to the impecunious state and the tribes based in the less well-developed rural areas. In turn this meant difficulties for the authorities in containing protest in the larger cities. However, apart from the spectacular growth of Tehran, the increase of the urban population over the rural was not as noticeable as elsewhere in the Middle East.[10]

Another way in which foreign intrusion affected society was in the shaping of resistance. Reaction against incursions and other forms of anti-imperialist struggle conferred legitimacy on popular protest, and at popular level reinforced religious authority during the period. Resistance to foreigners also became involved in internal battles between people, state and local powers, in which the last could be both winners and losers. However, the first stirrings of popular nationalism appeared in Iran even less than elsewhere in the Middle East for most of this period. Only in the last decade of the nineteenth century is it possible to detect the coming of a new relationship between people and state, and a new identity.

The population of Iran was between six and ten million during the nineteenth century. It was composed mainly of peasants, but between a quarter and a third of the people were tribal, and roughly 10–20 per cent lived in cities. Apart from Tehran, and to a lesser extent, Tabriz, the cities did not grow markedly over the period. The main reason for this was the absence of industrialisation together with fluctuations due to war, disease, famine arising from drought, crop failures, and the depredations of locusts. In a country with few passable roadways, it was difficult to move commodities, as a result of which urban communities were exposed to severe shortages.

Towns were also at the heart of the administration of the country. They were religious and administrative centres, and the focus of culture and learning, particularly through religious schools and the system of religious endowments. The commercial centre, the bazaar, provided facilities for financial exchange and for the storage in caravanserais of trading commodities, as well as quarters for the handicraft industries carried out by the guilds. As large and complex centres of population, vulnerable to economic change, towns presented the government with problems of order, and had to be carefully regulated as will be discussed further below.

The population of Iran has always included a large tribal component, but in the nineteenth century it became reconfigured in relation to the state with the creation of tribal confederations.[11] These confederations were formed partly as a defence mechanism in response to the development of the state bureaucracy and army, and partly as the result of state policy to regularise the control of the tribes, at the same time saving the cost of a standing army. As a result of this reconfiguration the major tribal khans became incorporated into the state system of control by the end of the century, so that, as Beck remarks, the distinction between the tribal and state political systems became blurred.[12] In the south the two most significant confederations were those of the Qashqa'i and the Bakhtiari, of which the first, Turkic speaking and Shi'i, were close to Shiraz and migrated through thickly settled agricultural areas. As part of the strategy of control of the tribes the Qajars invested the leaders of the Qashqa'i with not one but two titles, those of Ilkhani and Ilbegi. The government also manipulated the tribes by playing off one against another and fostering rivalries between tribal leaders. Nevertheless, in the nineteenth century the tribal leaders remained independently powerful, mainly because they had an armed support base, but also through the benefits they were able to dispense. A system of marriage alliances amongst themselves, and with other great tribal leaders, major landowners and members of the royal family, reinforced their position. Their landholdings and financial levies ensured that they had great wealth. The duties of the khans towards the government included the recognition of the royal authority on the part of their tribes, the raising of military levies, and the collection of taxes.

The towns and the bazaar community

As Abrahamian has observed, the bazaar was the granary, workshop, market-place, bank and religious and educational nucleus of society.[13] The centre of commercial activities only, the bazaar formed part of the centre of the city, along with residential areas. It consisted of a unified, self-contained complex of shops, passageways and caravanserais interspersed with squares, religious buildings and bathhouses and other public institutions.[14] The main political and religious centre was the Friday Mosque, which had significance as the main place of congregation for the Friday prayers.

People from the same trade worked in quarters, and those of similar ethnic, local and religious background tended to live in the same streets or localities, which contributed to a collective ethos. By contrast with western cities of the period, the Iranian city was not divided into areas by class, although some parts were recognisably wealthier or poorer than others. The relationship of the state with the bazaar was normally reciprocal, the former providing protection and the administration of justice, and the latter taxes, customs dues, and road tolls. A complex system of organisations and networks like the bazaar produced no one leader, which meant that the state management of cities, and especially bazaars, and the suppression of discontent, required considerable skill.

In conformity with the Islamic emphasis on order, the bazaar was very well organised through its regulations, sometimes down to the smallest detail. Each town or city had a mayor (*kalantar*) who was a local man of standing selected by the state in a process of consultation with leading members of the community, whose acquiescence was vital if he was to succeed in his duties.[15] Through the *kalantar* the state supervised the quality of products and merchandise in the bazaar, as well as the fairness of prices and the accuracy of weights. The bazaaris negotiated with the state collectively through the leading merchants, and the heads of guilds. The *kalantar* also supervised the management of the city quarters under local headmen (*kadkhudas*) whom he appointed. One of his principal duties was the allocation of taxes amongst city quarters, a subject which could generate protest and resentment. Finally, the *kalantar* was the shah's eyes and ears, while helping to alleviate the regime of despotism, making him a representative of the urban population as well as an agent of the state.[16] Perry has noted that from early times, sporadically, there was an official, initially entitled *vakil al-ru'aya* (representative of the subjects), who had the responsibility of ensuring justice for the underprivileged.[17] In the eighteenth century this function was specifically carried out by the *kalantar*. However, in the nineteenth century, whilst it probably came within his remit, it did not particularly characterise his office. Further, in the nineteenth century, as no doubt in the past, he not infrequently used his position to his own advantage.

The official in charge of law enforcement and police, the *darugha*, came under the mayor.[18] His job was to supervise the markets, regulate disputes in market affairs, and monitor weights and measure, as well as ensure orderliness. The *darugha* was often brutal and venal, and although shopkeepers paid a monthly rate to prevent robberies, the police officials themselves could be connected to the robbers.

The population of the bazaar was divided into different groups. At the top were the wealthier merchants, especially the wholesale agents and money lenders, and the leading members of the 'ulama. Then came the members of the guilds and the lesser 'ulama, and finally the mass of urban poor. Since the bazaar was the financial centre of the city, the great merchants and money-lenders exerted considerable influence, and lent large sums to the political elite, as well as small amounts to ordinary bazaaris. As a result, before the advent of modern banking, they conducted virtually all money transactions in Iran. The leading wholesalers (*bunakdars*) were also influential, profiting increasingly over the century from the import export trade. The merchants were expected to contribute from their wealth towards the well-being of the community, and they subsidised schools, ceremonies and processions, as well as making contributions to poor relief. As Lapidus has remarked, merchants had an institutionalised role in religious and political organisation through the funding of patronage and endowments.[19]

The guilds were highly organised and structured, each craft having its own guild, and each guild its own hierarchy and customs. The heads (*ustads*) and elders (*rishsifidan*) had a prestigious position in the bazaar hierarchy. Serving the guildsmasters, often under long apprenticeships, were the more junior members at various stages of training. The guilds leaders controlled and supervised the activities of other members and made sure that government instructions were implemented. They were responsible for finding the culprits of misdemeanours, settling disputes, collecting taxes, and fixing prices and wages. Many guildsmen were in debt either to the merchants or to wealthier fellow-members, who at times used this advantage to exert political influence over them.

The common people of the bazaar were largely engaged in unspecialised occupations, and were very poorly paid. They included petty traders, peddlers, minor craftsmen, dervishes, beggars, guards, entertainers, porters, animal handlers, manual workers and servants. As indicated in the chapter on *lutis*, some of the poor were more turbulent than others, organised in groups much like the gangs of eighteenth century Cairo, with links to a more respectable past with mystical aspirations.[20] In common with the *zu'ar* of cities of the Mamluke period, rival groups came from different quarters, which provided the boundaries for recruitment and organisation.[21]

In the relationship between state and society, whether the bazaar or elsewhere, the clergy enjoyed an intermediary position, and it was their recognised role to mediate between the two. In the social and political life of cities they had a central position in creating cohesion, as other groups did not have their authority, abilities or connections.[22] Their role was also enhanced by the minimal nature of the bureaucratic and legal structures. Indeed, their real authority derived from the significance of the shari'a, of which they had the knowledge, having taken long years of study to acquire it. In theory, in Ithna 'Ashari, Twelver Shi'ism (the branch of Islam to which most Iranians belonged), the temporal ruler had no legitimacy. The only legitimate ruler was considered to be the last of the Twelve Shi'i Imams, who vanished in the ninth century. The clergy had the right, through their knowledge, to implement the shari'a, but were not, at this period, considered to have the right to govern. In practice, most clergy acknowledged the shah as legitimate, provided he conformed to the shari'a, and to the rights and duties mentioned above. The clergy's knowledge of the shari'a was the main source of their status in the community of believers, but they owed their influence to other factors as well.

The roots of their position lay on the one hand in the Shi'i conception of the relationship of ordinary believer and clergy, and on the other, in the way clerical lives and institutions were funded. The senior clergy (*mujtahids*) provided guidance for the community on the basis of their learning and their example, which other believers were required to imitate. However, other believers could choose whom they wished to have as their example, so in practice the *mujtahid* was obliged to listen to his followers, and further their interests if he wanted to maintain his influence and prestige. Another factor was that the relationship between believer and *mujtahid* was reinforced financially. Much of their income came from religious endowments (*vaqf*) which they controlled, but a further substantial amount came from the contributions of the faithful in the form of the canonical taxes (*khums* and *zakat*) paid directly to the *mujtahid*. Such taxes helped to fund mosques and schools, as well as the whole establishment of lesser clergy and students who surrounded the *mujtahid*. Therefore the *mujtahid* was financially dependent on his following, and thus even further obliged to attend to their interests. The most faithful following tended to come from the bazaar, at all levels, but, of course, the most significant bazaaris were the wealthy merchants, who by their *largesse* both to the clergy and to fellow bazaaris had a considerable influence on the politics of the cities. It is therefore misleading to take at face value statements that such and such an event or movement was led by the clergy for although authoritative, they were in reality the spokesmen for the community or for the particular groups within it.

As Lapidus has indicated, the alliance between the bazaaris, particularly the merchants, and the 'ulama was assisted by the nature of Islamic institutions which gave a distinctive form to organised life in cities.[23] The institutions led by 'ulama and funded by bazaaris had substantial authority and value, given their religious functions, their revenue producing capacity and their commercial links, as well as their prime location. The system of religious endowments, as Inalcik has noted, was in particular a key institution in creating the urban structure and organisation.[24] They reinforced Islamic cohesion by contributing to an organisation of urban space which assisted the believer in leading a devout Muslim life in a community fully evolved for the purpose.

Lapidus has shown how, in numerous episodes in Sunni urban societies, the common people have shown solidarity with the 'ulama, and have engaged in mass demonstrations and fighting on their behalf. In the thirteenth and fourteenth centuries under the Mamlukes, such alliances were successful in bargaining with the authorities.[25] Yet if the bazaar-religious alliance has, at times, been strong in Sunni parts of the Muslim world, it has a formidable history in Iran.[26] Though the state was perceived as legitimate in practice, its illegitimacy in jurisprudence made its authority more vulnerable to question. Further, in Sunni lands the state has claims upon the religious contributions of the faithful, which in Twelver Shi'ism, as mentioned above, are bestowed on the 'ulama. These two points, combined in the nineteenth century with the weakness of the state, provided for a more close-knit alliance between the bazaar and the 'ulama than elsewhere.

Though the various groups of bazaar society intermingled there were also strict boundaries between them, which were difficult to cross and which limited mobility. Most people with any position came to it by inheritance, including state and religious officials and members of the trades guilds. The children of the more prosperous had advantages of skills, privileges, social contacts, lineage, and reputation, similar to those noted by Marcus for Aleppo.[27] Parents selected partners for their children who would fit into the family culture and customs, partly to reinforce its status and identity, and partly because the individual was very dependent on the family in time of need, in the absence of any support from the state. Although intermarriage within the bazaar was an extensive and preferred practice, it took place not between those of a particular level, but between those of a particular kind. In other words, members of the 'ulama married each other, a *mujtahid* for example, preferring to give his daughter to a lesser *mulla*, rather than a merchant.[28] On the whole the rigidities of the system worked to ensure stability, and clear delineation of divisions and enforcement of the *status quo* facilitated co-operation and cohesion. However, instances of protest occasionally brought on struggles between the different social groups at the popular levels of urban society, particularly between those with property and those without. Rivalries, as between different members of one group, could generate rivalries in the remainder of society.

Given Islam's crucial role in providing social organisation and cohesion, it is not surprising that it has also proved essential to resistance to the state. Islamic notions of justice have supplied the language of protest, mosques their physical centres, and processions their symbols. Beliefs in Islamic rights and boundaries have allowed the powerless to impose their will on policy.[29] Political will has thus been expressed through the mobilisation of bazaar communities. The complex networks of quarter and guild, of mosques and shrines, have at times of crisis served to unite the urban population against the state, though this phenomenon is not peculiarly Shi'i, nor even necessarily Islamic.

One stratagem of protest which has occurred in both Sunni and Shi'i countries for centuries is that of refusal to trade: the closing of part or in many Iranian examples, all of the bazaar.[30] Floor sums up the closing of the bazaar as an economic and political strike against the government. It involves a pattern whereby closure is followed by protest against harsh treatment, and the taking of sanctuary, ending in resolution through the intercession of a religious leader.[31] He notes that there have been similar events throughout Iranian history. Other methods of protest have included lengthy petitions, and the taking of sanctuary in such varied places as shrines and foreign consulates.

Personal and religious events such as marriages and funerals, as well as religious processions such as *ta'ziyya* and *sina zani*, have also been used as occasions on which to organise protest against oppressive acts against the community or the individual. They have thereby provided opportunities for the reinforcement of communal identity, and therefore unity.[32] Finally, in a society where policing was weak, and government regularly unfair, the populace could enforce their will through the threat of disorder by anonymous placards, malicious damage, and, of course, riot itself. Notably, the middle and lower classes of the urban religious community regularly collaborated in the organisation of such revolts, and the involvement of the former may explain why there were often particular targets and much of the violence was symbolic.

In practice, the politics of the cities was carried out mainly by negotiation and bargaining, often in the form of consultation, which took place between state officials, members of the 'ulama, leading merchants, members of the guilds, and even those of humbler position, depending on the occasion. Consultation was in accordance with Qur'anic injunctions, which placed it on the same footing as compliance with God's order, with prayer and with alms giving. Theoretical works, whether mirrors for princes, or legal compilations, were full of advice recommending consultation, and, as will be demonstrated, it was part of the process of decision making at most levels of Qajar society. Consultation was also a form of brokerage in which disputes, in particular over finance, property and taxation, were settled, and by which ways were found to persuade people to compromise.

As part of this culture, both the shah and his officials in the provinces had to ensure that they were open to complaints and requests, which often took the form of petitions, or documents where statements were witnessed. These petitions regularly requested that officials act according to the shari'a, that justice (*'adalat*) be done and that rights be implemented (*ihqaq-i haq*). One of the main stratagems of the plaintiffs was to imply that the actions of the officials were unlawful in shari'a terms. However, pressure on the government, particularly on the vexed question of taxation, was mainly brought about through the activation of networks, most significantly in the bazaar, and amongst the merchants and guilds. Also instrumental were extended family or tribal connections, and, vertically, the layers of networks in one particular quarter. So state and people were involved in a constant complex process of bargaining, which is epitomised in the following comment on the shah's forthcoming jubilee in 1896:

> People are looking forward to the celebration, like a show of any kind. They have persuaded themselves that the shah is likely to signal the event by remission of taxes and other marks of royal favour. It is however probable that the shah regards the matter from a different point of view, and though he will spend money in festivities, those who know him appear to think that the main feature of the year will be the collection of a large sum in the form of '*pishkish*' (gifts, usually in some way extracted).[33]

The Political and Economic Background

This work covers some sixty years of Qajar rule starting in 1835 at the beginning of the reign of Muhammad Shah (1834–1848), and ending in 1896 with the death of his son, Nasir al-Din Shah (1848–1896). The Qajar dynasty had come to power in 1785 when Aqa Muhammad Khan (1785–1797) finally united Iran after a long period of weakness. His heir, Fath 'Ali Shah (1797–1834) found himself reigning over a kingdom that was prospering and relatively secure, though he had a major task before him in trying to re-establish central government control in the remoter areas, particularly the Persian Gulf. The peace of the kingdom, however, was soon disturbed. Russia, having expanded through the Caucasus, aspired to a warm water port, and thus threatened Iran. Two wars were fought in the reign of Fath 'Ali Shah with the Russians, the first in 1811–1813, the second in 1826. Iran lost much of its territory in the Caucasus but managed, principally with first French and then British help, to hold on to Tabriz. The end of the second war was signalled by the Treaty of Turkomanchai in 1828, which granted extra-territorial privileges to Russian subjects, later extended to other nationals. In the meantime the rise of the British East India Company meant that a British presence was making itself felt on the south eastern borders and, more indirectly, in Afghanistan. In particular, the British established a consulate in Bushire, termed the British Residency, to guard its interests in the Persian Gulf and, more significantly, the trading route to India against piracy and any possible European marauders. Iran now found itself a buffer state between the British and the Russians, and was able to survive this predicament by playing them off against each other.

By the time Muhammad Shah came to throne in 1834, Iran was exhausted from the Russian wars, and the trade with India, which had from the latter part of the eighteenth century enriched the south dwindled, as that coming through the Ottoman Empire and Tabriz in the north prospered. Muhammad Shah felt a need to compensate for the losses to Russia under his predecessor, and although he lacked a strong economic position, embarked on a war over Herat. His ambitions collided with the desire of Britain to ensure that Russia did not acquire influence in Afghanistan, which would enable her to threaten British India. It was feared that Russia might exert control through consulates established in an Iranian dominated Herat, and further afield. The first Afghan war ensued in 1838–1841, ostensibly between Afghanistan and Iran, but really between Iran and Britain, with the result that Iran lost. The years following that war were probably the lowest point for southern Iran in the nineteenth century, and the reign of Muhammad Shah was characterised by insurrection and lawlessness, much of it connected to the country's weak economic situation.

When Nasir al-Din Shah succeeded in 1848, his principal minister, Mirza Taqi Khan, Amir Kabir, a reformer and an able and powerful personality, became his Prime Minister. Amir Kabir introduced a range of reforms, notably in education and the legal system, but in the process antagonised a variety of vested interests. He was brought down by a number of enemies at court, including the shah's mother, and put to death in 1851. The reform process stalled, and the country became involved in another conflict over Herat in 1856–7, which ended in Iranian defeat. By the 1860s however reform, encouraged by such notable figures as Mirza Malkum Khan, fitfully resumed. It was above all hampered by lack of funding, for the revenue of the central government was only £2 million, which was tiny even in nineteenth century terms. A saving was made by dispensing with a standing army and relying on bargaining and negotiation at a number of levels, and especially in balancing the interests of the British and the Russians. However, the failure to follow through on reform of the army forfeited the opportunity to develop a degree of efficiency through military modernisation.

Although Iran's balance of trade throughout this period remains something of a mystery, as there are no really reliable figures, there was seemingly an imbalance of imports over exports. The country nevertheless prospered, though at first very slowly, from the 1860s. In the south the trade with India picked up again, encouraged by the introduction of steam to the Persian Gulf in the early 1860s, the development of the telegraph line in the latter part of the decade, and the opening of the Suez Canal in 1869, which helped to develop trade with Europe by steamer. In 1877 a postal service was established between Tehran and Bushire. The involvement of southern Iran in the world economy now began to accelerate rapidly, as trade was facilitated by the development in communications. The decline in silk manufacture (mostly in the north) by the 1870s was offset by the rise in the carpet industry. The export of cash crops, particularly tobacco and opium, rose rapidly, with three hundred cases of the latter being exported in 1859, and eight thousand in 1886. However, the increasing import of European, and especially British, textiles and other manufactured produce damaged Iranian handicraft production. In 1871 a severe drought resulted in famine, which had an adverse effect on trade.

European capitalists, who had hitherto neglected Iran because of the communication and transportation problems, now began to consider the country more seriously with a view to introducing new enterprises. In 1872 a concession was granted to Reuter, a British subject, to build a railway system, which was to include a line from the Caspian to the Persian Gulf. It was opposed by the Russians and not supported by the British, in both cases because of their strategic interests. Faced also with heavy criticism by the 'ulama, who feared that it would undermine Islam, the shah was obliged to withdraw the concession, and dismiss his able reformist prime minister, the Sipah Salar. The issue of concessions came to a head in 1890–1, when the shah sold a monopoly of the collection, manufacture and export of tobacco to a British subject. The sale initiated widespread agitation, the first mass protest in modern Iran, culminating in a *fatva* (order) issued by the principal *mujtahid* of the Shi'i shrine cities in the 'Atabat (Mesopotamia) forbidding the smoking of tobacco until the concession was dropped. The *fatva* was observed throughout Iran, and as a result the shah had to withdraw the concession at a cost of £500,000 in compensation to the British company, which left him seriously indebted. The shah himself and the senior officials of the state suffered a severe loss of authority which, from the point of view of the south, was evident in both Shiraz and Isfahan.

Trade, however, continued to advance rapidly in the south, and (with fluctuations) went up overall from £1.7 million in 1875 in volume to £4.5 million in 1914. Carpet weaving, which had fallen into neglect in the Isfahan region, rapidly increased, especially in Sultanabad, between the 1870s and the 1890s. Transportation was further improved in 1888 with the opening up of the Karun river to steam shipping. From the 1860s there was deficit in the balance of trade though it is difficult to say by how much. An outflow of specie (coin) gathered momentum in the 1880s and 1890s, resulting in inflation. The problem was exacerbated by debasement of the coinage arising from maladministration of the mint, and by a drop in the world value of silver, which formed the basis of Iran's currency. The Iranian elite protected themselves by devices such as wheat rings, and the foreign banks by only accepting the copper coinage, the common currency, at a heavy discount. By the 1890s the connection between high inflation and popular unrest became increasingly clear, one of the outcomes being the dismissal of servants to reduce expenditure, thereby adding to unemployment.

A further problem from the 1880s, and more especially the 1890s, was the growth in the number of foreign-owned trading concerns, companies such as Gray Paul and Hotz, and institutions, such as the British-owned Imperial Bank of Persia. The advent of modern financial institutions facilitated commerce, and with improved communications, both exports and imports grew. The shah made an income out of this drive towards development by selling concessions to foreign firms. This augmented his meagre revenue, particularly at a time when the value of the principal tax, the *maliyat*, or land tax, was constantly falling because of inflation, and in any case difficult to collect. The shah's other considerable source of revenue was the sale of offices, most significantly provincial governorships, to the highest bidder. This resulted in the incumbent's attempting to cover his overheads with profit before he lost the post, often only a year later.

The growth in foreign firms caused social disturbance for more than one reason. The increasing involvement of foreign concerns meant that Iranian merchants, more precisely those of middle rank rather than the great traders such as Mu'in al-Tujjar, found their share of the market was falling, and that they were at a disadvantage in terms of their trading system in dealing with the increasingly dominant Imperial Bank. The local bankers (*sarrafs*) were hit by the new institutions, especially the Imperial Bank, which had the exclusive right of note issue in Iran, and offered loans at a lower rate of interest. Since it was linked to a long term capital market, it could offer greater security for deposits. Secondly, the number of Europeans grew, not massively but enough to make their presence more conspicuous. The 1890s especially marks a more aggressive approach on the part of Europeans towards their role in Iran, manifested in the conduct of the missionaries, backed by their counterparts at home. The British Church Missionary Society in Isfahan contrived to exasperate not only the local governor but also the British consul by insisting it had the right to proselytise in both Isfahan and Shiraz, thereby provoking the local clergy. Iranians at all levels felt a profound unease at the growth of foreign influence and interference in the affairs of the country, later accentuated by the shah (Muzaffar al-Din) taking out large foreign loans in the early twentieth century.

As indicated, a movement had begun, initially principally among the higher bureaucracy, to introduce reforms into the whole state administration. A renowned advocate of reform was the Crown Prince 'Abbas Mirza in Tabriz in the early nineteenth century, who briefly succeeded in creating a new model army. Reform was dogged by financial problems, and by the reluctance of vested interests to change, the forces which had brought down the Amir Kabir. In the latter part of the nineteenth century a series of treatises was written on reform by high ranking bureaucrats, such as Majd al-Mulk, and Malkum Khan. They advocated a proper code of laws, to which government officials should be made accountable, to end the inefficiency and corruption in the state system, thus creating greater security, and as a consequence, greater prosperity. Mirza Malkum Khan, an Armenian, wrote many treatises during his career, and tried to persuade the shah to introduce reform on European lines. Nasir al-Din Shah did encourage reform, for example by setting up a court to judge petitions for the redress of grievances in 1860, and provincial departments of justice in 1863. Justice-boxes called *sanduqha-yi 'adalat* were established in the main towns, as a means of checking arbitrary government, but the venture had little success because of the opposition of the provincial governors. Despite further attempts at reform in the 1890s, in practice there was little administrative change by the end of the nineteenth century by comparison with Egypt and the Ottoman Empire. However, many cases were decided by the people themselves in assemblies or informal councils convoked in the house of a clergyman or notable. A decision, usually in the nature of a compromise, would be reached, and accepted if reasonably fair.

There was gradual development in other institutions and administration during the reign of Nasir al-Din Shah, for example the introduction of a police force in Tehran, but the shah lacked the resources to carry out a major programme and was averse to any rationalisation which might curtail his own power. By the 1890s Malkum Khan, exiled in London and out of favour, demanded much more radical change. In his newspaper *Qanun* (Law), which was widely read in educated circles in Iran, he demanded the limitation of royal power by a Great National Consultative Assembly (*majlis-*

i shaura-yi kabir-i milli) to be composed of the leading members of society. This body was to draw up and implement legislation to cover all aspects of government, and was also to review the budget and make taxation accountable. Finally, an influential reformer of a different kind was Sayyid Jamal al-Din al-Afghani (so-called, though originally an Iranian), who advocated unity of Muslims against the encroachment of Europe in pan-Islamism, the regeneration of Islam by a return to its essential doctrines, and the reform of corrupt institutions.

A reformist press also sprang up, but principally among Iranians abroad because of the censorship in Iran itself. The papers, which evidently had some influence in the south either directly or indirectly, were *Akhtar* published by Iranians in Istanbul, and *Habl al-Matin*, published in Calcutta. They helped to criticise the policy of concessions, and generate opposition to it. The discussion and publicisation of the formation of new companies indicate that the readers were not only reformist bureaucrats, and members of the intelligentsia, but merchants and traders. *Akhtar* carried information on bond issues and market reports, as well as world events, to a community of merchants who were now travelling widely, learning foreign languages, and becoming familiar with new technology. Merchants were also now engaging in larger enterprises, for example, the ownership of steamships and the founding of factories, thus finding a new economic and political role.

Other topics discussed in the press were *millat* (a word essentially meaning community but coming to mean nation) and even more significantly, the establishment of a national consultative body where the leading members of society would make new laws to end oppression, poverty and backwardness. These views were also known to members of the clergy, notably in both Shiraz and Isfahan. It is not otherwise possible to divine the exact readership of these papers, but it must have extended beyond the numbers sold, not only in terms of reading but of debate and discussion, both in more westernised groups and in bazaar circles.

Although changes in social and political attitudes came gradually through most of the nineteenth century, in the last fifteen years or so, especially as the result of European influence, ideologically, politically and economically, they came precipitously. Neither the British nor the Persian sources of the 1890s give much sense of political development in Bushire. As a port, however, where newspapers were brought into the country, and as the centre of trade with India, where new ideas were also emerging, it is hard to see pressure for reform not making itself felt. Indeed, one of the pillars of the constitutional movement of 1905–6 was the merchant, Mu'in al-Tujjar Bushihri. However, the British interest in order and security, and the Iranian interest in ensuring there was no pretext for British interference meant that its presence was not openly demonstrated. Nevertheless, in Shiraz and Isfahan, where government authority had been seriously weakened as a result of the downfall of the Tobacco Concession, and the problems of inflation, the beginnings of a popular movement for reform could be discerned.

Notes

1 This discussion draws upon M. Khadduri, *The Islamic Conception of Justice*, Baltimore 1984; W. Friedmann, *Law in a Changing Society*, Cambridge 1973; L. Rosen, *The Justice of Islam*, Oxford 2000; A.K. Lambton, *State and Government in Medieval Islam*, Oxford 1981; 'Muhakama' and 'Mazalim' in *Encyclopaedia of Islam*, 2nd edition, Leiden 1991, IV, pp. 1–44 and 933–5 respectively; A. Houtum Schindler, 'Persia', *Encyclopaedia Britannica*, London 1902, 31, pp. 614–30; H. Enayat, *Modern Islamic Political Thought*, London 1982; R.S. Khare, *Perspectives on Islamic Law, Justice and Society*, Oxford 1999; C. Mallat, *Islam and Public Law*, London 1993; N.H. Barazangi, M.R. Zaman, and O. Afzal, eds, *Islamic Identity and the Struggle for Justice*, Florida 1996; A.R. Sheikholeslami, *The Structure of Central Authority in Qajar Iran 1871–1896*, Atlanta 1997; A. Amanat, *The Pivot of the Universe*, London 1997.
2 Quoted in A.K. Lambton, *State*, p. 283.
3 Ibid., p. 284. The specific duties of kings are set out by an earlier Islamic thinker of Persian origin, Fazlullah b. Ruzbihan Khunji, who stated that their obligations included protecting the religion according to fixed principles, settling disputes so that justice might be universal among Muslims, defending the lands of Islam from its enemies, collecting taxes, fixing stipends in a balanced fashion, appointing appropriate persons to office, and personally supervising affairs. He further stated:
> Man is a political being by nature and in gaining his livelihood he needs the society of his own kind to co-operate with him and to be his partners, but since the power of lust and passion stimulates violence and discord, there must be a just man who will abate violence – and the just man is he who finds what is congruous and equal among things which are incongruous, and justice is achieved for him who has the knowledge of 'the mean', and that which defines the mean is the divine law. Ibid., pp. 186–7.
4 Quoted in I. Safa'i, ed., *Asnad-i siyasi-yi daura-yi Qajariyya*, Tehran, 2535, p. 13.
5 See V.A.Martin, *Islam and Modernism*, London 1989, chapter 1.
6 Ibid. p. 31.
7 M. Tabataba'i, 'Nama'i az Haj Mulla Muhammad Sadiq Qumi bih Nasir al-Din Shah', *Vahid*, No.3, 1353, pp. 211–219; see also I. Schnedier, 'Religious and State Jurisdiction during Nasir al-Din Shah's Reign', in R. Gleave, ed., *Religion and Society in Qajar Iran*, London 2004 forthcoming.
8 Martin, *Islam*, p. 23.
9 See H. Inalcik, *Essays in Ottoman History*, Istanbul 1998, p. 173 ff.
10 See G. Baer, *Studies in the Social History of Egypt*, Chicago 1969, p. 138.
11 On tribes and the state in the Qajar period see in particular L. Beck, *The Qashqa'is of Iran*, New Haven 1986, and 'Tribes and the State in Nineteenth- and Twentieth-Century Iran' in P. S. Khoury and J. Kostiner, *Tribes and State Formation in the Modern Middle East*, Berkeley1990, pp. 185–225; and G. Garthwaite, *Khans and Shahs*, Cambridge 1983, pp. 4–16, 38–42.
12 Beck, 'Tribes', p. 191.
13 E. Abrahamian, 'The Crowd in the Persian Revolution', *Iranian Studies*, 2, No. 4, 1969, p. 129.
14 A full and informative account of the bazaar in Iran is given in sections by W. Floor and A. Ashraf, 'Bazar', *Encyclopaedia Iranica* IV, London and New York, 1990, pp. 25–30 and 30–44.

15 G. Hambly, 'The Traditional Iranian City in the Qajar Period', *Cambridge History of Iran*, Cambridge 1991, VII, pp. 565–7.
16 Ibid., pp. 566–8.
17 J.P. Perry, 'Justice for the Underprivileged: the Ombudsman Tradition of Iran', *Journal of Near Eastern Studies*, 37, 1978, pp. 203–215.
18 Hambly, 'City', pp. 569–70.
19 E. Burke and I.M. Lapidus, eds *Islam Politics and Social Movements*, Berkeley 1988, p. 146.
20 A. Raymond, 'Quartiers et mouvements populaires au Caire au VIIIeme siecle', in P. Holt, ed., *Political and Social Change in Modern Egypt*, London 1968, p. 111.
21 I. M. Lapidus, *Muslim Cities in the Later Middle Ages*, Cambridge 1984, pp. 154–5.
22 Ibid., pp. 113–4.
23 Burke and Lapidus, *Islam*, p. 28.
24 H. Inalcik, *Essays in Ottoman History*, Istanbul 1998, p. 268.
25 Lapidus, *Cities*, p. 113.
26 Ashraf, 'Bazar', p. 31.
27 A. Marcus, *The Middle East on the Eve of Modernity*, New York 1989, pp. 68–9.
28 This would appear to contrast with Ottoman Cairo, where the 'ulama were in two distinct groups. See G. Baer, 'Popular Revolt in Ottoman Cairo', *Der Islam*, 54' 1977, p. 213. Of the Iranian 'ulama only the Imam Jum'a, himself a state appointee, married into the elite.
29 For a similar role of beliefs and practice in Georgian England, though in a secular form, see D. Hay and N. Rogers, *Eighteenth Century English Society*, Oxford 1997, p. 135.
30 See Lapidus, *Cities*, p. 144, for examples from the Mamluke period.
31 Floor, 'Bazar' p. 29.
32 Again a comparison can be made with Georgian England where food riots were conducted with rituals, songs, parades, fiddlers, cornets and drums all borrowed from local loyalties. Hay and Rogers, *Society*, p. 137.
33 No. 22, 18.3.1896, FO 60/578.

2

THE PEOPLE, THE STATE AND THE BRITISH IN BUSHIRE AND KHARG ISLAND 1836–1850

The purpose of this chapter is to examine the relationship between the people at the more ordinary levels of society, and the state and the British in Bushire and Kharg Island in the period of the first Herat war. In effect it concentrates upon the merchants, small traders, 'ulama, boatmen, fishermen and pearl divers of the area – though inevitably the sources provide most information on the merchants. The role of more ordinary people is considered within the framework of elite struggles, the growth of the Qajar state, and the policies of the British, who dominated Bushire. The main aim of the chapter is to demonstrate that, although the Qajar state was oppressive and arbitrary, there were a variety of ways in which the people could negotiate with it and manage both to protect and advance their own interests. The chapter thus seeks to move away from the prevailing perception of the people as victims of the state and to see them as more assertive in pressing for their interests, particularly with regard to taxation. However, the sources also provide an opportunity to show how ordinary people sought to influence foreign relations, both by bringing pressure on the state and in collaboration with it, and also how they managed to use differences with a foreign power to their own advantage. It may finally be pointed out that it is unusual to find such a detailed account of the relationship between Iranian state and society at the lower levels at such an early period.

People and Trade in Bushire and Kharg Island

The population of Bushire in the earlier part of the nineteenth century cannot be known for sure, beyond the fact that it appears to have been somewhere between five to ten thousand, with the probability that it was around six to eight thousand.[1] Most of the population could speak Arabic, though Persian was also the common language.[2] According to Afzal al-Mulk there were four social groups each having their own *kadkhuda* (quarter leader or mayor), Kazerunis, Darisis, Behbehanis and Dehdashtis. Shushtaris and Shirazis did not have their own *kadkhuda* as they were too few.[3] The population was heterogeneous and the minority component grew larger towards the end of the nineteenth century.[4] Travellers tended to describe it with words such as 'mean' and 'wretched'. In 1825 Buckingham wrote that the only bathhouse was small, mean and filthy, whilst the bazaar consisted of benches covered by a roof of matted rafters.[5] In 1807 it was surrounded by a wall with a few bastions and had three *sarais* (courtyards with storage space).[6] The water of Bushire was scarce and salty, which meant that water had to be brought in from outside the town.[7] The economy of the hinterland was based on poor herdsmen, some cornfields and date gardens.[8] The people lived in *kappars* (houses made from mud, date sticks and leaves), the ceilings of which were so low that it was difficult to stand.[9]

Bushire was seen very much as an entrepreneurial centre, with the populace engaged in various forms of trade, though it also derived an income from fishing and pilotage.[10] It had originally been a fishing village, when it was chosen by Nadir Shah as his southern port and the dockyard for his prospective navy in the Persian Gulf.[11] In 1763 the East India Company transferred their factory from Bander Abbas to Bushire, and received a *farman* (order) from Karim Khan Zand, ruler of Fars, conferring trading privileges on them.[12] It allowed them to build a factory and dwellings at Bushire and to fortify them. The Company was excused customs duties, and a limited tax of 3% was imposed on British goods bought from Iranian merchants. Karim Khan hoped that in return Britain would grant him naval assistance in consolidating his authority in the Persian Gulf, and indeed on several occasions the navy co-operated with him in expeditions to quell the coastal tribes.

Trade between Iran and Britain, or rather British India, Iran's main trading partner in the south, tended to ebb and flow according to the political situation in Shiraz and Isfahan, the two principal commercial centres in Iran at that time. After a slow period, it grew rapidly in the early nineteenth century as a result of the establishment of order by the new Qajar state, combined with the increasing security provided by the presence of the British navy in the Persian Gulf. It was some years, however, before Fath 'Ali Shah was able to enforce his authority along the coast of Fars,[13] and even then only Bushire made practical acknowledgement of the authority of the central government by payment of tribute, fitfully, if the governor of Fars was able to extract payment.

Already in 1807, however, Bushire was beginning to experience the deleterious effects of the growth in trade in the north of Iran, as broadcloth imported from France by way of Russia was cheaper than that brought through Bushire from England.[14] This trend took further effect in the 1830s, as in 1830 the goods passing through Bushire amounted to £750,000 whereas by 1834 they had fallen off, as British trade itself was now going through Istanbul,[15] a tendency which continued for at least a further twenty years. Another disadvantage was that only about half the trade with India landed at Bushire, seemingly to avoid the exactions of the Iranian government. As a result much trade went through Basra, despite the more uncertain market there.[16] Trade exports included raw silk and bullion,[17] as well as opium, horses, old copper, dried fruits, carpets and rosewater,[18] and at least by the mid century, wool, silk, and grain in good years. Musket barrels, sword blades and spearheads made in Shiraz were sold throughout the Persian Gulf. Imports from India in the mid-century were cotton goods (making up two-fifths or more of the total), sugar, grain and metals.[19] The total trade of Iranian imports from India was estimated at 3,000,000 rupees at the beginning of the nineteenth century and exports at 1,500,000.[20] Trade was disadvantaged by a long series of exactions as elsewhere in Iran.[21]

The rulers, or rather, the hereditary governors of Bushire, were the Mazkur or Nasiri clan, who came originally from Oman, and the most formidable of whom, Shaikh Nasir, had defended his position with vigorous success on the rise of Karim Khan.[22] At the beginning of the nineteenth century, though tributary to the governor of Fars, Bushire was almost entirely under the control of the Mazkur, and the authority of the governor of Fars was rarely pressed, and never enforced.[23] They had early formed a close connection with the British, and encouraged trade with India, through which they became enriched. Shaikh Nasir's son proved less successful and lost much of his wealth to Lutf 'Ali Khan Zand in the eighteenth century, but the family nevertheless survived. Buckingham describes Shaikh 'Abd al-Rasul going around with about twenty men, and coming to the sea front before noon to sit on the bench of an unimpressive hut in order to observe: an indication of his watchfulness over his domain.[24] His forces, varying according to current need as was the practice of the time, were mostly provided by his tributaries. They furnished their arms and accoutrements at their own expense, carrying long guns and swords, and as many pistols and daggers as they could manage.[25] They manifested a frequent inclination to independence. Typically of the lesser Arab chiefs of the Persian Gulf coast, the Mazkur power and wealth depended on trade and their ships went as far away as those of Muscat in search of it.[26] Their rise was also linked to the emergence of wealthy merchants from whom they borrowed to fund their regime and to whom they were regularly in debt.[27] The senior member of the family in the period in question was another Shaikh Nasir. His main rival was Baqir Khan, the Arab chief of Tangestan, where he had a fortress, and was the principal local source for auxiliary forces to defend Bushire.[28] Baqir Khan was head of but one of a number of Arab tribes, who, from time to time, became involved in the affairs of Bushire.

Kharg Island, was mostly rocky, but capable of being cultivated on the eastern part, and possessed of abundant good water.[29] It was also held by this same Mazkur family, who had acquired it when it was conquered from the Dutch in 1766 by a Mir Muhunna of Bander Rig, who was connected to the contemporary Shaikh Nasir by marriage.[30] This being a period of weakness and uncertainty in Iran, the island was then conquered by the Imam of Muscat, and transferred to Shaikh Nasir, who then held it for him. Evidently the Imam did not consider it of particular value to him, and he lost interest in it, showing no tendency to become involved in its affairs. In time, as the authority of the Iranian government was re-established along the coast, the Mazkur transferred their allegiance from the Imam to the shah, acknowledging his ultimate authority over the island in 1815.[31] Strictly speaking they held no personal property on the island but were regarded as having the right to make use of the old Dutch fortification there. The second Shaikh Nasir also attempted to consolidate his connection with the shah by taking a wife from the Qajar family.[32] The Mazkur, however, could use their position on Kharg to thwart the Iranian government. In November 1837 the government replaced Shaikh Nasir with their own dependent nominee, Mirza Muhammad Riza, seemingly over non-payment of revenue. The Mazkur retreated to Kharg as a place of security and proceeded to harass trade until Shaikh Nasir was reinstated.[33]

The inhabitants of Kharg, who numbered three hundred houses, came from a different tribe, the Damuk, and were Sunni, whereas the Mazkur were Shi'a.[34] Shaikh Nasir was expected to keep one hundred soldiers on the island, though normally there were no more than thirty. The inhabitants of Kharg Island were not obliged to pay a land tax, but dues were levied on their revenues from pilotage. They had to pay one fifth of their earnings from the pearl fisheries, estimated at £10–12 per year, and taxes were also levied on fish, grain and vegetables.[35] Up till the time of the first Herat war their relations with Shaikh Nasir were not apparently difficult, even though they paid dues both to him and to the Iranian government.

The merchants of Bushire were about equally Iranian Muslim and Armenian.[36] At the beginning of the century there were no Jews of any note[37] but by the 1830s there was a Jewish quarter and synagogue, and at least two more substantial traders, Elias, the British Residency *sarraf* (banker), who was also engaged in the wine trade,[38] and Khojah Mourad, who had responsibilities with regard to their cargo.[39] Hindu merchants were treated with tolerance by the Iranians.[40] As in other towns, there was a Malik al-Tujjar (principal merchant), who acted as an intermediary between the merchant community and the state. The appointment of such an individual was also useful to the British, who found that settlement of commercial disputes was much facilitated by having an authorised person to deal with.[41] In Bushire one Haji Muhammad Baqir, surnamed Isfahani, was appointed by Firidun Mirza, governor of Fars, as Malik al-Tujjar, on account of being 'famed for his honour and rightness, respected by his peers and his fellows', and for whom respect and protection was also required of the British Resident.[42] A subsequent Malik al-Tujjar, Haji 'Abd al-Muhammad, had a prominent role in the arms trade and is mentioned as receiving a consignment of muskets for the Iranian government from Bombay.[43]

The attitude of the merchants of Bushire to both the Iranian government and the British was ambivalent, but principally characterised by the desire to eschew the exactions of both authorities. The strengthening of central government control over Bushire meant the local (al-Mazkur) governor and the town could no longer rebel against tax demands from Shiraz. As a result, the merchants diverted their goods through Bander Abbas, then under a long lease from the Iranian government by the Imam of Muscat, who seemingly charged lower customs duties. On the other hand, the merchants avoided using British ships for the transport of their merchandise, a source of annoyance to the British, who complained that native boats were taking over trade. Both ships from India and the local trade had established in the British view 'a system of dissent and falsehood regarding the times of sailing so as to baffle all conjecture as to when they depart.'[44]

In 1842 the British decided to investigate why their relations with the merchants of Bushire were not more productive.[45] It emerged that part of the problem was to do with trading practice. British merchants expected cash on delivery, whereas the local practice was to have an agent whose task was to distribute the goods, a mode of business more profitable to the local traders. They also disliked buying large consignments for fear, especially if there was more on the way, that the market would become overstocked and the goods would thus decrease in value. Further, the Iranians were accustomed to operating on credit, sometimes given for as long as three years, and did not have the cash available to pay up immediately, as British merchants required.[46] Ironically, also, British merchant shipping actually declined because of the repression of piracy. The safety of the seas permitted many small local boats to ply their trade to India more cheaply than the British carriers, and with a quantity of goods which suited delivery to the local markets.

Another prominent group in Bushire, as elsewhere, was the 'ulama, and the town appears to have had two prominent *mujtahids*, the Imam Jum'a and the *qazi* (religious judge), Shaikh Hasan. Whilst the former, as always was linked to the state, it was the latter, who, through his dependants and connections, particularly in the bazaar, was most active in representing popular feeling, whether against the depredations of the state or the intrusive foreign presence.[47] According to Amanat, Bushire was an active centre of Akhbarism, with connections with the 'ulama of Bahrein, among whom austerity and an interest in the occult sciences were practised.[48] The *qazi* of Bushire was a member of the 'Usfur family, who were Arab Shi'a originating from the western side of the Persian Gulf, renowned for their learning and distinction.[49]

To maintain control, the central government kept a garrison in Bushire, and in 1841 its troops amounted to two hundred men. Given the irregularities in their pay and conditions, it was not surprising that they occasionally plundered the local houses and terrorised the townsfolk to the point where they stayed indoors, and were thus another cause of ill-feeling between the authorities and the people.[50] In general the Iranian army suffered much from under-funding. Their clothing was such that they could hardly be recognised as soldiers, they had no hospitals or provisions for the sick and wounded, and their pay was constantly in arrears.[51]

The People of Bushire and the Herat War

The attitude of the populace of Bushire towards the British was ambivalent. They were dependent on the British protection for the prosperity of their trading activities, but they disliked the presence and influence of a foreign power in Iran. They were inclined both to support their own government against the British, bringing pressure on them to resist British demands, and to take advantage of ill-feeling between Iran and Britain. In 1836 relations between the two countries were entering a more difficult phase with Muhammad Shah's ambitions to regain the lost Iranian province of Herat, and British misgivings that the extension of Persian influence in Afghanistan would also mean the extension of Russian influence thus jeopardising the security of British India.[52] Even before the Herat war there were a number of anti-British incidents in Bushire, by which the populace sought to intimidate them and indirectly warn the Iranian authorities to keep them out of Iranian affairs. In December 1836 the passage on his way to Mecca of a radical member of the 'ulama through the town, inciting assassination of Europeans, stirred up anti-British feeling. An effigy of Griboedov, the Russian emissary who had been slain by a mob in Tehran in 1829, made in the bazaar of Shiraz, was suspended from a sort of gibbet in the bazaar for the edification of the British resident.[53] Not long afterwards, Elias, the *sarraf* of the Residency, was attacked for doing its business in the bazaar by Shaikh Salman, the *qazi*'s nephew.

In the late summer of 1837, Muhammad Shah marched on Herat with the hope of recovering it, despite British protests. The deterioration in relations gave the people a new opportunity to express their animosity towards the British, particularly when a fight broke out between a British apothecary and a dervish. Under popular pressure, the governor argued that the Briton should be tried in the *qazi*'s court (rather than in the Residency, as was usual), because the dervish was a *sayyid* (a descendant of the Prophet). The British Resident was reminded by the governor of the fate of a previous overbearing foreign official (meaning Griboedov), and of the fact that the shah had not consented to it.[54] Shaikh Nasir, the governor, was thereby indicating that he was subject to popular pressures that he could not control.

The British drew up a list of conditions for peace. The list included an equitable agreement over Herat, a commercial agreement placing British commercial agents on the same footing as Russian consuls, the relinquishment of the claim to punish the apothecary, the punishment of those who had made threats to the British Resident, and the removal of the governor of Bushire for failure to deal with them. The Iranian government itself responded to British complaints with a policy of stonewalling and evasion.[55] Frustrated, McNeill, the British Minister, broke off relations with the shah in June and gradually made his way to Erzurum in Ottoman territory. The British cast about for a bargaining counter to force the shah to accede to their view, and settled on the seizure of Kharg Island, which they invaded on 19th June 1838.

Meanwhile, a final full scale assault by Iranian troops on Herat on 23rd June 1838 did not succeed, and the shah raised the siege of Herat and withdrew. The cumulative effect of the failure over Herat and the British occupation of Kharg Island persuaded the shah to agree to a variety of British demands on 9th September, including punishment for the attack on the Residency *sarraf*, the dismissal of the governor of Bushire, the evacuation of the fort of Ghorian, and the conclusion of a commercial treaty: promises he did not keep.

In the meantime, the merchant community of Bushire was becoming alarmed at developments and their implications for trade, which was being damaged by the war. In addition, the community relied on the British to protect their trading vessels. When a local *buggalah* (sailing boat) was seized by the Arab chief of Qishm, they felt the Iranian government would be unable to control him and applied to the British for assistance and advice.[56] Directed to refer to their own authorities in the current circumstances, they evinced considerable alarm and sent a petition signed by the great majority to the new governor of Bushire emphasising that a breach with the British would jeopardise their merchandise, and hinting at drastic reductions in the customs revenues. The incident illustrates the contradiction in the interests and views of the Bushiris, for both state and society, whilst resenting the British, were dependent on them with regard to trade and security on the Persian Gulf coast.

These conflicting interests and differences in view among the merchants, and other sections of society in Bushire were illustrated by a further altercation in November 1838. A dispute arose between the merchants and the governor, Mirza 'Abbas, over the settlement of certain duties which the merchants claimed had already been paid to Shaikh Nasir when he was governor. As a result the bazaars closed, a fairly early recorded example in the nineteenth century of this strategy of protest, which was of course significant in both of Iran's revolutions.[57] Mirza 'Abbas sent *farrashes* (servants) to force the traders to open their shops. Shaikh Hasan, *qazi* of Bushire, clearly both representing the community over its grievance and guiding it, directed the bazaaris to refuse compliance and to assemble with arms at his house. Upon the pretext that one of the governor's *farrashes* had been discovered intoxicated, the *qazi* ordered that all the wine found in the Jewish quarter should be destroyed.[58] A crowd of poorer people organised into a mob, led by the *qazi*'s slaves and a *sayyid* (descendant of the Prophet) dependent on him, attacked the Jewish quarter, and most particularly the house of the British Residency *sarraf* (banker), where they assaulted him, and destroyed wine and spirits packed for export to the value of 40–50 tomans. In this action, on the one hand the people of Bushire were taking advantage of the rupture between the British and the Iranian government to resist payment of further taxation, and on the other they were protesting at British policies, notably the occupation of Kharg Island. They were also seeking to undermine British prestige. The British were not in a position to complain effectively, given that their Representative was not in the country. The governor of Bushire was likewise not in a position to protest, as the sale of alcoholic drink was prohibited, it being contrary to the shari'a. The British nevertheless made remonstrations to the governor of Fars, demanding the removal of Shaikh Hasan, his nephew Shaikh Salman, and his dependants from Bushire, together with the punishment of others involved.[59]

The governor of Fars responded by replacing Mirza 'Abbas with the much tougher (and more anti-British) Mirza Asadullah. He was welcomed by the merchants and tradesmen, who had also complained to the governor of Fars.[60] Hennell (the British Resident) commented that, 'This triumph was reached by the liberal disbursement of cash and influence of the merchants of Persia when they unite together.'

Mirza 'Abbas, in the interim, had proved himself unable to pay the dues expected of him, and had been sent to a garden house some miles from Bushire to reflect upon the matter.

The People, the State and the Occupation of Kharg Island

In December 1838 Mirza Asadullah, evidently encouraged by local support, embarked on a more vigorous anti-British policy. He cut off supplies to British ships, despite the fact that it would stop trade, and also meant a reduction of the customs revenues in Fars.[61] He followed up the measure with an embargo on supplies to the British occupying force on Kharg Island, using the pretext that everything was scarce and dear that year, and there was a need to regulate provisions in case of famine.[62] Further, Mirza Asadullah, on the authority of the shah, forbade stonemasons to accept work for the British on repairing the fort on Kharg Island. With these measures, he appears not only to have been trying to annoy the British, but also undermine their prestige in the Persian Gulf, because their protests were evidently fruitless. Loss of prestige meant attacks on British commerce, and thus more expenditure in protecting it.

The British Resident, Hennell, now had the options of either withdrawing or occupying Bushire itself, which he did not feel able to hold in view of popular hostility to the British. Matters finally came to a head in late March 1839, when a British admiral and fleet appeared at Bushire to demonstrate support for the Resident. When the admiral tried to land to meet the governor, the people of Bushire threw sticks and stones at the British. Then Iranian soldiers commanded by Baqir Khan Tangestani under the orders of Mirza Asadullah, fired on the British, who fired back, so the admiral was able to land. Later that evening the British Resident decided to withdraw the Residency to Kharg Island, and left Bushire on 30th March 1839.[63]

However, the views and interests of one part of the populace were not necessarily supported by all. Realising the implications for trade, some of the merchants of Bushire, and the *qazi*, wrote to the British Resident asking him to return. Later, the British on Kharg Island received a letter from the Imam Jum'a of Bushire, presumably prompted by the trading community there, inquiring about the health of the admiral, and remarking that the governor (Mirza Asadullah) was not used to dealing with the English. Since in a forty year friendship matters of greater moment than this had been adjusted, he hoped that this too might be settled.[64] The contrast between these letters and the welcome extended to Asadullah on his appointment indicate divisions both of interest and of opinion on the foreign presence in Iran among the community of Bushire, and demonstrate their different tactics in trying to influence the situation.

Muhammad Shah, however, did not share the more conciliatory view and, realising the implications for British prestige, seized the opportunity to embarrass them. *Farmans* (commendations), dresses of honour and decorations were sent to Baqir Khan, his companions and Mirza Asadullah on 5th June. The incident coincided with the news that the British had been repulsed at Kandahar. The British were furious, since they felt that the event had weakened Britain in the eyes of Iranians.[65]

The Persian government's version of the events in Bushire was reported to the British as follows:

> An English admiral had arrived in a ship of eighty guns and by a stratagem had obtained possession of Bushire. Baqir Khan with the troops of the Dashtestan attacked and defeated the English with great loss, and drove out of Bushire the admiral, the resident and the English flag, and had sent a large quantity of English heads to Shiraz.

In practice the Iranian authorities realised it was unwise to annoy the British too much. Asadullah was removed from his position by the governor of Fars, who evidently felt he had acted precipitately towards the British. The governor also needed their support against the Ottomans, who had ambitions to extend their influence in the Persian Gulf. The removal of Asadullah provoked a petition to the governor from the *qazi* of Bushire and the merchants associated with him demanding Asadullah's reinstatement. On the other side, at least one prominent merchant, Sayyid Muhammad Baqir, favoured the Mazkur family, and with them the return of the British.[66] The shah, on the other hand, wrote to the governor of Fars fully supporting what he believed to be his policy in expelling the British from Bushire.

The shah also made his version of events known throughout Iran and the Persian Gulf,[67] undermining British prestige with consequent injury to the British.[68] He continued to humiliate them by showing favours to the anti-British *qazi*, and his nephew, the first being received in several private audiences, and praised for his good services in the matter of the admiral, and the second being granted a pension in the autumn of 1840.[69]

The conflict duly took its toll on trade, which was affected in various ways, principally with regard to the export of horses to India, over which the British made numerous complaints on behalf of their interests.[70] Mirza Asadullah dealt harshly with anyone who had contact with the British, which meant the merchants were afraid of using British bills of exchange, and consequently had to obtain funds from Basra.[71] At one point the people of Bushire, being largely tradesmen and money-makers, were contemplating leaving the place because of the disturbed situation.[72] In nineteen months there were eight governors of Bushire, principally as a result of elite struggles for the post of governor against a background of increasing disorder in Fars in the wake of the conflict in Afghanistan.[73] The troops had not been paid and so became more than usually unruly.[74]

The British occupation of Kharg also marked a distinct downward turn in the fortunes of Shaikh Nasir. His family's long connection with the British, combined with his problems in remitting the expected amount of revenue, had led to his being removed from the governorship. He was obliged to leave Kharg Island by the British, who found him an embarrassment there.[75]

Palmerston finally succeeded in restoring relations between Britain and Iran by the treaty of 28th October 1841, in accordance with which the British evacuated Kharg Island in February 1842. The *karguzar* (foreign agent) of Bushire reported to the Ministry of Foreign Affairs that they had set up their own police, and replaced the Iranian flag with their own. Optimistically, the *karguzar* hoped that a proper court of justice (*mahkama*) and a reliable garrison would be established, properly provisioned and with adequate cannon and ammunition. Soon afterwards an Iranian garrison arrived and raised the Iranian flag.[76] In the course of time the garrison in Kharg was to be stabilised and better run.

The British returned to Bushire, but not to the welcome they had anticipated. The Residency *sarraf*, Mr Essai, an Armenian merchant, informed his fellow traders of the British Resident's return, but only two, also Armenian, appeared to meet him.[77] It would seem that this slight was organised by some of the leading Iranian merchants, including Haji Muhammad Baqir, 'Abd al-Muhammad and Mirza 'Ali (who was the current agent of the governor of Fars for collecting the revenue).[78] As ever sensitive on the subject of British prestige, Hennell retaliated by subsequently refusing to see those merchants who tried to meet him. He noted the 'mean spirit' of the Armenian merchants in not greeting him as they gained advantage from the British presence, but it is possible that pressure had been brought to bear on them not to attend. Later, the majority of the merchants, excluding only three Iranians, felt able to call on him, and there can be little doubt that most benefited from the British return.

Lower down the social scale the advantages of the connection were not so clearly felt. The British received a chilly welcome from the *sarbaz* (soldiers), who stoned the Residency doctor and attempted to set fire to a merchant vessel flying the British flag, possibly with the connivance of the *darugha* (local magistrate). He in turn had to seek protection by taking refuge in the *qazi*'s house.[79] Shaikh Salman was also active in inciting expressions of contempt for the British, and those who set fire to the ship evaded punishment.[80] Shaikh Hasan and Shaikh Salman further made trouble for the perceived ally of the British, Shaikh Nasir, by petitioning the governor of Shiraz for 1600 tomans worth of their stipends from Shaikh Nasir, which had not been paid.[81] The people of Bushire later kept up their vigilance against further infiltration of British interests by demonstrating hostility to the Resident's construction of a second house in a cooler district above the town.[82] It was forbidden for foreigners to own property, and the merchants and clergy of Bushire not only reported the new house to the governor of Fars, they also magnified its extent.

The Kharg Islanders and the War

In the meantime the inhabitants of Kharg Island had made full use of the opportunities provided by the war. Firstly, they had paid little in the way of taxes for three years, their main dues normally being paid to Shaikh Nasir to support the island garrison through the pilotage tax.[83] Secondly, they restructured their administration. In the absence of Shaikh Nasir they had grown used to managing their own affairs by council and were now adamant that they did not wish for his return. One of the principal problems confronting them at this time was that, with the extension of central control, they were increasingly having to pay dues both to the centre through the governor of Fars, and to the established standing power, the Mazkur family.[84] The inhabitants managed their affairs by assembly and consultation, which probably reflected existing practice since Shaikh Nasir was rarely on the island, though his relations may have previously participated. The intricacy of the arrangements dealing with the collection of money to pay various government agents suggests a measure of experience.[85] The participants were described as the principal men of the place, merchants, members of the 'ulama, and many others.[86]

Struggling to assert their rights between the contending powers of the shah, the governor of Fars, and the local powers, particularly Shaikh Nasir, the inhabitants of Kharg negotiated to try to cut out the local and regional depredating authorities and to send their remuneration to Tehran themselves. They apparently even succeeded in obtaining a *farman* (order) from the shah separating Kharg from the government of Fars.[87] The governor of Fars, meanwhile, on a visit to Bushire recognised Shaikh Nasir's right. Shaikh Nasir and the governor of Shiraz agreed an assessment of 3600 Muhammad Shah rupees for Kharg to be levied by the Shaikh. In addition, the governor was to issue an order to Shaikh Nasir to pay fifteen tomans annually to the Mutavali (guardian) of the local Imamzada (shrine) for prayers to be offered for the shah's well-being,[88] a donation which was presumably a conciliatory gesture to the islanders. However, Shaikh Nasir's ambitions to restore his unfettered rights did not accord with the emerging central policy on Kharg. The shah's agent and the commander of the garrison made it clear that there was to be no charge on the islanders involving Shaikh Nasir. Pressing the shah's agent, the islanders tried to have the expenses of the garrison borne by Shaikh Nasir as governor of Bushire. In addition they obtained from the shah a *farman* specifically protecting the Damuk tribe of Arabs, and enjoining the Khan of Laristan to ensure the Lari garrison did not oppress the people.

The inhabitants were initially pleased with the shah's new arrangements for them to manage their own affairs, and with the Lari garrison. However, differences which were largely financial at root soon began to emerge. They maintained that the commander, Lutf 'Ali Khan, was trying to milk them, although he owed his position to the shah's order to defend them from oppression.[89] They discovered allies in Lutf 'Ali's own troops, who complained that he purloined their salaries. The two groups joined together and expelled Lutf 'Ali,[90] who departed to Bushire, where he claimed to have been ejected by both mutiny and rebellion.[91] Both the *qazi* of Bushire, and the governor sent emissaries to Kharg to discover the facts. These were subjected to undignified treatment, and dispatched with messages to their respective masters to attend to their own concerns. Kharg Island, it was explained to them, was under the chief of Lar (by royal edict), and therefore not obliged to listen to views from Bushire.

The authorities of Bushire responded by advising Lutf 'Ali to raise a body of Shi'a to punish the Sunnis of Kharg Island, presumably as a form of jihad. Thus Lutf 'Ali sailed with thirty unemployed 'Shi'a', but his force was soon repulsed by the Lari garrison. The acting commander of the garrison had in the meantime written to the chief of Lar, who replied expressing disapproval of Lutf 'Ali Khan, and indignation at the *qazi* of Bushire. The garrison was relieved on the command of their chief and the Kharg Islanders were delighted to be free of oppression. Financial realities, however, soon made themselves clear. The Lari soldiers departed as the islanders could not support them, and the troops' provisions from Bushire had been stopped. The Khargis were now faced with new, rapacious, troops from either Bushire or Fars, or the return of Shaikh Nasir, whom they vehemently opposed. They had the right of appeal to the shah, but the expense was too great for a poor person such as a Khargi fisherman, who thus had to endure oppression rather than go to Shiraz for redress.

When a new contingent of soldiers was duly sent to Kharg in 1843, the inhabitants demonstrated their discontent by abandoning the island *en masse*, leaving behind their homes, cattle and donkeys, a manoeuvre intended to imply to the authorities that their regime was unjust and unlawful.[92] Their departure deprived the country of its livelihood, and the government of revenue, and may be accounted a form of strike. The island had never before been garrisoned by government troops, with their habit of plunder, and the islanders were too few and too poor to provision the garrison. Whatever the demands of the Mazkur family, they had also, like many notables, protected their people to some extent by acting as intermediaries in negotiating with the state. The soldiers, presumably acting under orders on this occasion, destroyed the homes of the islanders, and threatened to destroy their livestock if they did not return.[93] Various complaints about the garrison of Kharg Island were duly lodged in Tehran, and the shah requested the governor of Fars to ensure that 'there is peace and quiet and the inhabitants are happy', that is to say, to arbitrate as appropriate to secure tranquillity.[94]

The Decline of the Mazkur

As part of the ongoing trend of the assertion of central control, the *yavar* (major) at Bushire was taking an increasing role in acting as a confidential agent of the governor of Fars, and was given responsibility for settling all disputes. The captain of the garrison on Kharg also assumed more authority, taking responsibility from the *yavar* at Bushire.[95] When the inhabitants of Kharg Island returned home in March 1844 from their places of refuge in Basra and Kuwait, they found that the administration of Kharg Island had become more regularised. The changes thus brought about undoubtedly owed much to the British presence and administrative practice. It also developed from the Iranian government's determination not to give the British an opportunity to interfere.

In the interim Shaikh Nasir, having lost all but a foothold in the fort of Kharg Island, retained his position fitfully as governor of Bushire. Even after being re-appointed governor in 1842, Shaikh Nasir was largely powerless, partly because he owed money to three of the merchants, Haji Muhammad Baqir, Aqa 'Abd al-Muhammad and Aqa Mir Baqir, as well as supposedly 6000 tomans to the governor of Fars.[96] As a result, he soon lost his position again, but returned in September 1845. His situation was precarious, however, principally because he could not raise the expected revenues as a result of the fall off in the customs dues discussed above.[97] At the same time, relations between the merchant community and the Mazkur had soured as Shaikh Nasir was always overcharging them, or asking for loans, which he failed to repay. The consequent antagonisation of the merchants contributed to the decline in the fortunes of the Mazkur.[98] Yet Bushire was a prosperous place, and the decline of Shaikh Nasir saw the concomitant rise of Haji 'Abd al-Muhammad, the Malik al-Tujjar. This was part of a gradual process whereby the merchant community grew richer while the state administration became increasingly pressed, both as a result of growing expectations and of the difficulty of enforcing the application of increased tax rates. Trade was producing not so much the emergence of a new class as the enrichment, and consequent growth of influence, of an old one.

The influence of the Malik al-Tujjar incurred the animosity of Shaikh Nasir, and the merchant in his turn became involved in the process whereby the Iranian government undermined the position of the Mazkur family, mainly because of their long-standing connection with the British, but also partly as a result of the growth of state control. At one point, in May 1849, when the Malik al-Tujjar's life was threatened by Shaikh Nasir, and his uncle, Shaikh Husain, some of the principal merchants of Bushire remained in his house night and day to protect him.[99] The Malik al-Tujjar was influential because he was able to command the markets and exercise a degree of control over his less prosperous fellows, and also because he had connections in both Shiraz and Tehran. Hennell considered it was thus unwise of Shaikh Nasir to engage in a dispute with the merchant, because he could receive more support from the Malik al-Tujjar than all the other merchants put together, the Malik al-Tujjar's position being enhanced by his link with the state and the consequently important role he played in the settlement of disagreements.

Despite two rebellions by the Mazkur family against the government policy of removing Shaikh Nasir from Bushire, including a rebellion led by his uncle, Shaikh Husain,[100] Shaikh Nasir finally lost his position in the autumn of 1850. This last rebellion was crushed partly by a government army, and partly by the people of Bushire who forced Shaikh Husain to flee with his family.[101] The merchant community of Bushire became disturbed by this manifestation of the extension of state control, and of a Persian as opposed to an Arab governor. They complained to the governor of Shiraz, but to no avail.[102] It was not long, however, before they settled down under the new administration.

*　*　*

The people of Bushire asserted their interests against the Iranian state in a number of ways. The network of 'ulama (Shaikh Hasan and Shaikh Salman), merchants and poorer people consistently resisted the attempts of a series of governors to impose taxation, using traditional organisation based on the bazaar, and stratagems of undermining the legitimacy of the authority of the governor, as in the attack on the wine dealer in 1838. With regard to foreign relations, such methods were also used to undermine British prestige, as in the incident over the admiral, and to resist British pressure to extend their influence in Bushire – for example in the acquisition of property. Resistance by the people in collaboration with the state thus succeeded in embarrassing the British, and at the same time brought pressure on the state to keep them out. The potential for disorder they caused also created a disincentive for the British to invade the mainland. In Kharg Island the use of consultation to achieve the best interests of the inhabitants is notable in the ousting of the local power during and after the Herat War, and in dealing with the pecuniary demands of government officials. The people of both Bushire and Kharg Island were also adept at playing the local authorities, specifically the governors of Fars and Bushire, against one another, and in complaining of the one to the other, or to the central government itself. A further method of coping with an impecunious but rapacious power was to flee, leaving the government without income because there was nothing to tax, as the Khargis demonstrated. As at the time of the Constitutional Revolution, the people, in this case on Kharg Island, successfully used the disruption in foreign relations as part of their strategy to secure fairer government and to reduce the power of the Mazkur.

With regard more specifically to the merchants, their relationships with one another and with both the authorities and the British were inevitably complex. The merchants acted together in certain common interests, one of which was to evade or to exclude from detailed knowledge of their affairs both the local authorities and the British. For example, they avoided the higher Iranian customs dues at Bushire by trading through Bander Abbas. The availed themselves of British trade protection, whilst preferring transportation of goods by cheaper local vessels rather than seemingly dominant British ones. There is some evidence that the merchants were becoming more prosperous, and therefore more assertive as against the Iranian state system.

The merchant community clearly also had its divisions, some of which would have been due to individual commercial rivalries. Others obviously depended on their status vis à vis the British, on whose goodwill nearly all were more or less dependent for trade down the Persian Gulf as well as with India. The Armenians had more connections in India, which meant their interests were closer to those of the British and also that the British tended to use them, as well as the Jews, for services such as banking. It must be supposed that differences would have arisen from the nature of the trade the merchants were involved in, whether it was more internal or external, whether it was very closely connected with India (e.g. the horse trade) or related more to other parts of the Persian Gulf (e.g. weapons from Shiraz), but lack of detailed information about the various merchants prohibits us from being more precise. The growth in state power over local notables caused certain merchants, particularly the Malik al-Tujjar to become wealthier and more dominant. All could be caught between the interests of the two states, as the difficulties caused by the return of the British to

Bushire demonstrated, and for that reason they could each have more than one position or identity.

Notes

1 Macdonald Kinneir put the population at around 5000 in 1813, see J. Macdonald Kinneir, *A Geographical Memoir of the Persian Empire*, London 1813, p. 70; J. Buckingham assessed it as under 1,500 dwellings in *Travels in Assyria, Media and Persia*, London 1829, p. 347. By 1868 it was estimated to be 18,000, see C. Issawi, *The Economic History of Iran 1800–1914*, Chicago 1971. Looking back at the end of the nineteenth century, Curzon considered it had probably been 6000–8000 at the beginning of that century, see G.N. Curzon, *Persia and the Persian Question*, London 1892, II, p. 231. Afzal al-Mulk, who passed through in 1256/1840–1, said the population was not more than a thousand families, giving an estimate of 5000–8000. Mirza Ghulam Husain Afzal al-Mulk, 'Safarnama-yi Isfahan' *Du safarnama-yi junub-i Iran*, ed. S.A. Al-i Davud, Tehran 1368, p. 71. It had not grown very much by the mid-century, owing to the movement of the trade routes. Binning, passing through in 1857, estimated it at 11,000, R.B. Binning, *A Journal of Two Years Travel in Persia, Ceylon, etc*, London 1857, p. 144.
2 Buckingham, *Travels*, p. 350. According to Semino the population was mixed. He also says that there were eight hundred families, which was similar to the population of Kharg Island, a figure that does not accord with the other sources. See *General Semino dar khidmat-i Iran 'asr-i Qajar va jang-i Harat*, eds M. Ettehadieh and S. Mir Muhammad Sadiq, Tehran 1375, p. 189.
3 Afzal al-Mulk, 'Safarnama', p. 72.
4 X. de Planhol, 'Bushehr', in *Encyclopaedia Iranica*, IV, London and New York, 1990, p. 571.
5 Buckingham, *Travels*, p. 348.
6 Scott Waring, *A Tour to Sheeraz*, London 1807, p. 2.
7 Macdonald Kinneir, *Memoir*, p. 70.
8 No. 72, 1.9.1837, FO 60/50.
9 Binning, *Persia*, p. 140.
10 Buckingham, *Travels*, p. 349.
11 Curzon, *Persia*, II, p. 231.
12 J.B. Kelly, *Britain and the Persian Gulf 1785–1880*, Oxford 1968, p. 52.
13 Kelly, *Persian Gulf*, p. 42.
14 Scott Waring, *Sheeraz*, p. 2.
15 Willock to Canning, Report on the Trade of Persia, FO 78/241, 1834, p. 214.
16 See Buckingham, *Travels*, p. 352, where he says that about fifteen merchant ships traded with India in 1825 but only half landed at Bushire. The Iranian government further appropriated goods and then either delayed payment for them or used them against duties to be paid (p. 354).
17 Macdonald Kinneir, *Memoir*, p. 70; Scott Waring, *Sheeraz*, p. 8.
18 Kelly, *Persian Gulf*, p. 44.
19 Issawi, *Iran*, p. 83.
20 Ibid., p. 83.
21 Buckingham, *Travels*, p. 352.
22 Scott Waring, *Sheeraz*, pp. 7–8. See also Kelly, *Persian Gulf*, pp. 42–3.
23 No. 18, 8.3.1839, FO 60/65.
24 Buckingham, *Travels*, p. 351.
25 Binning, *Persia*, p. 144. He reports that the other natives of Bushire were poorly dressed so as not to have money squeezed from them.

26 Buckingham, *Travels*, p. 351.
27 S.R. Grummon, *The Rise and Fall of the Arab Shaikhdom of Bushire 1750–1850*, Ph.D. John Hopkins University, 1985, translated by H. Zanganeh as *Chalish barayi qudrat va thirvat dar junub-i Iran as 1750–1850*, Qum 1378, p. 185.
28 See for example No. 42, 25.6.1838, FO 60/60.
29 Macdonald Kinneir, *Memoir*, p. 18.
30 Robertson to Sheil, 4.1.1843, FO 248/108.
31 Robertson to Sheil, 4.1.1843, FO 248/108.
32 Hennell to Sheil, 16.7.1846, FO 248/113.
33 Hennell to Willoughby, 9.11.1837, FO 248/85.
34 Robertson to Sheil, 4.1.1843, FO 248/108. It is not clear how many people were considered to inhabit a 'house', but James Morier, in his calculations of the population of Shiraz, comes out with a figure between four and five, see *A Second Journey through Persia, Armenia and Asia Minor*, London 1818, p. 110. On this estimate the population of Kharg Island would be probably around 1200–1500. Kemball to Sheil, 21.9.1843, FO 248/113, refers to 300 men. The sources agree that was certainly higher at the time of the Dutch occupation (see for example Macdonald Kinneir, *Memoir*, p. 18, which states the population was 2000–3000 under the Dutch, and John Malcolm, who believes it to have been a rather surprising 12,000, *The History of Persia*, London 1839, II, p. 80.)
35 Robertson to Sheil, 19.1.1843, FO 248/108.
36 Buckingham, *Travels*, p. 350. According to Semino, all the Armenians in Bushire were pro-British, except Yusif Malikian, who possibly helped the French. See Ettehadieh and Mir Muhammad Sadiq, eds, *Semino*, p. 189.
37 Buckingham, *Travels*, p. 350.
38 Hennell to McNeill, 21.11.1838, FO 248/85.
39 Hennell to Sheil, 6.1.1852, FO 248/150.
40 Scott Waring, *Sheeraz*, p. 3. There were also Hindu trading communities in Yazd and Kerman, who occasionally found themselves in difficulties.
41 Hennell to Farrant, 20.8.1849, FO 248/138.
42 IO R/15/1/75, p. 78, July 1837.
43 Hennell to Farrant, 15.11.1848, FO 248/132.
44 Hennell to Sheil, 15.12.1836, FO 248/83.
45 Robertson to Sheil, 23.7.1842, FO 248/108.
46 Robertson to Sheil, 23.7.1842, FO 248/108.
47 On Shaikh Hasan see FO 248/85 Hennell to McNeill, 3.12.36. Hennell referred to him as Shaikh Husain, but the British also called him Shaikh Hasan (see Mackenzie to the government of Bombay 17.9.1840 and 17.10.1840 clearly writing about the same person). Since he is called Shaikh Hasan in H. Busse, *History of Persia under Qajar Rule* (trans. of Hasan Fasa'i's *Farsnama-yi Nasiri*), Columbus 1972, p. 260, this name has been preferred.
48 A. Amanat, *Resurrection and Renewal*, London 1989, p. 134.
49 Ibid., p. 63. Shaikh Muhammad Husain Sa'adat, *Tarikh-i Bushihr*, Tehran 1340, handwritten Ms, TU Adabiyyat 95 Hikmat, p. 53. For mention of Shaikh Hasan's family name see also H. Busse, *Qajar Rule*, p. 260. This being the case it is worth noting that Shaikh Hasan's role in the socio-political events of his town is not discernibly different from the role of Usuli *mujtahids* elsewhere. His Akhbarism is not mentioned in the British sources, suggesting that it was not particularly significant in local politics, though the British were disinclined to comment on religious-theoretical disputes unless they disturbed order. Ya Hosseini, who says the leaders of the Usulis in Bushire were the Baladi family, comments that they both came from Bahrein in 1801, and that Shaikh Hasan did much to build up Bushire as a religious centre. He died in 1271/1854–5 aged 92. Sayyid Qasem Ya Hosseini, *Pishgaman-i mubariza ba Britania dar junub-i Iran*, Bushire 1373,

pp. 10,12,14,20. Khurmuji, however, who also comments on his great learning, says that he died in 1263/1846–7 aged 63, Mirza Ja'far Khan Khurmuji, *Nuzhat al-akhbar*, ed. 'Ali Al-i Davud, Tehran 1380, p. 589. For his works see Sayyid Muhammad Hasan Nabavi, *Ulama va nivisandigan-i Bushihr*, ed. A. Mashayekhi, Bushire 1377, p. 16. According to Sa'adat, the people of Bushire had formerly been mostly Akhbari, but by the early twentieth century were largely Usuli, *Bushihr*, p. 54.
50 Hennell to Sheil, 6.6.1840, FO 248/99.
51 No. 73, 28.7.1847, FO 60/131.
52 For discussion of Anglo-Iranian relations at this time see Kelly, *Persian Gulf*, and M.E. Yapp, *Strategies of British India*, Oxford 1980.
53 Mackenzie to McNeill, 3.12.1836, FO 248/85.
54 Mackenzie to McNeill, 27.12.1837, FO 248/85.
55 Kelly, *Persian Gulf*, pp. 295–6.
56 Encl. in No. 44, 7.9.1838, FO 60/59. No. 43, 26.6.1838.
57 As mentioned in the introduction, refusal to trade had a history not only in Iran, but in other parts of the Middle East, see Lapidus, *Cities*, p. 144, and Raymond, 'Caire', p. 113.
58 The imbibing of wine among Muslims as well as non-Muslims in Qajar Iran was large for a Muslim country, although it was prohibited. See J. Malcolm, *The History of Persia*, London 1839, II, p. 423; R.G. Watson, *A History of Persia*, London 1866. Its trade was in the hands of non-Muslims, i.e. Jews and Armenians. In this instance Hennell tried to get round the problem of the illegal activities of the British *sarraf* by saying that he traded only with non-Muslims, though there is no evidence this made the business legal, just more accepted.
59 Hennell to McNeill, 21.11.1838, FO 248/85.
60 Hennell to McNeill, 12.12.1838, FO 248/85.
61 Hennell to McNeill, 28.12.1838, FO 248/85.
62 No. 17, 5.3.1839, FO 60/63. It was a duty of an Islamic government to ensure the regular and adequate supply of food, particularly grain, principally as a result of its obligation to maintain order. The Iranian government, like the Ottoman, was especially sensitive over the movement of grain supplies to and from the towns, bread being the main staple of diet. For this purpose the government had its own granaries. Attempts to foresee and provide for conditions of famine were sometimes confused with, or mistaken for, grain hoarding. One of the more pernicious activities of the British in Iran arose from a general failure to understand the management of the food supply and the problems it presented for the government. Thus they would still insist at times of famine on the rights of British merchants to export food.
63 No. 35, 26.5.1839, FO 60/66.
64 IO R/15/1/81, No. 80, p. 33.
65 No. 42, 6.6.1839, FO 60/66.
66 No. 64, 24.9.1839, FO 60/67.
67 It was recorded in Hasan Fasa'i's *Farsnama-yi Nasiri* that Shaikh Hasan, the *mujtahid* of the 'Usfur tribe, his nephew, Shaikh Salman and Baqir Khan, had risen in rebellion with the inhabitants of Bushire and expelled the British regular soldiers and Resident from the town. See H. Busse, *Qajar Rule*, p. 260.
68 IO R/15/1/87, Mackenzie to the government of India, 17.9.1840. British fury is demonstrated by Sheil to Palmerston in FO 60/73, No.13, 7.4.1840.
69 IO R/15/1/87, Mackenzie to the government of India, 17.9.1840 and 7.10.1840. In addition, Baqir Khan Tangestani was honoured for saving Bushire.
70 See for example Hennell to Sheil, 18.6.1840, and Mackenzie to Bombay 11.9.1840, FO 248/99.

71 No. 47, 22.6.1839, FO 60/66.
72 Hennell to Sheil, 12.3.1840, FO 248/99.
73 See for example No. 6, 4.2.1840, FO 60/73; No. 13, 7.4.1840, FO 60/73.
74 IO R/15/1/91, Shiraz Agent to Resident, 1.3.1841.
75 IO/R/11/1/79, p. 137, 10.4.1839: FO 60/65, No. 26, 16.4.1839. IO/R/1/81 p. 26, No. 69, 5.4.1839. No. 59, 15.8.1839, FO 60/67.
76 M. Nijhadirshadi, ed., *Asnad-i Khalij-i Fars*, 5, Idara-yi Intishar-i Asnad, 1375, pp. 468–471.
77 Robertson to McNeill, 10.5.1842, FO 248/108. FO 248/108, 13.5.1842.
78 Robertson to McNeill, 13.5.1842, FO 248/108.
79 No. 61, 16.9.1842, FO 60/90; FO 60/67, No. 92, 10.12.1842.
80 No. 92, 10.12.1842, FO 60/91.
81 Robertson to Sheil, 21.6.1842, FO 248/108.
82 No. 93, 25.8.1845, FO 60/115.
83 Robertson to Sheil, 21.6.1842, FO 248/108.
84 Kemball to Robertson in Robertson to Sheil, 19.1.1843, FO 248/108.
85 Robertson to Sheil, 1.1.1844, FO 248/113.
86 Robertson to Sheil, 1.1.1844, FO 248/113.
87 Robertson to McNeill, 14.4.1842, FO 60 248/99.
88 No 41, 6.4.1842, FO 60/87.
89 Robertson to Sheil, 2.8.1842, FO 248/108.
90 Robertson to Sheil, 29.6.1842, FO 248/108.
91 Robertson to Sheil, 3.11.1842, FO 248/108.
92 Kemball to Sheil, 21.9.1843, FO 248/113.
93 Kemball to Sheil, 6.10.1843, FO 248/113.
94 No. 89, 6.11.1843, FO 60/99.
95 Hennell to Sheil, 27.3.1844, FO 248/113.
96 Robertson to McNeill, 13.5.1842, FO 248/108.
97 Hennell to Farrant, 15.12.1848, FO 248/129
98 Grummon, *Chalesh*, pp. 193–4.
99 Kemball to Farrant, 15.5.1849, FO 248/138.
100 Hennell to Sheil, 8.1.1850, FO 248/138; No. 124, 19.10.1850, FO 60/153; Busse, *Qajar Rule*, pp. 294–5.
101 Mirza Muhammad Taqi Lisan al-Mulk Sipihr, *Nasikh al-tavarikh*, ed. J. Qa'im Maqami, Tehran 1337, III, pp. 124–5; Muhammad Ja'far Khurmuji, *Haqa'iq-i akhbar-i Nasiri*, ed. S.H. Khadiv Jam, 1363 edition Tehran, p. 87; Sa'adat, *Bushihr*, p. 124.
102 Hennell to Sheil, 16.10.1850, FO 248/138.

3

SHIRAZ: URBAN PROTEST AND THE BALANCE OF POWER IN FARS

In the course of the period under study, Shiraz changed. The growth in new communications systems – particularly the arrival of steam in the Persian Gulf in the 1860s, the opening of the Suez Canal in 1869, and the opening up of the Karun River to trade in 1888, together with the introduction of the telegraph in the 1860s – began to undermine the existing political configuration. Politics in Shiraz consisted of intermittent state control through manipulation of elite rivalries, the dominance of the family of Qavam al-Mulk in the city, and the Khans of the Qashqa'i in much of the countryside. Although state control was only marginally more secure by 1896, and Shiraz was only just beginning to be part of the world economy, the old consensus of city and tribes, town and country elites, was beginning to break down. This chapter looks at how urban politics, and more particularly urban protest, came to challenge that consensus and balance of power by the end of the nineteenth century.

Shiraz in the Nineteenth Century

As an urban centre, Shiraz has a long and distinguished history, above all as the birth place of the poets Sa'di and Hafez, but also of the mystic, Ruzbihan, and the philosopher, Mulla Sadra. At its apogee in the thirteenth century, it was a famous centre of the arts and learning, and it continued to prosper under the Safavids. Like other parts of Iran it suffered at the time of the Afghan invasion in 1722, but in the mid eighteenth century was so fortunate as to have an enlightened ruler, Karim Khan Zand, who ruled from 1752 to 1779. He chose it principally because it was centrally situated amongst the pasture-lands of the tribes on which he depended for his power.[1] Karim Khan embarked on a programme of public works, which included a citadel, administrative buildings, a mosque and an impressive covered bazaar. With the rise of the Qajars, the capital moved to Tehran, but Shiraz maintained a significant position as the centre of Fars province, and as a trade link between the Persian Gulf and the interior.

The fortunes of Shiraz fluctuated with those of the country in the nineteenth century, a fact reflected in the travellers' accounts, especially the estimates for the population. In the early nineteenth century, one informed guess was 40,000.[2] According to Morier, Shiraz had 7780 houses in all,[3] and he thought the population was 3800 households, a family constituting five people, making a total of 19,000. He then produced a calculation of 18,000 based on the level of consumption of bread. The estimate of 40,000 seems high for an urban centre in Iran at this period, even though Shiraz had been the capital under Karim Khan, so Morier's figure is likely to be closer to the truth, but it is impossible to say for sure. By the mid-nineteenth century Shiraz was estimated at 5,000 families or 30,000 people (a family in this case evidently being considered as about six people).[4] Afzal al-Mulk, who visited Shiraz in 1841, mentions the population as being around 30,000.[5] The British put the figure at 25,000, which seems low, in 1868.[6] A census carried out in 1883 estimated the population as 53,607,[7] and it would seem reasonable to assume that it went up in the 1870s and 1880s because of the huge growth of trade in that period. Sobotsinski put it at 30,000 in 1913,[8] an estimate which again might not be so far wrong because of the breakdown of order and the decline of trade after the Constitutional Revolution. From this picture it is not possible to draw firm conclusions, but it suggests that for the period under study the population was generally around 20,000–30,000, perhaps rising in the latter part of the nineteenth century.

The character of the city also varied over the period. At the beginning of the nineteenth century, Scott Waring, in what was probably an optimistic view, portrayed Shiraz as a lively place, on the whole well-regulated,[9] which had seen a revival in the local trade and agriculture of Fars, making it second only to Azarbaijan in terms of provincial prosperity.[10] He observed that, whereas in Britain men of rank could escape debts to tradesmen, because it was so difficult to bring a case against them, under the shari'a debtors were obliged to pay without regard to rank.[11] Shiraz was otherwise a city of streets so narrow that it was not possible to pass a donkey carrying wood on horseback, and the populace was too poor to be fashionable, a view shared by another traveller.[12] Morier, in 1818, was struck by Shiraz being less strict in its attitudes than other towns, giving as an example the fact that he was admitted to the bathhouse.[13] By chance he arrived in Shiraz at a time of discontent when there was unrest over the increased price of bread, the cause being a raised tax levy by the central government, so that the bazaars closed in protest.[14] The bazaaris then requested the Shaikh al-Islam to issue a *fatva* which might make it lawful to assassinate the shah's emissary, and conducted demonstrations outside the governor's palace.[15] The price of grain was lowered, but the bakers of the city were publicly bastinadoed. Such a style of pressure and unrest over prices marked the politics of the entire nineteenth century in Shiraz.

By the mid-century the streets of Shiraz were still reported as narrow and filthy, but the town was presented as more disorderly. The population was described as turbulent, and long accustomed to insurrection against governors who displeased it.[16] Wine was sold openly by the Armenians and drunk by some Muslims. According to Usscher there were ten theological schools and about fourteen large mosques, and Afzal al-Mulk mentions that there were ten districts, five Haidari and five Ni'mati, and that all had to pay an equal amount of tax of 4000 tomans under the seal of their *kadkhudas* (heads of quarters).[17] He says the houses were of stone, plaster and brick, and fruit trees grew in their courtyards. Abbott observed that the walls at this time were in bad condition, and much was ruined.[18] He counted 53 mosques, 64 bathhouses, 9 theological schools, and 15 caravanserais. Health was undermined by the stagnant water in the ditch surrounding the town, which was particularly putrid in summer. The living conditions were especially inimical to the health of Europeans, so that few were resident there for any length of time.

At this time there were hardly any manufactured goods, the principal ones being swords, daggers and knives, with a small amount of superior *khatamkari*.[19] Another source of trade for Fars in general was the export of horses to India, and Shiraz especially was much dependent on the Indian trade. Curzon, passing through at the end of the nineteenth century, commented on the lively bazaars, benefiting from the increased trade activity in Iran, and Shiraz in particular, as it was on a major trade route. He gave the chief imports as cotton fabrics from Britain, and exports as opium, noting also that local merchants were worried about the opening up of the Karun river.[20]

The Local Powers and Shiraz

Under the Qajars, Shiraz was generally ruled by a son of the shah as prince-governor, with the assistance of a vizier, also appointed from Tehran, an office held through much of this time by Abu'l Hasan Khan Mushir al-Mulk. Power, in the sense of command of the provincial military forces, was in the hands of the governor, whilst the vizier had responsibility for the tax administration. As elsewhere there was also a variety of local powers including, in the town, the mayor (*kalantar*), and the headmen of the quarters, (*kadkhuda*), as well as the 'ulama and merchants, supported by the guilds organisation. The office of mayor, at this period hereditary in the family of Qavam al-Mulk, was highly significant as its responsibilities included not only the collection of taxes but also the overseeing of the town administration, and above all, the curtailing of the influence of the tribes in Shiraz itself. There is no real evidence that he had any particular duties in providing justice for the underprivileged, but his general administrative responsibilities would have involved curbing oppression in response to complaints.

The countryside, especially the Zagros mountains, was dominated by another type of local power: the tribes, under the leadership of their khans. They had autonomous management of their affairs and, being composed of numbers of armed men, had a crucial role in the politics of

Fars. The most notable of the tribes was the great Qashqa'i confederation, which included among its clients many villages and other tribes, mostly Turkic speaking, like itself. Like other tribal confederations, that of the Qashqa'i had developed partly in response to the growth of the state bureaucracy to protect its interests, and partly as a matter of administrative convenience for the state itself. The leading Qashqa'i family, the Janikhani, owed its prominence to the privileges bestowed on it by Karim Khan Zand who dominated Shiraz from 1756 to 1779.[21] A second confederation was to make its appearance in the period in question, that of the Ilat-i Khamseh, (the Five Tribes, from the Arabic for five), that is the Arab tribes of central and south-eastern Fars, the Basiri (who were Persian speaking), and the Inalu, the Nafar and the Baharlu (all three of which spoke Turkic languages).[22]

However, the most detailed source on Shiraz during the nineteenth century – the reports of the British Agent in Shiraz – indicate that the Ilkhani (paramount chief) of the Qashqa'i did not hold much influence in Shiraz itself, although he had an urban base. On the one hand, the Ilkhani was expected to spend a considerable amount of time attending to the business of his tribe in the countryside. On the other hand, the government was wary of tribal influence in Shiraz itself. To some extent also the townsfolk controlled it themselves. In 1850, when the then Ilkhani died, the bazaars of Chaharsuq Sultani closed primarily on the orders of one of the *mujtahids* (leading clergy).[23] The Ilkhani's rivalry with Qavam and with the official governors, as well as the determination of the central government to curtail the power of the tribal leaders, nevertheless had a bearing on the politics of Shiraz. However, this impact is not always clear at the popular level, and is to some extent outside the scope of this study, which is not directly concerned with elite rivalry.

The Family of Qavam al-Mulk

The pivotal figure in the politics of Shiraz was the *kalantar* (mayor), Qavam al-Mulk, who had a highly significant role in managing popular pressure and protest. It is therefore perhaps useful to consider the origins of this family. As far as is known, one Haji Hashim became such a prominent man of affairs, seemingly a merchant, in Shiraz in the eighteenth century, that Nadir Shah held him in high regard.[24] After the death of Nadir Shah, Haji Hashim's son, Haj Muhammad Ibrahim became first an elder of the Haidari quarter of Shiraz, and then rose to the rank of *kalantar* (mayor) at the time of the Zands. At the fall of Lutfali Khan Zand, Haj Muhammad secured Shiraz for his rival, Aqa Muhammad Khan Qajar, for which he was made governor of Fars with the title of Beglerbegi. After the fall of Kerman, and on his ascension to the throne in 1785, Aqa Muhammad Khan appointed him Sadr-i 'Azam with the title of I'timad al-Daula. Fath 'Ali Shah, his successor in 1797, retained I'timad al-Daula as Sadr-i 'Azam, but with specific responsibilities. His family was granted land, and his brother and sons made heads of districts. For fourteen years he prospered as a servant of the state, until, because of criticism and jealousy, according to some, and oppression and extortion, according to others, he was removed from power in 1215/1800–1801 and executed. Other members of his family suffered the same fate, or were severely mutilated, so that they could not regain power. His eleven year old son, 'Ali Akbar, however survived, it is said because he was severely ill at the time of the disaster and not expected to live. For reasons that are not clear, 'Ali Akbar was subsequently appointed to a government post in Fars, and then became *kalantar* of Shiraz. In 1830, the title of Qavam al-Mulk was conferred on him, but he does not emerge as the main influence at popular level at this stage, possibly because of the role of one of the *mujtahids*, Haji Mirza Ibrahim. He proceeded to rebuild the family wealth, and it may be that lack of substantial means also explains his lesser influence before the 1840s. 'Ali Akbar Qavam al-Mulk played a considerable role in the politics of the city, principally by using the *lutis* to intimidate others of the populace, as will be discussed below.

In 1865 'Ali Akbar Qavam died, he of whom Khurmuji wrote that he was in shrewdness without equal, and in the execution of most matters, irreplaceable.[25] Indeed, subsequent Qavam al-Mulks were to uphold the family values and traditions, but were not to match 'Ali Akbar in sagacity. He had additionally profited since 1274/1857–8 from connections with the court in Tehran,[26] and at the time of his death he was reported to own 104 villages between Tehran and Bushire. The crowd which gathered for the funeral was the largest in living memory for such an occasion in Shiraz, a testimony to his power and influence,[27] if perhaps not entirely to the affection in which he was held.

At this time, the house of Qavam al-Mulk extended the threads of its influence into the countryside. 'Ali Akbar was succeeded by his fourth son, 'Ali Muhammad, who in 1868 was made governor of Darab and the Baharlu and Inalu tribes.[28] The appointment was primarily a result of Qavam's own ambitions, and of his rivalry with Mushir al-Mulk, Vizier of Fars. The latter was used by the central government both to control them and to mulct them by of eliciting *pishkish* (gifts) to secure its support. The appointment of 'Ali Muhammad Qavam al-Mulk was to lead to a long standing connection between Qavam al-Mulk and the so-called Khamseh tribes. From then on, they were his responsibility, though not continuously and permanently.[29] It should be noted, however, that the nineteenth century sources usually refer to the tribes associated with Qavam as 'the Arab tribes' or 'the Baharlu', the first clear reference to the Khamseh tribal confederation being in 1876.[30]

Thus it was that 'Ali Muhammad Qavam al-Mulk won power and authority through leadership of a substantial tribal group, whose members could be recruited into a personal armed and mounted militia that was independent of the various social and political factions in Shiraz.[31] The militia was employed at once to control Shiraz, and to outmanoeuvre his rivals, the Ilkhani of the Qashqa'i, and Mushir al-Mulk, vizier of the time. He had come a long way from the time, in the mid-nineteenth century, when 'Ali Akbar, Qavam al-Mulk was dependent on the roughs (*lutis*) of Shiraz for sufficient might to intimidate the populace and negotiate with other notables. He had further strengthened his position through marriage alliances.[32] In December 1883 'Ali Muhammad died, to be succeeded by his son, Muhammad Riza.[33]

Finance and Taxation

As elsewhere in Iran, relations between people and the various local authorities have to be understood against the background of an impecunious government endeavouring to extort as much taxation as possible from an indignant and reluctant populace. Although Fars was supposed to supply a substantial portion of the state revenue, there is not much evidence that anything like the expected amount came in. Battles over taxes were at the heart of many disorders, examples being in 1840–41, and 1850, when 27,000 tomans of taxes were due, and only 6000 collected.[34] Sheil commented that the state of the revenue was in general an excellent criterion of the authority of the government and of the condition of the provinces.[35]

By 1851, under the improvements in administration brought in by Amir Kabir, particularly the implementation of more regularity and order in the financial system, various chiefs in Fars who had never before contributed to state expenditure now paid taxes and the province was tranquil. Two years later, however, in 1853, irregularity and disorder had once again descended. By 1867–8 the customs of Shiraz and Bushire were in arrears and the central government was threatening to extort 6000 tomans from the local authorities.[36]

Problems over taxation were an integral part of the link between town and countryside, as is illustrated by the financial difficulties of 1874, when there was also a spate of robberies. The taxes demanded by the Shiraz authorities were beyond the means of the tribal chiefs, who thus took to the roads as their only way of retaliating against the local government, and also drawing the attention of the central authorities in a bid to bring the local ones to account. Of course the local authorities were under pressure from the capital to levy these very taxes, but from this financial system, trade and the townspeople suffered.

The burden of taxation also fell upon those it was easiest to squeeze: the merchants and tradesmen of the cities. In 1853 a group of them took sanctuary in protest in the Nau Mosque in Shiraz.[37] The governor tried in vain to negotiate an agreement on taxes with the bazaar community, who, however, refused to comply without an allocation to repair what they termed their ruined houses.[38] The governor next turned his attention to Qavam al-Mulk, who was at that point in charge of the administration of the coastal area and wished to resign from it. The governor refused to accept his resignation knowing full well that he could get 14000 tomans a year from him, but there was little chance of obtaining that amount from the impecunious tribal khans.[39]

Taxation became a particularly serious issue in the last decade of the century. In 1890 the remission of taxes of Fars was brought down to 30%, but the governor requested Amin al-Sultan to cancel this order, and taxes were demanded as usual.[40] By 1893, 200,000 tomans were due to the government on account of the taxes from Shiraz. The governor owed the Imperial Bank 80,000 tomans, and Haji Mirza Karim *sarraf* 60,000. The governor was embarrassed as to what to send the shah as his annual *pishkish* (gift), because the people[41] had refused to lend him 12,000 tomans and the bank had refused him an advance. In 1893 the Ilkhani had not remitted more than 900 tomans of the 20,000 that he owed, and a list of taxes owed by petty governors was required from Tehran.[42] The *sarrafs* (bankers) also had exchange problems because of the debasement of the coinage, a particular cause of popular unrest.[43] Prices continued high throughout the period, and one correspondent of the Ministry of Foreign Affairs reported that a lot of money had to be given to the 'ulama and *sayyids* (descendants of the Prophet), and that many people came to eat in his house.[44]

The financial situation in the period was exacerbated by occurrences of famine, plague and locusts. In 1871 famine brought dire problems to southern Iran. Nearly all the springs dried up, there was a bad harvest, and no bread, and the opium crop was an almost total failure. The bazaars closed and people were dying in large numbers.[45] As a result robbery, in itself a form of rebellion under such conditions, became an almost daily occurrence both inside and outside Shiraz, and desperate tribesmen drove off flocks of sheep and cattle or beasts of burden. The population was so devastated and debilitated, however, that there were no serious incidents of protest, and indeed at such times the government was wont to reduce or waive taxation. In 1891 much damage was done by locusts,[46] and the economic situation was also exacerbated by an excessive rainfall, which destroyed the summer crops.[47] In early 1892, the deputy governor took bonds from the bakers to sell bread at a lower rate. Bread then became unavailable for twentyfour hours until its price was restored.[48]

Popular Protest in the Middle of the Nineteenth Century

It was perhaps the tribal element in the population which made struggles over resources in Fars so formidable. Few cities in Iran despatched governors with such tumultuous regularity as Shiraz. Elsewhere, the turnover in governors tended to arise from the royal displeasure at the failure to remit the expected revenues, but in Shiraz, although taxation was also part of the problem, governors simply went because they could not control the city. As Hennell explained in 1840, on the arrival of a new governor, Nurallah, in Shiraz:

> So long as he refrains from interfering with the populace and priesthood of the city, he may perhaps be able to carry on the government, but I have little doubt of his experiencing the same treatment as all former governors have done, the instant his proceedings run counter to this influential body.[49]

Like Isfahan, and other places in the south, Shiraz was particularly disturbed in the late 1830s and 1840s, at the time of the first Herat war. In August 1839, for example, rebelliousness against government control manifested itself in a quarrel between the people of the city and the Azarbaijani soldiery linked to Mirza Ahmad Khan, principal administrator of Fars.[50] A highly organised rebellion began, including amongst others a sword-cutler, a dyer and a musket-maker,[51] and resulted in Mirza Ahmad Khan being driven from the town.[52] On 9th August 1839 a tumultuous crowd assembled in objection to his return and detained all the minor government officials, *mirzas*, *kadkhudas* and *mullas*, on their way to see the governor, tearing up papers and throwing away inkstands. In desperation, the prince-governor, specially dressed in military uniform, gave an order that the town should be destroyed and the people massacred, obliging two officials to point out that such a punishment was unjust, as the innocent would suffer with the guilty, and that would be against the wishes of the shah. Thereafter they were forced to leave the city,[53] leaving the people victorious in this particular round of negotiations, especially as the new governor had no power.

It was at this time that Muhammad Shah decided to crack down on disorders in the south, and marched to Isfahan. As part of the same design he summoned the chief *mujtahid* of Shiraz, Shaikh Abu Turab, to his presence. The *mujtahid* refused, and also declined to take himself to Kerbala. When the governor then ordered troops to eject him from Shiraz, the city elders objected, and the governor was obliged to desist.[54] Eventually Shaikh Abu Turab was brought to see the shah, and allowed in the end, as a compromise, to spend some time in Qum.[55]

It is to be noted that in accounts of the resistance of the community to the government during the previous two years, no mention is made of Haji Qavam, bearing out Hennell's comment that the people (i.e. principally the bazaar community) and the 'ulama had the influence to protest against the state and to resist it on their own account, rather than through any one individual. It would seem that the greatest influence over the populace in the period up to this point had been Haji Mirza Ibrahim *mujtahid*, who died in Rabi' I 1255/May–June1839.[56]

Meanwhile taxes were still well in arrears,[57] and in 1841 the shah appointed Farhad Mirza, his brother – and known for his stern measures –

as governor.[58] The *kadkhuda* of the quarter in which one affray took place was brought before the prince and summarily strangled, a form of punishment known as *'ibrat*, and intending to deter by example.[59] When Qavam al-Mulk failed to produce the culprits, he was beaten, imprisoned, his property and stable taken away, and his family confined to his house.[60] Hennell commented that the prince was now unlikely to be able to keep order in Fars without Azerbaijani soldiers, as his position would be weakened by the anger of Qavam.[61] However, Qavam was shortly restored to his position.[62] Taxes were still in arrears, and the vizier of Fars was ordered to pay 50,000 tomans in revenue, and, being unable to do so, took sanctuary.[63] In addition, the principal government accountant of Fars, Nasir al-Mulk, was taken to Tehran, because of failure to balance his accounts. The system oppressed the oppressors as well as the poor.

By 1846 Shiraz was quiet, amongst other reasons because it had acquired a reasonably able governor in Mirza Husain Khan, who, however, favoured the middle over the poorer social groups, and was strong on protecting property. He dealt firmly and severely with robberies, but was accessible, and listened to grievances with exemplary patience. With regard to taxation, he was of course oppressive, but 'given the large sums paid as presents for his appointment, . . . other than this could hardly be expected'. As Hennell commented, 'No chief or head of district thinks of paying even the legitimate dues of government until he has undergone a certain degree of pressure.'[64]

From 1848 the poorer social groups, neglected by the governor, had found a champion in 'Ali Akbar Qavam al-Mulk, who began to emerge as the major force in Shirazi politics. In the immediately succeeding years it was he, probably through distribution of largesse, rather than the 'ulama, who exerted greatest influence over the poor. Qavam used his followers to embarrass the governor of Fars, Husain Khan Nizam al-Daula. He condoned their plunder of the property of the wealthier groups and they used him to secure them protection from the state, particularly its taxes.[65] The shopkeepers, on the other hand, had no one to look to for protection, but were afraid of the rougher elements of society.[66] Nizam al-Daula had further incurred the displeasure of the Ilbegi of the Qashqa'i (another major khan owing his appointment to the government), who was encamped seven miles from Shiraz with a tribal force, and had a grievance over taxation.[67] Qavam and his unruly collaborators made common cause with the Ilbegi, and, with his tacit support, the chiefs of the town roughs surrounded the governor, and demanded his removal. Another governor was rapidly appointed, so town and tribe, for once united, managed to dispose of an unpopular government official.[68]

As a result of the weakness of the government, a village named Siwund was plundered by the Qashqa'i. The villagers, realising that this arose from the alliance of the Ilbegi and Qavam, came to Shiraz seeking justice, led by their headman, Mulla Rahim.[69] The shah's emissary, Ahmad Khan, said this was unnecessary and that he would rectify the matter, at which point the following dialogue ensued:

> Mulla Rahim: Neither you nor Haji Qavam have the power to recover our property.
>
> Qavam: Have you sown your seed that you (have the time to) come here to talk nonsense?
>
> Mulla Rahim: Where do we get the seed?[70]
>
> Qavam: Do not be impertinent.
>
> Mulla Rahim: When can we speak out? We have nothing to lose. If you kill us, it will be just what we want.

Qavam was on the point of having him bastinadoed, when his fellow villagers seized the pole and stick from the *farashes*.[71]

> Ahmad Khan (shah's messenger): It is not right to beat them.

This story illustrates a point made by Malcolm, that for all the oppressive nature of the system, there existed a certain openness of speech:

> A stranger, unacquainted with the nature of the government and the latitude of speech it permits in the persons it oppresses, is surprised to hear the meanest inhabitant of a town venting imprecations against his superiors, even against the shah. These extraordinary ebullitions of passion, which are very common among the lower orders, generally pass unheeded.[72]

Qavam, however, was not oblivious to the discontent of the merchants, who by this time felt unable to leave their houses, nor to its significance. Having used the poorer class to establish his influence over the situation, he began securing and restoring some of the lost property, thereby intending no doubt to secure the goodwill of merchants and tradesmen.[73] By January 1850, Qavam was effectively master of Shiraz, and it was reported that he and the Ilkhani of the Qashqa'i had each agreed to give the governor 1000 tomans a month, in an arrangement by which Qavam was acknowledged as controlling the city, and the Ilkhani the countryside.[74]

Qavam's influence depended much on his ability to mediate between the populace and the government. For example, on one occasion he prepared a receipt to be sealed by the different traders to the effect that they had received 4000 tomans from the prince on account of recent plunder of the bazaars of Charsuq Sultani, (which some signed and some did not).[75] He also mediated between social groups, so that when some shops were attacked and damaged by *lutis*, complaints were made to Qavam, and he promised to restore the property if the claimants swore to the amount.[76] An attempt by Qavam to win favour with the shah, by illuminating the bazaars of Shiraz at the capture of Mashhad, was defeated by all the tradesmen shutting up shop and taking *bast* (sanctuary) in the Nau Mosque, complaining of his exaction (as Mayor).[77] The cleric Shaikh Abu Turab intervened and achieved a compromise whereby one bazaar only was illuminated. Thus when he attempted to ingratiate himself with the government the populace used the opportunity to make points of their own.

The Impact of the Growing Foreign Presence

By the 1880s the economic picture in the south of Iran had changed completely. The volume of trade had grown greatly since the mid-nineteenth century. Between the 1860s and 1913, the total trade of Iran quadrupled,[78] whilst imports for Shiraz increased massively between 1887–1896, though exports seem to have fallen.[79] Prices rose by nearly double between 1880 and 1890, but they caused much more unrest in the 1890s than in the 1880s, suggesting that the major rise took place in the later decades, particularly after the Iranian economy got into difficulty over its dependency on silver, at a time when the world value of that commodity declined.[80] Trade via the Persian Gulf greatly expanded following the opening of the Karun River in 1888.[81] Whilst Iranian merchants profited from trade to the extent that many of them became substantially wealthy by between 1870 and 1900, they were also conscious during this period that foreign merchants were making even greater profits, a source of growing discontent during the period. They complained vociferously to the government of the problems confronting Iranian merchants in competing with foreigners, and of their lack of legal rights by comparison.[82]

From the mid-nineteenth century the European presence in Iran had grown, particularly as a result of the introduction of the telegraph in the 1860s.[83] It produced a rise in suspicion of foreigners and a sense that Shi'i religion and culture were threatened, though such sentiments were not new. From the beginning of the nineteenth century at least many of the 'ulama had opposed contact between Iranians and infidels, a means at once of guarding Islam, and of raising their prestige with the poorer classes. In 1850 in Shiraz a contretemps occurred when six European men were allowed to inspect the Hamam-i Vakil (Vakil Baths) in Shiraz, which led to complaints to both the governor and to Qavam, by Shaikh Abu Turab, the Imam Jum'a.[84]

In 1867, there was an attack on the British interpreter on his way home. The assailant was an *akhund* (cleric) who abused the interpreter in terms, 'though current – I understand – among Persian men and women', he considered too bad to repeat.[85] The attack was linked to the cleric's annoyance at a group of Armenians playing lively music in their house, and his instigation of an assault on them by a group of soldiers. The governor chastised the soldiers involved, but admitted to being afraid to punish a cleric as it would cause a riot, and disturb public order, demonstrating how the 'ulama were able to voice their opinions, and those of their following, and impose their views on the government. Alison commented that there had been a growth in ill-feeling in Shiraz recently towards foreigners and Christians in general.[86] He also observed that the mob of Shiraz was violent and the clerics beyond the control of any authority. It would seem that suggests that the influence of Qavam over the lower social classes had weakened, and that of the 'ulama had grown, probably as a result of Qavam's increased dependence on the tribes of which he was leader, as opposed to the *lutis*.

This fear and suspicion of foreigners and their intentions continued to grow, mixed with worries about the changes that technology was bringing. In 1889, at least some of the people of Shiraz were concerned over the opening of the Karun River and the appointment of a Russian Consul General in Mashhad, believing it would be to the disadvantage of Iran.[87] This concern for the fate of Iran at the hands of foreigners led over the period to a number of attacks on those more closely associated with them: the Armenians, and more particularly, the Jews. In 1889, after the murderer of a Jew was punished by Muhammad Riza Qavam al-Mulk, Sayyid 'Ali Akbar, the principal scourge of the minorities, sent some men to the house of one of the inhabitants of Shiraz, and seized some Jewish musicians whose instruments were then destroyed. Sayyid 'Ali Akbar, the favoured *mujtahid* of the poorer classes, was, however, the only one who ill-treated the Jews.[88]

Sayyid 'Ali Akbar was also active in resisting missionary activity in Shiraz. This emanated originally from the Church Missionary Society in Isfahan, and he applied to the governor to have its members expelled. A large crowd milled through the bazaars and streets, causing fear of disorder.[89] Although attempts at restraint were made by both Iranian and British authorities, both sides refused to moderate their zeal. The missionaries declared themselves ready for martyrdom, and Haji Muhammad Isam'il, the *sarraf* (banker) incited the Shirazis to jihad, for which he was bastinadoed by Qavam al-Mulk.

The Crisis over the Tobacco Concession 1891–2

On the eve of the political crisis over the Tobacco Concession, all the features of that crisis were present in the politics of Shiraz before it occurred. The merchants were complaining about foreign entrepreneurs securing special privileges. The 'ulama were angry and concerned about the implications for Islam of the growing foreign presence and influence in the country. The authorities were caught between obdurate local opinion and equally obdurate foreign pressure to disregard local sensibilities. Both sides were organised, the Iranians through the bazaar networks, even in the face of the most powerful personage in Shiraz. Both sides were using modern technology, i.e. the telegraph, to advance their cause.

The first clear report of disquiet over the Tobacco Concession in Shiraz itself came in early 1891, when the merchants expressed unease over the Concession granted to the British.[90] By April, evidently at the instigation of the merchants, there was much agitation amongst the 'ulama, particularly Sayyid 'Ali Akbar, who was openly preaching against the British.[91] Letters telling the 'ulama to act to prevent the implementation of the Concession had also been sent to them from Tehran. These were reportedly from the connections of Malkum Khan, and placards had been put up in Shiraz evidently under the influence of his paper, *Qanun*. A number of merchants, already seriously in debt, were threatened by the Tobacco Concession agent, and Sayyid 'Ali Akbar presented their case from the pulpit with great feeling. He called for a jihad, weeping, and then abruptly descended from the pulpit because he was too moved to continue.[92] His sermons were reported to be inspired by articles in *Akhtar*.[93]

The problem facing the shah was that if he came down hard, he risked a popular uprising, but if he acted irresolutely, the people would take it as a sign of weakness and grow bolder.[94] There was considerable support for the cause against the tobacco company from the poorer classes. The pressure against the Concession built up to the point where there was riot, with threats against the telegraph officials, and Sayyid 'Ali Akbar was expelled from Shiraz. He was in fact kidnapped by Qavam on the orders of the chief minister, 'Ali Asghar Amin al-Sultan, set on a horse and dispatched to Basra. There he encountered Jamal al-Din al-Afghani, with whom he is said to have collaborated, before he went on to Samarra to the home of his father-in-law, Mirza Hasan Shirazi, the principal *mujtahid* of the 'Atabat.[95]

The Government also had problems because of the crowd intercepting its telegrams. When news came that Sayyid 'Ali Akbar was to be exiled, the bazaars closed and placards were posted protesting at his banishment.[96] As a result of an order from Shirazi in September 1891 that people should not let their houses to Europeans, nor have any dealings with them over tobacco, both the governor of Shiraz and Qavam al-Mulk threatened the 'ulama and the bazaaris not to go to a meeting to hear that order read. Rukn al-Daula, the governor, was by now informing the central government that much of the trouble emanated from Qavam, and his handling of the political problems of Shiraz. It should be added that Qavam was in danger of seeing his own revenues as a grower of tobacco diminish.[97]

When Shirazi's ban reached Shiraz it was placarded on the walls round the city. Caught between people and government, Qavam tried to placate and propitiate elements of the population. On 13 January 1892 the Concession was abolished. The people of Shiraz, like those in other cities, had joined a movement against what they perceived as giving the country's resources to foreigners, and had successfully reversed government policy. The withdrawal of the Concession was marked by demonstrations against foreigners, and requests that Christians be expelled from the town, especially the theological students.[98] In the event, the principal victims were a group of Russian rope-dancers, and a photographer who had taken photos of women. They were forced to leave town.[99]

The Fall of Qavam al-Mulk

In March 1892 Sayyid 'Ali Akbar passed through Isfahan on his way back to Shiraz from the 'Atabat. His imminent arrival having been announced from the pulpit in all the mosques, a procession of people, consisting of notables, 'ulama, merchants, tradesmen, and women, as well as men, went to meet him.[100] His prestige was much enhanced by the *fatva*, which was attributed by the people to his influence, since Shirazi was his father-in-law.[101] He was effectively the chosen leader of a large proportion of the people of Shiraz. The ongoing struggle between Qavam and Sayyid 'Ali Akbar and the people of Shiraz now began in earnest, with a great many complaints lodged against Qavam with the governor, Rukn al-Daula, as the populace played on the rivalry between the governor and Qavam. Qavam threatened to have Sayyid 'Ali Akbar killed if he preached against him, whereupon the *sayyid* promptly gave a sermon saying Qavam was from an infidel family and in the pay of foreigners.[102]

In May 1892, Muhammad Riza Qavam al-Mulk, fearing for his position, put 300 riflemen round his house to protect himself.[103] It was in vain. He was seized by Rukn al-Daula, imprisoned and then bastinadoed, with the intention of extorting money from him.[104] He was released on the orders of the shah, and departed at once to Tehran bearing gifts to express his gratitude. Many of the merchants and small traders of Shiraz wrote to the shah expressing their satisfaction with the governor for relieving them from Qavam's oppression.[105] Qavam, however, still had his supporters in Shiraz, and on his release from prison and return home, he had been received with acclamation by the women of his quarter.[106]

The fall of Qavam al-Mulk destabilised the tribes of Fars. The precise financial connections of Qavam al-Mulk and the tribes he administered are not known, but with his position in Shiraz and links with the court in Tehran, he acted probably as a beneficial intermediary between them and the state, especially over tribal levies and taxation. Since they formed a significant part of his power base it is also likely that he used his vast wealth to provide them with gainful occupation, for example, acting as his bodyguard and personal militia.[107] Riza Khan and Husain Khan, two powerful chiefs of the Arab tribes, went into revolt, and looted the country to the east and north east of Shiraz.[108] Their revolt in turn brought down the prince-governor of Fars, Rukn al-Daula, who was recalled to Tehran on the grounds of maladministration. The provinces of Kerman and Bushire were drawn into the conflict, as the governors became occupied with pursuing the Arabs, and also the Baharlu, who had been driven into rebellion, and the roads from the coast to the interior were closed.

In March 1893 Qavam al-Mulk was reported as returning to Shiraz to exert his influence to restore order.[109] From the time of his return he made himself unpopular by raising the price of bread (possibly a necessity), fining the inhabitants and billeting his Baharlu horsemen in people's houses.[110] Within a few weeks, the population was so discontented that on 12th May a major revolt broke out. Three days later all of Shiraz were in the telegraph office complaining of the ill-treatment by Qavam al-Mulk, and demanding his removal.[111] The crowd, numbering fifteen to twenty thousand men and women, remained weeping, beating their breasts and crying, 'Ya 'Ali' (Oh 'Ali!) and 'Ya Sayyid al-Shahada' (referring to Imam Husain). They also suspended copies of the Qur'an from the telegraph office crying out, 'We are Muslims (i.e. the government is unrighteous).'[112] They swore that they were not in revolt against the government, but against Qavam, but if the new governor, Nizam al-Saltana, was determined to protect him, they did not want him either.

The governor felt he dared not fire on them because of the presence of *sayyids* and *mullas*, foreigners and Jews, and so tried to placate them by promising to lower the price of bread (then high), raise the value of silver, and expel the Arabs and the Baharlu, who had returned with Qavam.[113] However, the people unanimously ignored these promises and insisted they did not want Qavam as mayor, thereby forcing the governor to remove him. They also asked that he be exiled from Shiraz, but the shah ordered that they be dispersed by force. However, when the Kazzaz and Khalij regiments[114] were ordered to attack on 18th May, they sided with the people, saying as long as they respected the shah, the soldiers would not fight them for the sake of Qavam al-Mulk and the Arabs and the Baharlu.

Qavam brought in his tribal militia to quash the revolt, but they were promptly dispersed by the mutinous regular troops. However, though the rebels were armed, and many riflemen had joined them, they pointedly refrained from using their arms. An attempt by the governor to use the 'ulama to persuade the people to disperse also failed, and the governor therefore had to promise to exile Qavam. A final telegram arrived from the shah promising that the price of bread would come down, that of silver coin would be fixed, and Qavam would be expelled from the province of Fars. The crowd stayed at the telegraph office until he had left Shiraz. At the instigation of Nizam al-Saltana, representation was made to Sayyid 'Ali Akbar, and a letter obtained from him asking the people to disperse.[115] This protest had in effect been a victory for the people.

The government was faced with the problem of finding someone to take responsibility for the Khamseh tribes in the absence of Qavam. Saham al-Mulk was summoned from Tehran to be appointed governor of the Baharlu, the Arab tribes and Darab, in succession to Qavam, but the Arab tribes refused to accept his authority.[116] This was probably because he did not bring either the financial advantages or the connections, which could improve their lot. Riza Khan reverted to rebellion and government forces were sent in pursuit, eventually killing him and restoring order.[117]

Qavam was also missed in Shiraz, where at least some of the people began to feel the uncomfortable burden of dealing with the central government without their broker and mediator, especially as the governor, Nizam al-Saltana, was a strict tax collector. In March of 1894 they petitioned the shah to send Qavam back, and were immediately punished and expelled by Nizam al-Saltana.[118] The central government, however, did not feel able to bring back Qavam, and he was sent as governor to the Persian Gulf ports.

Nizam al-Saltana continued to struggle to raise taxes from the populace of Fars. In order to shame the Shaikh al-Islam, who had failed to pay his dues, he sent a band[119] to play at his door, proximity to popular music being abhorrent to a member of the clergy. In addition, the petty governors and also the bakers together owed 70,000 tomans in taxes, whereas the tribes were refusing to pay 35,000 tomans of what they owed. As a result, Nizam al-Saltana was recalled as governor, and replaced by Rukn al-Daula (previously removed). After the latter's arrival in 1894, he appointed his stepson as governor of Neyriz. However, as soon as taxes in the form of a *pishkish* (gift) were requested, a number of inhabitants fled to Yazd and Kerman, so he had to be recalled.[120] The people of Neyriz also refused to pay their taxes, and dispatched seven governors in seven months.[121]

The Emergence of Reform

In Shiraz itself a new form of foreign intrusion was causing the inhabitants to mobilise. The *sarrafs* had become much dissatisfied at the establishment of a branch of the Imperial Bank in Shiraz, and the merchants of Isfahan, where there was similar trouble, had written to those of Shiraz asking them to boycott the bank.[122] The right to issue bank notes was much resented,[123] affecting as it did the *sarrafs* and suggesting control of the economy was passing to foreigners. The Shiraz merchants formed their own company to establish a bank, and some considered that the Imperial Bank issue was causing more trouble than the Tobacco Concession.[124] These problems over the Imperial Bank came to a head in December 1895, in particular because it was blamed for the economic crisis,[125] which in reality derived largely from the fall in the price of silver. There was fierce resistance to the Bank both by local bankers and merchants whose interests were affected, and more broadly, through a wider popular perception that the economy of the country was passing out of Iranian control.[126]

In an attempt to manage the situation a council, known as the Majlis-i Istintaq (the Council of Interrogation) of 'ulama and notables was established by the governor Nazim al-Daula, and met each week for three days to look into the people's problems.[127] The governor chose Sa'id al-Saltana, Amir Tuman (divisional commander), as head of the Council, whilst 'Azar al-Saltana was elected by the people (doubtless meaning mainly merchants) and Haji Mirza Muhammad Taqi Fasa'i by the 'ulama. The commercial community attempted a response by establishing its own trading companies, encouraged by the Calcutta based newspaper, *Habl al-Matin*, which promoted mergers between the companies to ward off foreign control.[128] The Council, known as the *'adalatkhana* (House of Justice) of Fars attended to the problems of the people. *Habl al-Matin* described it as a new initiative inspired by European practice to investigate people's problems.[129] In the 1880s there had been a Council for the Redress of Grievances functioning in Tehran but that had been more of a government initiative, and had both a wider and more personal remit.[130] However, the Shiraz Council would have been perceived as at least partially having the function to redress grievances.

The movement for reform kept up its momentum. The governor was praised for organising repairs, the cleaning of the town, and also for *rifah* (welfare), a novel term for those days.[131] The Council now had other members including Mas'ud al-Daula for the *nizam*,[132] Aqa Beglerbegi for the *divan-i 'ala*,[133] and, most significantly Haji Mirza Mahmud Mu'in al-Tujjar and Aqa Sayyid Mihdi Tajir for the *millat*, (a term meaning community, or people, which later came to mean the nation). Mu'in al-Tujjar was, of course, one of the leading figures of the Constitutional movement of 1906. Sa'id al-Saltana was reported as working conscientiously on the wages of the soldiers specifically, and the endeavours of the Council met with general approval, their courtesy being especially commended.[134] However, progress was interrupted when the shah died in May 1896, and Shiraz went into a state of confusion and disorder.[135] Eventually Qavam now restored to his role of mediator as the most effective agent between the government and the troublesome populace of Shiraz, persuaded the people to disperse from the mosque on the shah's orders.[136]

At this stage the assembly appears to have acquired a new incarnation, the Majlis-i Muhtarram (the Honourable Assembly), still composed of 'ulama, notables and merchants. Twelve of its leaders took an oath not to spare life or property in an attempt to carry out its purpose, which was seemingly to restore order.[137] The assembly caused the removal once more of the governor, Rukh al-Daula, and the British Shiraz Agent implied that it had other plans, not clarified. It rapidly acquired support from the poorer classes in the expectation that it would alleviate demands for taxes.[138] Effective management of the city remained, however, with Qavam. When the bazaars closed in August because some soldiers caused disorder, it was Qavam who punished the soldiers, forced the bazaars to open and arranged compensation.[139]

Qavam thus survived because the state and populace still needed him, principally to broker their financial disagreement. From the point of view of the state Qavam was useful as a balance against other local powers, whose rivalry with him both reduced their authority and provided opportunities to extract further taxes in the form of gifts for the retention of office. Qavam also kept the influence of the Qashqa'i khans to a minimum in Shiraz itself. His association with the Baharlu and the Arab tribes, from the government point of view, released him from dependence on disorderly *lutis* to buttress his position in Shiraz. Paradoxically, however, it weakened his hold on the people of Shiraz because he was less entrenched in local politics, less vulnerable to pressure from them, and therefore less sensitive to their concerns. To say that the comparatively small and loose Khamseh was properly a counterweight to the Qashqa'i in the politics of Fars would be to fatally overestimate their significance in the districts.

* * *

The relationship of people and state in Shiraz was one of a subtle process of relentless negotiation and bargaining, which occasionally broke down in the form of urban protest. The government strove to raise the maximum in taxation by whatever means it could, or at least to avoid lowering the price of bread. The people protested when the burden became in their view intolerable, with the implicit threat of worse to come if the government did not desist. The relentless non-payment of expected taxes and departure in quick succession of the governors who had failed to raise them bear testimony to the power of popular protest. In the course of the struggle various lower social groups together or singly made use of elite power struggles, and particularly the weaknesses of the state or local notables, to negotiate better conditions for themselves. Sometimes the government was forced to bring in troops, but more often the situation was resolved by some sort of compromise, whereby, for example, the more lawless members of the populace were punished, the government lowered the price of bread (at least for a while), and the member of the 'ulama who had acted as spokesman was despatched to Kerbala or Mashhad but did not get further than Qum.

In the course of these protests the populace could evoke the events of Kerbala to imply that the government was oppressive and illegitimate and therefore not worthy of obedience (thereby mobilising support, implying that they would resort to even more troublesome, costly disorder and hinting that the government might be overthrown). A major example of the use of the language and imagery of Kerbala occurs in the revolt in Shiraz in 1893. There may well have been others, but the elite and British sources on which so much depends for study of the subject were little concerned with reporting popular language.

At the end of the nineteenth century, into this struggle of state and society, crept the beginnings of the influence of modernity, in the sense of new style economic and political systems, and organisation and technology. Rapid growth in trade brought novel commercial methods, and their implementation caused dislocation in a society accustomed to different and long established practices. In particular the wealth gained for Shiraz from being on a main trade route began to slip away from the opening of the Karun in 1888, as the transportation of goods to some extent by-passed the city. Foreign banks and the establishment of foreign firms put the bulk of the trade in the hands of Europeans. Europeans also appeared in the form of bank and Tobacco Concession officials, and missionaries. If the telegraph changed the rules in the sense that the shah was able to make his officials immediately accountable, it also enabled the populace to circumvent the local authorities and appeal directly to Tehran, as they did during the Tobacco Concession.

The revolt in Shiraz in 1893–4 in particular demonstrated the emergence of modernity, influenced no doubt through the reading of such publications as *Akhtar* and *Qanun*, but taking more than one form. On the one hand the attitude towards the Jews and Armenians demonstrates a wider sense of community than the local religious one on the part of some of the participants, probably those associated with educated state officials, as well as a more secular point of view. The unusually organised and active role of women would seem to be part of this development. On the other hand a new sense of identity and political direction had for some time been developing in the notion of Islam in danger, of the need to protect the shari'a and providing the force to support it. This militant more totalist view shows in the notable rise in the attacks on the playing of music, the drinking of alcohol, and upon the Jews – hitherto largely victimised at the time of political crisis but now singled out as a link with foreigners.

Both these forces and all social groups contributed to the creation of the Majlis, at once a fusion of customs of consultation to be observed as regularly practised throughout the nineteenth century at the popular level in Iran, and of new ideas on political organisation and representation coming from Europe. Its configuration and preoccupations with the need for collaboration and discussion, with the problems of mismanagement, particularly of the finances, of finding ways to change the old system, prefigure much of the agenda of the early participants in the Constitutional Revolution. Particularly significant is the role of Mu'in al-Tujjar in both organisations, and the use of the term *'adalatkhana* (house of justice).[140]

Finally, the fall of Qavam al-Mulk in 1893–4 was significant in that it represented an early major challenge by the forces of modernity to the old order. His opponents recognised his pivotal role in the established system of control, and in the delicate structure of checks and balances by which the Qajars ruled Fars. In the end it was too early to replace him. On the one hand, at the local level there was no one else with his connections and skills to manage Shiraz and to balance the needs of the different groups in the city, on the other, the centre was not strong enough to rule without the assistance of local powers. It would take till the 1920s before state and people finally dispensed with Qavam, and his functions became gradually replaced by modern institutions. In the meantime, by 1911 he had acquired the title of Ilkhani of the Khamseh and was on very good terms with the British.

Notes

1. Malcolm, *The History of Persia*, London 1839, II, p. 84. According to one estimate the population of Shiraz had been around 50,000 in the later eighteenth century. See Issawi, *Iran*, p. 26.
2. Macdonald Kinneir, *Memoir*, p. 64.
3. Morier, *A Second Journey through Persia, Armenia and Asia Minor*, London 1818, p. 110.
4. Brugsch, *Reise der K. Preussischen Gesandtschaft nach Persien 1860–61*, Leipzig 1862, p. 180. Abbott put it at 30,000 in 1840. FO 251/42, p. 83.
5. Mirza Ghulam Husain, Afzal al-Mulk, 'Safarnama-yi Isfahan', in *Dau safarnama-yi junub-i Iran*, ed. S.A. Al-i Davud, Tehran 1368, p. 48.
6. Issawi, *Iran*, p. 28, quoting Thomson to Alison 18.4.1868, see also Abbott in FO 60/165.
7. See discussion in C.E. Davies, *A History of the Province of Fars during the Later Nineteenth Century*, D.Phil. Oxford 1984, p. 507 quoting Fasa'i, *Farsnama*, and Shiraz Agent 24 July 1893, FO 248/577, and 21 Jan. 1894, FO 248/601.
8. Issawi, *Iran*, p. 33.
9. Scott Waring *Sheeraz*, pp. 64, 68–9, 72.
10. Amanat, *Resurrection*, p. 21.
11. Scott Waring, *Sheeraz*, pp. 30, 56. He also noted the lines of a popular chant sung by the porters: If you can, say 'Ya 'Ali', If you are weary in spirit, say 'Ya 'Ali' *Sheeraz*, p. 43.
12. Macdonald Kinneir, *Memoir*, p. 62.
13. Morier, *Journey*, p. 59.
14. Morier, *Journey*, p. 102. Note that this is an unusually early reference to such closure of the bazaars, which Morier describes as a common practice in the east.
15. He was considered to be in league with the mother of the prince-governor, one of the shah's wives, who lived in Shiraz and greatly enriched herself through commerce and monopolies. Every now and then she negotiated a visit to Tehran, for which she was required to make a generous gift to the shah, who 'permits her to return and reside with him as his wife'. Scott Waring, *Sheeraz*, pp. 61, 102.
16. Ussher, J., *A Journey from London to Persepolis*, London 1865, p. 510–12.; Abbott, Shiraz, FO 251/42, p. 85.
17. Afzal al-Mulk, 'Safarnama', p. 48.
18. Abbott, FO 251/42 pp. 81–5 The decayed fortifications are also noted in No. 72, 1.9.1837, FO 60/50.
19. Veneer made up of mosaic patterns in tiny pieces.
20. G.N. Curzon, *Persia*, II, pp. 99–100.
21. Beck, 'Tribes', p. 204.
22. On the Khamseh generally see A.M. Najafi, *Vaqayi'-i ilat-i Khamsa*, Tehran 1380. Darab was the main urban centre and winter quarters of this particular tribal area.
23. Shiraz Agent, encl. in No. 383, 16.10.1850, FO 248/138.
24. Muhammad Ja'far Khurmuji, *Haqa'iq-i akhbar-i Nasiri*, ed. S.H. Khadiv Jam,

Tehran 1363, p. 309–12, and *Nuzhat al-Akhbar, tarikh va jughrafiyya-yi Fars*, ed. S.A. Al-i Davud, Tehran 1380., p. 553. See also Busse, *Qajar Rule*, pp. 219 ff.
25 Khurmuji, *Haqa'iq*, p. 312.
26 Ibid., p. 235.
27 No. 83, 11.8.1865, FO 60/290. Brugsch described him as the most influential and dangerous subject in the whole province, saying that he held the people in fear of him, and pursued his goals with great surety of purpose. *Persien*, p. 196.
28 He had had some previous connection with the Baharlu and Inalu, as, by 1868, the local *kalantars* and *kadkhudas* were agitating against his administration (which doubtless involved disagreements over taxes) Hasan Husaini Fasa'i, *Farsnama-yi Nasiri*, ed. M. Rastgar Fasa'i, Tehran 1367, I, p. 831–2. The governorship was taken from Qavam and given to 'Ali Akbar Khan, the son-in-law of his enemy Mushir al-Mulk. However, a *pishkish* to the government in Tehran secured its return to Qavam. See also Khurmuji, *Haqa'iq*, p. 312. The account in this chapter of Qavam's connections with the Khamseh is taken from the contemporary nineteenth century sources.
29 He was removed from his governorship, for example in 1291/1874, A.K. Saidi Sirjani, *Vaqayi'-i ittifaqiyya*, Tehran 1362, p. 28, and restored by Mu'tamid al-Daula in 1876, Busse, *Qajar Rule*, p. 387.
30 Busse, *Qajar Rule*, p. 387. Many secondary sources in both Persian and English state that his appointment to the governorship of the Khamseh was an attempt by the government of Nasir al-Din Shah to create a counterweight to the Qashqa'i, as part of a policy of balancing power in Fars (see for example and most notably P. Oberling *The Qashqa'i Nomads of Fars*, The Hague 1974, p. 65). I have not been able to find a single primary source from the period that refers to an appointment for this year or puts Oberling's construction on the role of the Khamseh, though doubtless the government of Fars from time to time played the tribal groups, and, more particularly, their leaders, off against one another.
31 See Shiraz Agent, No. 109, 18.6.1891, FO 248/533 for an example. On his connections with the tribes see Shiraz Agent, No. 182, 21.11.1889, FO 248/492; Shiraz Agent, No. 188, 13.12.1890, FO 248/513; Shiraz Agent, No. 174, 14.11.1890, FO 248/513; and No. 89, 18.5.1891, FO 248/533; see also No. 6, 18.1.1891, FO 248/533.
32 C.J. Wills, *In the Land of the Lion and the Sun*, London 1883, p. 272.
33 Sirjani, *Vaqayi'*, p. 204–5, and index p. 750.
34 Shiraz Agent, encl. in No. 191, 16.5.1850, FO 248/138.
35 No. 22, 12.2.1851, FO 60/158.
36 SAM 295003369, 1,AB675, dated 184/11867–8.
37 Shiraz Agent, encl. in No. 267, 15.9.1853, FO 248/150. There were at this time about ten leading merchants in Shiraz, all of those listed being Muslim. There were English merchants in Shiraz, but the foreign presence was not to grow until the 1880s.
38 Shiraz Agent, encl. in No. 321, 15.10.1853, FO 248/150
39 Shiraz Agent, encl. in No. 383, 15.12.1853, FO 248/150.
40 Shiraz Agent, No.134, 15.8.1890, FO 248/513.
41 Probably meaning the merchants and possibly notables.
42 No. 477, 15.3.1893, FO 248/576.
43 Nizam al-Saltana, *Khatirat*, I, p. 183.
44 MFA 1314 B28 F2 N128, unknown (but possibly Nazim al-Daula) to unknown, 2 Jamadi I 1314/9 October 1896.
45 No. 399, 18.4.1871, FO 248/271.
46 Shiraz Agent, No. 109, 18.6.1891, and No. 124, 14.7.1891, FO 248/533.
47 Shiraz Agent, No.193, 14.10.1891, FO 248/534

48 Shiraz Agent, No. 277, 14.3.1892, FO 248/555
49 IO, R/15/1/93, Hennell to the governor of India, No. 76, 15.6.1840.
50 Busse, *Qajar Rule*, p. 262ff. Encl. in No. 58, 15.8.1839, FO 60/67. Both administration and payment of dues were a problem elsewhere in Fars. The shah was requested to order tenants who leased *vaqf* (religiously endowed) land to pay their rent according to a previous rescript, as it was much in arrears. SAM, 295004997 1,A3B719, Zhi al-Hajja 1252/March-April 1837. In 1259/1842–3 landowners were complaining about the taxes on the villages near Shiraz. SAM 240023275, 1AB2ZCh716.
51 Ibid., p. 265–6.
52 Encl. in No. 72, 17.10.1839, FO 60/67.
53 Busse, *Qajar Rule*, p. 266.
54 Shiraz Agent, encl. in Hennell to Sheil, 17.3.1840, and 11.5.1840, FO 248/99.
55 Shiraz Agent, encl. in Hennell to Sheil, 11.9.1840, FO 248/99.
56 Busse, *Qajar Rule*, pp. 262–3.
57 Shiraz Agent, encl. in Hennell to Sheil, 18.11.1840, FO 248/99.
58 Hennell to Sheil, 11.1.1841, and 27.1.1841, FO 248/99.
59 Davies, *Province of Fars*, p. 11.
60 Hennell to Sheil, 6.10.1841, FO 248/99.
61 Hennell to Sheil, 11.1.1841, and 27.1.1841, FO 248/99.
62 Hennell to Sheil, 1.2.1841, FO 248/99.
63 Shiraz Agent, encl. in Hennell to Sheil, 6.10.1841, FO 248/99.
64 Hennell to Sheil, 14.5.1846, FO 248/113.
65 See, for example, Shiraz Agent, encl. in No. 348, 12.10.1848, FO 248/132.
66 Shiraz Agent, encl. in No. 386, 20.11.1848, FO 248/132.
67 Shiraz Agent, encl. in No. 199, 24.6.1848, FO 248/129.
68 Shiraz Agent, encl. in No. 386, 20.11.1848 ,No. 409, 8.12.1848, No. 411, 12.12.1848, FO 248/132.
69 Shiraz Agent, encl. in No. 8, 11.1. 1849, FO 248/138.
70 Presumably he was implying that the landlord, probably meaning Qavam himself, should have provided it but had failed to do so. This probably refers to *arbabi* land, the holders of which, usually persons of consequence, were obliged to furnish seed to the cultivator, afterwards taking a major part of the produce themselves. See A.K.S. Lambton, *Landlord and Peasant in Persia*, Oxford 1953, p. 146.
71 Later the people of Siwund applied to the governor for someone to be sent with them to receive the property which had been plundered. A royal *muhassil* (a tax collector) was eventually sent from Tehran to receive the property. Shiraz Agent, encl. in No. 61, 15.2.1850, FO 248/138.
72 Malcolm, *Persia*, II, p. 460. He then goes on to quote a dialogue between the governor of Isfahan and a seller of vegetables in that city. An extra-ordinary tax having been levied on every shop, the vegetable seller forced himself into the presence of the governor when he was giving public audience, and explained he was unable to pay tax.

Governor: You must pay it or leave the city.

Grocer: I cannot pay it, and to what other place can I go?

Governor: You may proceed either to Shiraz or Kashan if you like those towns better than this.

Grocer: Your brother is in power in one of these cities and your nephew in the other: what relief can I expect in either?

Governor: You may proceed to court and complain to the shah, if you think I have committed an injustice.

Grocer: Your brother, the Haji, is Prime Minister.

Governor: Then go to hell, and do not trouble me any more!

Grocer: The holy man, your deceased father, is perhaps there.
And so he was let off.

On the one hand, by contrast, according to Marcus, the culture of Aleppo stressed obedience, conformity and deference to hierarchy, and discouraged individualist views. See *Middle East*, p. 329. On the other hand such manifestations of passion are not uncommon in Iran at the present time.

73 Shiraz Agent, encl. in No. 8, 11.1.1849, FO 248/138.
74 Shiraz Agent, encl. in No. 6, 8.1.1850, FO 248/138. It should be noted that in 1846 Mirza Muhammad 'Ali Mushir al-Mulk died aged 80 and was succeeded by his son, Mirza Abu'l Hasan Khan. However, the influence of this family was for a time in eclipse compared to the earlier part of the century, and it was to be some time before he exercised considerable influence in the districts of Fars. See Busse, *Qajar Rule*, pp. 376, 305, 318, 339, 347, 386.
75 Shiraz Agent, encl. in No. 61, 15.2.1850, FO 248/138.
76 Shiraz Agent, encl. in No. 61, 15.2.1850, FO 248/138.
77 Shiraz Agent, encl. in No. 191, 16.5.1850, FO 248/138.
78 Issawi, *Iran*, p. 131.
79 Davies, *Province of Fars*, pp. 296–301, quoting from Accounts and Papers for Bushire 1890 to 1898.
80 On price rises see, G. Gilbar, 'Trends in the Development of Prices in Late Qajar Iran 1870–1906', *Iranian Studies*, 16, Nos 3–4, 1983, pp. 177–98. For the effects of the world economy see J. Foran, 'The Concept of Dependent Development as a Key to the Political Economy of Qajar Iran', *Iranian Studies*, 22, Nos 2–3, 1989–90, pp. 5–56; V.F. Nowshirvani, 'The Beginnings of Commercialised Agriculture in Iran', *The Islamic Middle East*, ed. A.L. Udovitch, Princeton1981, pp. 547–91. For the problems over the currency see P.W. Avery and J.B. Simmons, 'Persia on a Cross of Silver 1880–1890', E. Kedourie and S. Haim, eds, *Towards a Modern Iran*, London 1980, pp. 1–37; Davies, *Province of Fars*, cites increasingly unfavourable rates of exchange over the period 1885–1895, p. 309.
81 C. Issawi, 'Iranian Trade 1800–1914', *Iranian Studies*, 16, Nos 3–4, 1983, p. 236.
82 Asif al-Daula, *Asnad-i Mirza 'Abd al-Vahab Khan, Asif al-Daula, guzida-yi asnad-i Khurasan*, ed., A.H. Nava'i and N. Kasra, Tehran 1377, p. 30; Mirza Taqi Khan to Zill al-Sultan, 23 Safar 1299/14 Jan. 1892, in I. Safa'i *Asnad-i nau Yafta*, Tehran 1349, pp. 105ff. With the encouragement of the government the merchants had established councils to discuss their affairs in the 1880s. They particularly wanted a stronger voice in government policy, and the strengthening of support for trading interests, as well as more rational administration, including *ihqaq-i huquq* (implementation of their rights). Security of property was one of their major concerns, in addition to the establishment of an Iranian bank to protect their interests against foreigners. See F. Adamiyyat and H. Natiq, *Afkar-i ijtima'i va siyasi va iqtisadi dar athar-i muntashir nashuda-yi daura-yi Qajar*, Tehran 1356
83 A further advantage was provided by an organised postal service, which was set up in 1876, and brought some improvements in communications. *Akhtar* noted that it would advance the interests of trade. Year 2, No. 41, 13 March 1876.
84 Shiraz Agent, encl. in No. 224, 15.6.1850, FO 248/138. Imam Jum'a was a title conferred on one of the *mujtahids* by the state.
85 No. 84, 27.8.1867, FO 248/305.

86 No. 87, 28.8.1867, FO 248/305.
87 Shiraz Agent, No. 38, 25.2.1889, FO 248/491.
88 Shiraz Agent, No. 107, 27.7.1889, 248/491. It seems there was also a certain tolerance of the different customs of the Jews. According to the British Agent, they regularly played music and gambled all night in their houses, but did not attract the ire of the clergy. Shiraz Agent, No. 123, 21.8.1889, 248/491. This tolerance was not necessarily extended to Muslims. On one occasion a party involving drinking and music was invaded by theological students, who broke all the instruments. The guests were servants of Qavam al-Mulk. Shiraz Agent, No. 126, 26.8.1889, FO 248/491.
89 Shiraz Agent, No. 159, 16.10.1889, FO 248/492; No. 193, 29.10.1889, FO 60/502.
90 Shiraz Agent, No. 47, 14.3.1891, FO 248/533. For accounts of the tobacco protest, see N. Keddie, *Religion and Rebellion in Iran*, London 1966; H. Abadian, 'Junbish-i tanbaku: nigahi bih darun', *Tarikh Mu'asir-i Iran*, 8, Autumn 1374, pp. 43–69; Khan Malik Sasani, *Siyasatgaran-i daura-yi Qajar*, Tehran, Intisharat-i Babak, 1338, II, p. 212ff. In fact the tobacco merchants made a big profit through buying cheap and selling dear, and the cultivators would have secured a better rate from the Company. When the French Ambassador asked Talbot, the concessionaire, how he justified his enterprise, Talbot answered that it benefited the cultivator by dealing with him directly. 'And what,' asked de Balloy, 'are you going to do about the tobacco merchants?' MAE, Ambassades/Teheran/62, No. 5, 18.3.1891.
91 Shiraz Agent, No. 63, 18.4.1891, FO 248/533.
92 Shiraz Agent, No. 74, 29.4.1891, FO 248/533.
93 MAE, Ambassades/Teheran/62, No. 25, 12.6.1891.
94 MAE, Ambassades/Teheran/62, No. 14, 30.4.1891.
95 Bamdad says that the *sayyid*, who was known as Sayyid 'Ali Akbar Falasiri-yi Shirazi from the place of his birth, near Kangan, was seized while walking outside the town on the orders of Qavam al-Mulk, bundled onto a horse and sent to Bushire, and thence to Basra. M. Bamdad, *Sharh-i hal-i rijal-i Iran*, Tehran, 1347, II, pp. 430–1; see also Nizam al-Saltana, *Khatirat va asnad-i Husain Quli Khan Nizam al-Saltana Mafi*, eds. M.Mafi, M. Ettehadieh, S. Sa'dvandiyan, H. Ram Pisha, Tehran 1361, I, p. 182. Afghani was in Shiraz in 1886, see Keddie, *Religion*, p. 16.
96 Encl. in No. 129, 20.5.1891, FO 60/523. On 16th September another placard appeared at the entrances to the inns, a copy of which is in the PRO. It recommended the killing of 'these dogs' (company officials), so that they went to hell, and the perpetrators would be recompensed by God. Shiraz Agent, 23.9.91, FO 248/534.
97 No. 95, 13.10.1892, FO 248/544; No. 105, 9.6.1892, FO 60/532.
98 Shiraz Agent, No. 265, 25.2.1892, and No. 330, 22.6.1892, FO 248/555. The late 1880s and 1890s are notable for the frequent references to *tullab* (theological students), as being involved in political demonstrations. Their politicisation, the result of increased foreign influence, is a sign of the early stages of the Islamist impact on the young, and the growth of political Islam. There would also seem to have been more students in the theological schools in the latter decades of the century, probably as a consequence of the enrichment of the leading bazaaris through trade, and their customary duty of funding religious institutions. Examples of student activity included rivalry over a *ta'ziyya* performance in 1893, see Shiraz Agent, No. 548, 19.2.1893, FO 248/576, and No. 563, 20.8.1893, FO 248/577, No. 792, 16.10.1894, FO 248/602. The growth in the number of students and their involvement in popular disturbances by the mid-1890s indicates the situation may have taken another

turn. The money to fund the theological schools may have been drying up, and this increased source of income for poor men was proving less fruitful than in the past decades, resulting in a higher number of battles between the 'ulama involving students. See encl. in No. 221, 29.10.1894, FO 60/559.
99 Shiraz Agent, No. 277, 14.3.1892, FO 248/555.
100 No. 15, 10.3.92, 248/548.
101 Bamdad, *Rijal-i Iran*, II, p. 431.
102 MAE, Ambassades/Teheran/63, No. 33, 12.5.1892. There is a myth that the family of Qavam was originally Jewish, but none of the nineteenth century sources mentions it. It may, however, have sprung up at this time.
103 Shiraz Agent, No. 313, 17.5.1892, FO 248/555.
104 No. 105, 9.6.1892, FO 60/532; Nizam al-Saltana, *Khatirat*, I, p. 173.
105 Shiraz Agent, No. 324, 13.6.1892, FO 248/555. I'timad al-Saltana, Muhammad Hasan Khan, *Ruznama-yi khatirat-i I'timad al-Saltana*, ed. I. Afshar, Tehran 1377, p. 821. I'timad al-Saltana commented that Rukn al-Daula's treatment of Qavam was wholly inappropriate as he was the nephew of the Sahib Divan, and further, this era was not like that of Fath 'Ali Shah, when people were ransomed, and that the foreigners would complain.
106 Shiraz lAgent, No. 332, 22.6.1892, FO 248/555.
107 Compare with the relationship between the Hashemites of Jordan and the Bedouin tribes, where a bond of loyalty developed on a military basis, although there was no other close link.
108 Shiraz Agent, No. 181, 24.11.1892, FO 248/532; Nizam al-Saltana, *Khatirat*, I, p. 173.
109 No. 38, 13.3.1893, FO 60/542.
110 No. 513, 19.5.1893, FO 248/576.
111 Tel. 15.5.1893, FO 248/578; Nizam al-Saltana, *Khatirat*, I, pp. 183–5.
112 Sykes to Lascelles 31.5.1893, FO 248/578; Nizam al-Saltana, *Khatirat*, I, pp. 184–5.
113 Shiraz Agent, No. 513, 19.5.1893, FO 248/576; Nizam al-Saltana, *Khatirat*, I, p. 185.
114 They were not from Shiraz, see H. Picot, 'Report on the Persian Army', FO 881/7364, p. 102.
115 Shiraz Agent No. 516, 24.5.1893, FO 248/576. He was seemingly a major influence on the revolt, along with government officials, Fath al-Mulk and the *lashkarnivis bashi*, Sykes to Lascelles, 31.5.1893, FO 248/578, and Shiraz Agent, No. 513, 19.5.1893, FO 248/576.
116 Shiraz Agent, No. 531, 11.6.1893, and No. 554, 12.6.1893, FO 248/577.
117 Shiraz Agent, No. 563, 20.8.1893, and No. 575, 6.9.1893, FO 248/577.
118 Shiraz Agent, No. 664, 17.3.1894, FO 248/601.
119 Shiraz Agent, No. 664, 17.3.1894, FO 248/601. Bands of music were becoming increasingly popular, one preceding the deputy governor on his arrival in Shiraz in September 1896. See Shiraz Agent, No. 153, 18.9.96, FO 248/639. For a discussion of the development of military music in Iran, see A. Bulookbashi and Y. Shahidi, *Musiqi va sazha-yi musiqi-yi nizami-yi daura-yi Qajar*, Tehran 1381.
120 Shiraz Agent, No. 778, 20.9.1894, FO 248/602.
121 Shiraz Agent, No. 823, 21.12.1894, FO 248/602.
122 Shiraz Agent, No. 26, 15.2.1891, FO 248/533.
123 Keddie, *Religion*, p. 68.
124 Shiraz Agent, No.149, 13.6.1891, FO 60/523.
125 *Habl al-Matin*, No. 7, Year 4, 29 Rajab 1313/15 Jan 1896.
126 *Habl al-Matin*, No. 9, Year 4, 13 Sha'ban 1313/29 Jan 1896
127 *Habl al-Matin*, No. 10, Year 4, 21 Sha'ban 1313/6 Feb. 1896.

128 *Habl al-Matin*, No. 11, Year 4, 28 Sha'ban 1313/13 Feb. 1896. At least one local company had already been established, in 1892. *Akhtar*, Year 18, No. 22, 9 Feb. 1892.
129 *Habl al-Matin*, No. 13, Year 4, 12 Ramazan 1313/27 Feb. 1896, and No. 23, Year 4, 30 Zhi al-Qa'da 1313/13 May 1896. Merchant councils had been previously associated with reforms, see F. Adamiyyat and H. Nateq, *Afkhar-i ijtima'i va siyasi va iqtisadi*, Tehran 1356.
130 M. Ettehadieh, 'The Council for the Investigation of Grievances', *Iranian Studies*, 22, No. 1, 1989, pp. 51–61.
131 *Habl al-Matin*, No. 23, Year 4, 30 Zhi al-Qa'da 1313/13 May 1896. The paper said that Shiraz was the first town after Tehran to have such facilities.
132 It is not clear whether this term would refer to the state bureaucracy or the military, or both.
133 The highest council of the local government system in Fars.
134 *Habl al-Matin*, Year 4, No. 27, 28 Zhi al-Hajja, 1313/11 June 1896.
135 Shiraz Agent, No. 70, 13.5.1896, FO 248/639.
136 Shiraz Agent, No. 114, 17.7.1896, FO 248/639.
137 Shiraz Agent, No. 130, 5.8.1896, FO 248/639.
138 Shiraz Agent, No. 130, 5.8.1896, and No. 131, 15.8.1896, FO 248/639. A *sanduq-i 'adalat* (chest of justice) had been introduced in 1874 in response to countrywide reforms, but had been only partially effective because of the interference of the notables. It did, however, succeed in bringing about a reduction in the levy on the guilds, contrary to the practice of their tax agent, Qavam al-Mulk. See Busse, *Qajar Rule*, pp. 381–2, and Davies, *Province of Fars*, pp. 97–99.
139 Shiraz Agent, No. 131, 15.8.1896, FO 248/639. It does not appear to have lasted, possibly because it was not regarded fondly by either the Iranian government or the British, who tended to see it as a potential cause of further disorder.
140 By contrast with Daulatabadi's *divan-i 'adalat*, see V.A. Martin, *Islam and Modernism*, London 1989, p. 78. The social configuration of this *majlis* was very similar to that in Tehran 1905–6, which eventually secured the Constitutional assembly.

4

ISFAHAN: POPULAR PROTEST, SOCIAL CONTROL AND THE EMERGENCE OF COLLABORATION

This chapter looks at the relationship between religion and state from a different perspective, that of the government, and demonstrates the means by which it tried to negotiate with society. It is argued that force tended to be more limited than is normally understood, and was used in a specific context for a particular purpose, successful governors bringing other, more peaceful, means to ensure control. The chapter refers to three disturbances at different periods, namely in 1849–50, in 1879 – the early period of the governorship of Zill al-Sultan – and the prolonged struggle between 1889–1896 (and after) between Zill al-Sultan and the prominent cleric, Shaikh Muhammad Taqi, known as Aqa Najafi. The discussion of the period at the very end of the century also brings out the emergence of new organisation, ideas and language in response to the pressure of foreign trade on life in Isfahan, in the face of which governor and people began to collaborate.

Isfahan – City and People

Isfahan was a flourishing centre of architecture, the arts, learning, philosophy and commerce even before the Safavid Shah 'Abbas (1586–1629) made it the capital of his dynasty at the end of the sixteenth century. Isfahan reached its apogee during his reign in the early seventeenth century. Prosperous trade, military success and a strong administrative system were accompanied by a programme of magnificent building, public works and town planning, earning the comment that 'Isfahan is half the world'. From the latter part of the 17th century Isfahan declined as a result of the development of maritime commerce by European merchants. In 1722 the Safavid dynasty ended when the city fell to an Afghan invasion and was sacked. Though Nadir Shah (1736–47) drove out the Afghans in 1729–30, the country was unsettled and Isfahan continued in a state of decay, except for some years after Karim Khan took it in 1758–9. From the end of the eighteenth century, it, like other cities, began to benefit from the greater security provided by the Qajars, who, however, made Tehran their capital.

The population, which at its height in the seventeenth century had been estimated at several hundred thousand (though on no very reliable basis), was greatly reduced.[1] Morier, who passed through the city in the early nineteenth century, considered the population to be 60,000, and said it was much renovated and wearing a general air of prosperity, though he thought it had probably declined to a quarter of its size in the seventeenth century.[2] Macdonald Kinneir, who visited the city at the same period, gives a figure of 200,000 for its population, which is almost certainly an over-estimate.[3] By 1848 Isfahan had again experienced a measure of decline, and in common with other cities of Iran was troubled by disturbances, though it was still one of the biggest cities in the country. Abbott, passing through in the autumn of 1848, mentions its exports as cotton twist, canvas, felt, copper utensils, loaf sugar and damascene swords.[4] Already, however, Isfahan's principal manufacture, textiles, was suffering from the popularity and importation of European goods which were to bedevil it for the remainder of the nineteenth century. By this period the population was estimated at 60,000,[5] and the state of city was still dilapidated. In 1872, the population was also put at 60,000.[6]

In 1877 Husain Khan Tahvildar calculated the population to be 50,000, basing his view on food consumption and the reports he gathered from the heads of the city's quarters. His estimate is approximately in line with the previous one, but likely to be more accurate.[7] He commented on the decline of the guilds generally, and noted in particular that the makers of printed cloth had been much affected by foreign imports.[8] However, he put the fall in population down to the rise in the influence of Tehran as the capital of Iran. By the end of the nineteenth century raw cotton was exported from Isfahan to Russia.[9] At this period also the increase in foreigners in Isfahan and the growth of banking are a testimony to the growth in trade, though much of it was in foreign hands. Curzon refers to it as the second largest trading emporium in Iran (after Tabriz), and estimates the population at 70–80,000, following a recent revival in commercial activity.[10] He lists its main imports as Manchester clothing, copper sheets from UK, and tin and zinc from Java, and its exports as being opium (widely grown in the Isfahan district, and a major export of Iran at this period), tobacco, and carpets. By 1913 the population was estimated at 80,000,[11] which concurs with Curzon and, given the increase in trade to and from Iran in the later nineteenth century, seems a reasonable estimate.

Economic Decline and Popular Disturbance

In the mid-century Isfahan was prey to serious disturbances, involving discontented members of the poorer social groups and many roughs, whose ranks were evidently swelled by the unemployed.[12] There was a revolt in 1840, which was so serious that the shah himself had to come and repress it. Another took place in 1849–50, in the time of Amir Kabir, against a background of serious decline in trade in the first part of the century, and the disruptions of the Herat war, involving long-term high unemployment. The insurrection originated in a dispute over taxation, in which the government, declaring itself unhappy over the amount returned, summoned the governor to Tehran and replaced him.[13]

The new governor, Ghulam Husain Khan Sipahdar, arrived in Isfahan in July 1849. Among the problems that faced him was the corruption and inefficiency of the officials of the previous regime, three of whom, in particular, descendants of the Safavid dynasty, were intent on fomenting discontent. One of these, Mirza 'Abd al-Husain, was vizier of Isfahan, and another, Ahmad Mirza, had wide connections at all levels of society. The first serious sign of trouble occurred in December 1849 as the Imam Jum'a led a large crowd at prayer in the main mosque. One of his companions became involved in a fight with a government soldier, which escalated into an attack on the Imam Jum'a himself. The situation was further enflamed by the Safavid descendants, who stirred up the bazaaris to support the Imam Jum'a. The deputy governor, Muhammad Hasan Khan, was sent by the governor to discuss calming the situation with the Imam Jum'a, he was thrown in a mosque pool by the town roughs, and subsequently died. As a consequence, the house of Ahmad Mirza was demolished, and Mirza 'Abd al-Husain took sanctuary in the home of Zain al-'Abidin, the son of a late leading *mujtahid*.

The people of Isfahan, particularly the so-called *lutis*,[14] or poorer, rougher element, now went into revolt. Forming a crowd of as many as 3000, they intersected the streets with numerous barricades,[15] which were protected by marksmen posted on the roofs of the adjacent houses. Then they launched a violent attack on the governor's house, into which he had barricaded himself, but were dispersed. On 3rd December/18th Muharram troops were brought in to attack the barricades and fire was exchanged, but they were defeated, reportedly with high casualties. More troops were requested from Tehran, and the situation was at a standstill, with the people reinforcing their barricades. All commercial contact with Isfahan stopped. Those citizens who did not wish to be involved moved with their property to another part of the town.

In early January 1850 the chief *mujtahid* of Isfahan, Aqa Sayyid Asadullah, returned from a pilgrimage, and the 'ulama began to assume their traditional role of intermediaries between people and state. The Imam Jum'a and Sayyid Asadullah denounced the insurgents from the pulpit, and warned them of high casualties and the destruction of property if they did not desist, with the result that the fighting stopped. A meeting with the governor followed, and it was agreed that the ringleaders, especially the Safavid descendants, should be allowed sanctuary in the house of Sayyid Asadullah, whence they would petition the shah, and that otherwise lives should be spared. The *sayyid* then told the people to leave the barricades, and a public crier was sent round the bazaar, saying woe to those who did not open their shops. Altogether between four hundred and five hundred people were killed.

A large party of 'ulama and insurgents, including members of the guilds and poorer people, led by Sayyid Asadullah, left Isfahan for Tehran to demand that the government restore peace, order and just law (*qanun-i 'adil*), in other words that it practise fair government. By way of retribution, the governor of Isfahan sent troops, who routed and pillaged some of the departed, and forced them to return to Isfahan. The Safavid descendants also fled, and the *lutis* were seized and sent to Tehran for execution, after which order was restored.

Managing Popular Protest

The means used by the governor to deal with the populace included a variety of tactics. In particular it should be noted that Sipahdar responded with restraint to the initial disturbance and attempted to negotiate with the Imam Jum'a. Even after the death of his deputy governor he did not retaliate against the townspeople as a whole, but confined himself to attacking the principal insurgents. In the event he had to settle through the mediation of the 'ulama which proved remarkably effective. Afterwards, despite apparent acquiescence to pleas for mercy for all, punishment was meted out, but only on the principal insurgents. Ultimately, despite a few weeks when he lost authority, the governor was able to handle the situation mainly through negotiation. He did this without calling in the shah, and, although he had asked for reinforcements, without troops from Tehran. Force was used, but to a specific purpose, whilst overall reliance was placed on discussion and co-operation by such means as were possible.

Isfahan appears to have been quiet on the whole in the period following this revolt, as the government, having removed the Safavid descendants and to some degree reformed the administration, was better able to regulate both economy and society.[16] However, another insurrection took place in Isfahan in 1879, this time in the age of the telegraph, and it might be fruitful to compare management of the two. The account that follows is based on a series of telegrams between Tehran, particularly from one of the shah's ministers, Mustaufi al-Mamalik, and his son, the prince Mas'ud Mirza Zill al-Sultan, then governor of Isfahan. In the exchange Mustaufi al-Mamalik, and those involved in Isfahan, came in person to the telegraph office, so that discussion could be closer and more direct.[17] By contrast with the view that prevails in much of the literature on the Qajars, and more especially on Zill al-Sultan, that they governed by tyranny, oppression and arbitrary methods, the telegrams demonstrate the complexity and variety of the strategies of social control that were used.

Not all the reasons for the insurrection are known, but it is evident that the price of bread had gone up, causing serious popular discontent. The disturbance was stirred, according to Zill al-Sultan, by the Imam Jum'a of Isfahan, who was in dispute with the governor over his tax returns, and by his brother-in-law, the Na'ib al-Sadr, whom Zill al-Sultan believed was intriguing against him with the Mirza Husain Khan Sipah Salar, Minister of War.[18] The telegrams reveal Zill al-Sultan's intense insecurity over the possibility of losing his position. He later built up his own army, but it is clear that at this period he did not have much of a force at his disposal. In the course of the insurrection, the bakers refused to produce bread, the bazaars closed and the people assembled in large numbers in the mosques. The Imam Jum'a and Shaikh Muhammad Baqir, the two leading 'ulama in the city, were summoned to the telegraph office to account for themselves. The central government began moving in troops and threatening punishment, but the governor succeeded in negotiating a solution to the crisis without resorting to force.

The exchange of telegrams which took place in late April 1879, centres on the subject of the closing of the bazaars, and the 'ulama's refusal to attend public prayers, a typical tactic at times of discontent, implying that the government had no rightful authority. When Zill al-Sultan asked why everything had closed, the 'ulama answered that it was their *shar'* duty to stay at home (implying that their action was lawful and his unlawful).[19] Zill al-Sultan attempted to diffuse the crisis (which seems to have been precipitated by hoarding) by giving grain to the bakers.[20] Mustaufi al-Mamalik complained on 23th April 1879 that such a policy undermined the prestige of the government, presumably meaning that it was made to appear weak and vulnerable to pressure.

Zill al-Sultan explained that he had given the grain so that bread could be sold more cheaply to undermine the opposition, and particularly the influence of his opponents among the 'ulama. However, the reduction in the price of bread failed to satisfy the people, who went on telling the bakers to close, being evidently dissatisfied with the management of the city. A further attempt to discredit the government was being made by some people who were putting about rumours that control of the city had been given to foreigners, and that the security of Muslims was in their hands.[21] Although foreigners were not involved at all, it was a useful way of slandering the governor.

Since Zill al-Sultan was struggling to control the city, and his stratagem of trying to buy off the majority of the population by reducing the price of bread had evidently so far failed, Mustaufi al-Mamalik presented himself at the telegraph office and suggested that the Imam Jum'a and Shaikh Muhammad Baqir come to the office in Isfahan. Zill al-Sultan replied that so far no one had been killed, so the situation was not yet dire, but the Mustaufi then announced that he would not leave the telegraph office until he was sure that everything in Isfahan had been put right, and the people had gone home. He ordered that the two 'ulama should tell the people to disperse, and report to him in detail.

On the same day the Imam Jum'a appeared at the telegraph office and informed the Mustaufi that the people were demanding new reforms (*islahat-i jadid*), and that the government should promise no more oppression (*zulm*) (something only a member of the 'ulama could say without fear for his life). It would thus appear from the above expression that there was a reformist element in an insurrection that was chiefly concerned with the cost of living, a feature which the event shares with the constitutional revolution. The Mustaufi duly became irate and demanded to know what was meant by oppression.

The Imam Jum'a then proceeded to give quite a different view from Zill al-Sultan. He explained that for three days the 'ulama had refused to go to their mosques, and for two the shops had been closed, indicating the seriousness of popular disquiet. That day the crowd in his mosque had been huge, and turbulent, complaining of oppression (meaning by Zill al-Sultan).[22] He also reported that the people were very unhappy over the security of their property and families.[23] The Mustaufi now resorted to threats, and said this was a disturbance caused by roughs and *lutis*, and only bad could come of it to all concerned, unless the people calmed down and went home.[24] He suggested the traditional remedy for such a situation, which was to petition the shah, thereby no doubt hoping that the problem would subside in the time it took for the shah to deal with it. The Imam Jum'a was not to be intimidated or diverted, and pointed out that two hundred mosques were closed, indicating that the whole of Isfahan was involved, not just his quarter. The implication was that if the government did not listen to him, it would have a major rebellion on its hands, bloodshed, antagonism and resentment, with all the dreaded trouble and expense that involved.

The Imam Jum'a then evidently departed,[25] but he must have made some attempt to win round the people, since in the afternoon he sent an emissary to ask if the grain given to the bakers was to be taken back or remain with them. Zill al-Sultan, reporting the query to Tehran, said he had answered that it did not matter, they could do what they liked with it. He went on to say that he thought they were becoming apprehensive, and asked that no one be sent officially to investigate the problem, as it could once again embolden the people. He presumably meant that it would lead them to believe they were in a position to play off the governor against the central government. Further, according to Zill al-Sultan, the Imam Jum'a was not being entirely sincere, as his son had been preaching to his congregation that they must stand up for themselves and not be like the people of Kufa. Clearly, the opposition was using Shi'i examples to incite resistance to Zill al-Sultan.

A telegram now arrived signed Husain (probably the Sipah Salar, Minister of War). It said that an order had been sent to the commander of the Khamseh regiment, which was near Kashan and marching to Fars, to reroute to Isfahan, where they were to report to Zill al-Sultan. The measure, confirmed the following day was regarded as precautionary, and Zill al-Sultan was to inform the sender as soon as Isfahan was quiet and orderly, so that the regiment could be sent elsewhere.[26] The same source sent another message to Zill al-Sultan, which was in effect really a warning to the people of Isfahan, reminding them of the last time they caused trouble, and saying the shah was thinking of destroying Isfahan and killing all its people.

At about this time a further exchange took place between both the Mustaufi al- Mamalik and the Sipah Salar and the 'ulama of Isfahan, in which the ministers said that the people were too foolish to understand the situation, but that the 'ulama were better informed. They were failing in their duty of admonishing the people, thus avoiding their responsibilities, and should be held accountable for the consequences.[27] They should petition the shah, and not encourage disturbance. Resisting the implied threat to themselves, and the attempt to divide and rule, the 'ulama answered that they were under pressure from the people, and their efforts at admonition had been futile. The cleric Shaikh Muhammad Baqir reported that the people were tired of extortionate government. The government complained of his obstinacy in refusing to co-operate when they were trying to grant the people their rights (*risidigi bih huquq-i mardum*), that is to say, to carry out their expected duty, and threatened him with the army, which would be there in two days. The Imam Jum'a was ordered to Tehran, and the others told to go home, otherwise their salaries would be cut and the *ru'aya* (subjects) punished.

According to Zill al-Sultan's recollections, after a few days of withdrawal by the 'ulama and the closing of the shops, people realised there was no unrighteous response to justify their campaign and therefore their action had been in vain.[28] Members of the poorer social group, however, particularly the *lutis*, who represented the thrust of popular discontent, continued to demonstrate. They collected a large number of women and children, who chanted that they did not want so-and-so (meaning Zill al-Sultan himself), and that he should leave Isfahan. Mustaufi al-Mamalik gave Zill al-Sultan the authority to fire on the people if necessary, when the troops came.[29] However, he declined to do so, even restraining his Azarbaijani soldiery.[30] Zill al-Sultan reported the *luti* disturbance in a telegram to Tehran, saying that it was over, and the security of the town was good, after which he rapidly sent the additional troops on to Fars.[31] At the request of Zill al-Sultan, the Imam Jum'a was sent to Tehran and lost his office.[32] In early May 1879, the shah landed the bill for the military expedition on Zill al-Sultan, and he was also being pursued by the government for the arrears of taxes for Isfahan,[33] once more indicating the problems of the position of governor.

Many of the stratagems of popular bargaining with the government are evident in this incident, as well as typical government manoeuvres to maintain control. The people used their weight of numbers, the implied threat of economic and political disruption, and the hint of illegitimacy to obtain their main goal, a fall in the price of bread. The government responded to them through their representatives among the 'ulama, preached mercy and understanding, and threatened force. It gave in on the grain, but did not remove the governor, Zill al-Sultan. The overall situation was clearly not as dire as that in 1840 and 1850, which was the real reason why the incident ended with little or no bloodshed. The use of the telegram permitted much more cohesion in government policy, as well as rapid response, and the precautionary use of force in good time. In other words, the government could pursue a number of strategies simultaneously. In this incident the people had seemingly not learnt the lesson they had absorbed by the time of the Shiraz demonstrations, namely that they could use the telegraph office to try to play off the governor against the local authorities.

Zill al-Sultan and the Loss of His Military Force

Zill al-Sultan survived and thrived as governor of Isfahan, sustained in part by the growth in trade, particularly opium. In the early 1880s he is reported as undertaking a number of projects to embellish the city, which included the encouragement of the founding of a school with a modernised curriculum, the establishment of a learned society, the building of a hospital, the fostering of trade and agriculture, and the restoration of the dilapidated areas.[34] By 1882 his list of provinces amounted to a third of Iran, and he had been given seventeen regiments under his independent control with a good supply of arms and ammunition.[35] In February 1888 however, this force, which had grown to 21,000, was suddenly removed from him, leaving him with only 400–500 men. This was because the shah feared that he had aspirations to the throne, threatening the rights of the Crown Prince.[36] On the consequent loss of influence, Zill al-Sultan subsequently commented:

> There are two sorts of influence, one of which is moral, such as the Prophet enjoyed, and the other consists in possession of material force. I do not pretend to be a prophet, and my material force has been taken away from me.[37]

Zill al-Sultan's position in Isfahan was therefore much weakened from 1889 onwards, and the politics of Isfahan became dominated by one *mujtahid*, Shaikh Muhammad Taqi, Aqa Najafi, the son of Shaikh Muhammad Baqir.[38] He owed his pre-eminence to great wealth and family prestige, as well as his position as the prayer leader in the principal mosque, the Masjid-i Shah. However, his power was also rooted in an exceptionally astute ability to divine the views and wishes of the ordinary people of Isfahan. According to Mahdavi, he was firstly very good at gleaning what the common people were saying, and what they wanted, even when their inclinations were ambiguous or unclear. He saw it as his obligation to support their view, and devised a policy to attain their objectives, all the while assessing whether it was gaining public acceptance. Once he was completely sure of the grounds of his strategy, he pursued it, winning the support of the majority of the population. For this reason, he always succeeded in his objectives, in contrast to the other 'ulama, who lacked his perspicacity.[39] Aqa Najafi was also perceived as thinking about the community, as having a social conscience, and of being a sincere and just man, impervious to bribes, although avaricious.[40] The sources do not permit close analysis of the popular view, but it may traced through the manoeuvres of Aqa Najafi, and it is from this perspective that the relations between people and governor will be studied in the final section of this chapter.

The Response to Foreign Influence – Aqa Najafi

The huge growth in trade and foreign influence in the country was making itself felt in Isfahan by the later 1880s in a much larger and more evident foreign presence. In the 1890s four major concerns were to shape political opinion and configuration: the first was the Tobacco Concession of 1891, the second, the price of piece goods, the third the attempt to form a local tobacco company in 1894, and the fourth, the creation of the Imperial Bank of Persia in 1889, which was followed by the establishment of a branch in Isfahan. As elsewhere, Isfahan also suffered in the 1890s from the inflation caused by the decline in the value of silver.

First of all, the heightened activity of foreign concerns produced a negative reaction, which manifested itself among other ways in persecution of Babis, Jews and foreign Christians. In this popular response, Aqa Najafi took the lead.[41] He conducted a crusade against Babism in 1889, obliging hundreds to take refuge in the stables of Zill al-Sultan, and promulgated eight measures against the Jews, including prohibition from riding into town, and eating in the presence of a Muslim during Ramadan.[42] The Babis were again attacked in 1892, and their execution demanded.[43] Following a fight between two women, one of them a Jew and the other a Lur, the town was in ferment, the Jews were beaten and soldiers had to be positioned in the bazaar for three days.[44] Missionaries were both an incitement and a target, since they proselytised amongst Muslims, as well as Christians and Jews. Aqa Najafi declared European goods unclean, as part of a campaign to keep missionaries out of Isfahan.[45] When a Miss the missionary Mary Bird was attacked by a mob threatening to throw her into a water course, Aqa Najafi protected the culprits.[46]

Needless to say, Aqa Najafi was most relentless in his pursuit of apostates, and a Muslim of Isfahan who had converted in Christianity in Baghdad was forced into hiding because Aqa Najafi wanted him tried for it.[47] He complained to Zill al-Sultan that Qajar princes were reading books from a foreign culture, and would end up wanting to be like foreigners.[48] Drinking of wine and music were further subjects of discontent,[49] and in 1895 he contrived to have the coffee houses closed, because they were centres of wine drinking and gambling.[50] So, to sustain orthodoxy, he was vigilant in his opposition to all forms of deviancy. Overall, such attacks were part of a growing resistance to foreign influence, but they were also more frequent, better organised and more clearly formulated than in the past. At the heart of the problem lay a struggle over the control of trade and resources between British and foreign merchants that would ultimately force Iranians to reshape their identity. The xenophobic attacks were the very first stage of its emergence at popular level. It was not simply incited by the 'ulama, but represented genuine popular disquiet, as is exemplified in a mob attack on the opium house of the agent of Hotz and Co, when popular pressure got out of control.[51]

In March 1890 the shah himself summoned Aqa Najafi to Tehran in an attempt to try and curb the disturbances he was causing, not least because they were annoying the British. He told him that, since he had heard so much of his excellent qualities from Zill al-Sultan, he had a strong desire to talk to him in person, and to hear views on the mutual consolidation of (the interests of) religion and state, and also the essential points regarding those who had been led astray by the devil and fallen into the wilderness of error from him personally. And he (the shah) would also like to discuss the solutions necessary to restore well-being.[52]

Aqa Najafi duly went to Tehran in July 1890, and spent some months away, but, as might be expected, the admonition did not deter him from further engagement in opposition to the government policies.

Prince-governor and *mulla* also collaborated in more than one way, but particularly in social control. After someone had defamed the 'ulama and been reprimanded by Zill al-Sultan, Aqa Najafi wrote to thank him, and promised to inform him if it happened again.[53] He praised the prince-governor for the security he maintained in Isfahan,[54] and also reminded him of his duties as a ruler, in accordance with Islamic principle: 'The people are a trust, which God has bestowed on you.'[55] Sometimes, indeed, collaboration worked to their mutual personal advantage, as when Aqa Najafi suggested to Zill al-Sultan:

> Dih-i Nau village is part of a *khalasa* (crown land). Either you and I together buy it, or I buy it all and give you half as a present.'[56]

He also tried to cajole the governor with promises of good conduct on the part of the people, promising that in return for protection, agricultural produce would be delivered on time.[57] In addition, emphasis was placed on consultation (*mashvarat*), with the 'ulama promising to confer with the governor as they had always done.[58] It was observed that there was no trouble from Aqa Najafi when Zill al-Sultan was away,[59] as though he depended on the governor to set boundaries to the disturbances he fomented.

Isfahan went into insurrection over the Tobacco Concession on 21st November 1891, although there were already rumblings in September.[60] The people gathered in Mussala Square but Aqa Najafi was himself summoned to the presence of Zill al-Sultan and threatened to the point where he could not go to the mosque, but the crowd went anyway. The people went round pillaging *qaliyans* (hubble bubbles), realising they could do what they liked for as long as they liked. Zill al-Sultan telegrammed the shah in desperation, saying he dared not disperse the crowd as the whole town would erupt in revolt.[61] The shah responded the following day, telling him to suppress the uprising by whatever means.[62] The governor sent a message to Aqa Najafi asking why he made such a fuss over tobacco and so little over wine, when the latter was much more unclean, to which the *mujtahid* replied: 'This is our shari'a duty, you keep to your *'urf* duty,'[63] thereby taking advantage of the occasion to maintain the position of the 'ulama with regard to legal jurisdiction. Yet despite his agitated telegram, prompted also, no doubt, by the desire to regain some of his army, Zill al-Sultan kept order in Isfahan throughout the period of disturbance by a mixture of acquiescence, threats and cajolery, and probably bribery as well.

Following the abolition of the Concession in January 1892, Isfahan became quiet. The evident weakness of the state was encouraging to the reformers, and they were reported as being willing to support the 'ulama, as a way of using them to undermine the existing system, and then to attain their own ends,[64] in effect the policy of Malkum Khan. Emboldened by the success of the campaign, Aqa Najafi and other 'ulama now turned on the Imperial Bank and wrote to complain of it to Tehran, as well as to 'ulama throughout the country, inciting the overthrow of all other European institutions in Iran.[65] Zill al-Sultan meanwhile complained of the boldness of the 'ulama and their popular following, who were demanding the return of their money from the tobacco company: 'Every day I have to read thirty interceding and threatening notes from the 'ulama and fifty petitions from the subjects (*ru'aya*).'[66] Having failed to secure troops from his father, he endeavoured to use the situation to obtain money from the British. The business of the Concession would settle, he told them if they paid a substantial bribe to the prominent citizens of Isfahan, including his sister, which offer was declined.[67]

The 'ulama were also engaged in a struggle with the state over their respective spheres of legal jurisdiction, the state having for some time been endeavouring to extend its legal authority at the expense of the 'ulama, though to little avail. Aqa Najafi now countered by attempting to enlarge his sphere of authority, specifically by getting all questions referred to his court, and by inciting Iranians to renege on their debts to Europeans.[68] He also tried to undermine the legal rights of Europeans. In June 1892 a major case arose concerning a merchant who was a British subject, on which Aqa Najafi produced a most interesting opinion.

Therein it is possible to discern the very early beginnings of Iranian religious nationalism, as well as the traditional view of religion and state being the twin pillars of Islamic rule:[69]

> According to the law of the government of Islam, any order which is issued by the national[70] religious law has to be carried out. Religion and government are twins and there is no difference. In any case where the religious judge has given decisions, the government has to carry them out and there is nothing beyond this. In reality, both (litigants) are subject to the government of Islam, and their case is to be decided by religious law . . . Even if Malthos Aqa is a British subject, according to English law also, the subject of any nation must obey the laws of the country in which he is. Here it is the government of Islam, and people must obey its law.[71]

Thus a territorial aspect comes into Islamic practice, which was not previously present, and we see the beginning of absorption of the concept that law relates to territorial jurisdiction. So religious responses to imperial influence began to reflect the wider development of territorial loyalties in the shaping of national identity traced by Kashani Sabet.[72]

In 1893 a major issue between Aqa Najafi and the governor of Isfahan was the desire of the British Consul, Preece, to move into the centre of the city. With popular support Aqa Najafi tried to persuade other 'ulama to join him, but they were cautious for fear of the shah. 'The shah is a fool,' said Aqa Najafi, 'and I am not afraid of him.'[73] The support of Zill al-Sultan he considered unnecessary, and he tore up a petition to the governor which his students had drafted, as inappropriately deferential. Preece duly moved into the centre of town, his landlord being an army officer. There were demonstrations against Zill al-Sultan, and as a sop to the populace, he dismissed the officer from his job, leaving Preece where he was.[74] The incident shows both how the governor negotiated with popular discontent, and also, the continued pressure from the British.

The main source of contention at this point, however, was a rise in the cost of piece goods due to the heavy depreciation in the value of silver currency, which had a deleterious effect on the sale of European merchandise.[75] People went to Aqa Najafi and his brother, Shaikh Muhammad 'Ali to complain of the prices, and brought pressure on the local dealers not to collect the goods from the European merchants, in protest. They complied despite the fact it meant that they would lose money. As a result the foreign merchants were forced by an effective embargo on their goods, to bring down their prices by 6%, though not without objection, and the local merchants were also resentful of Aqa Najafi.[76] Thus popular pressure was, at least for a while, able to secure a change in the market. Zill al-Sultan judiciously kept out of the whole issue, in order to maintain good relations with both sides.

Economic problems were again to the fore at the end of the year, when there was a scarcity of bread, causing much discontent in city and villages. There were rumours of Aqa Najafi and Zill al-Sultan cornering wheat, though it cannot be known for certain. It would seem though, that some agreement had been reached between the *mujtahid* and the governor on the price of wheat, the basis of which is not clear. Placards appeared in the bazaar abusing Aqa Najafi, and calling him a 'wheat merchant'.[77] He was forced by a crowd, mostly of women, to go and remonstrate on their behalf with Zill al-Sultan and oblige him to bring down the price.[78] Zill al-Sultan stated that it was not possible, but having no troops to quell the riot, had to give way to a request for consultation on the subject. An assembly (*majlis*) duly met, which consisted of five hundred members representing different classes. After consultation, they agreed a price for wheat, a little above that originally requested, and for retailed bread.[79]

The troubles of the tobacco trade continued after the demise of the Concession. The Ottoman Empire, the main market for Iranian tobacco, placed restraints on its import by granting a monopoly to the Societe de Tombac, which greatly reduced the purchase of Iranian tobacco.[80] The effects of the change were felt in Isfahan by 1893 to 94, and various attempts were made to establish Iranian tobacco companies to market the product, including one by Aqa Najafi.[81] The cultivators of tobacco petitioned Zill al-Sultan on the failure of their agent to sell their tobacco, and on the fact that they were being taxed when they had not made a sale.[82] Zill al-Sultan tried to shift the burden to the merchants by forcing them to purchase the tobacco, so that he could obtain his taxes. The merchants explained that they had a backlog of tobacco, and would be ruined if they bought more, but suggested instead that a company be formed which would have sole rights to buy the tobacco from the cultivators. Its primary aim was to prevent damage to tobacco cultivation, and further loss to those engaged in the trade. Its proposal was that less tobacco should be grown, so that the Societe de tombac was squeezed out, and that the cultivators did not sell tobacco for export, but only for the internal market. Zill al-Sultan was persuaded to grant the company officially the sole right of export from Isfahan. A document was produced detailing the arrangements for the company, and signed by Zill al-Sultan and several 'ulama, thus establishing a new degree of co-operation and organisation in Isfahan in the face of an outside threat. The Prime Minister, Amin al-Sultan, also supported the venture, and the 'ulama preached that Iranians should stop doing business with foreigners. The company had 100,000 tomans in shares for which purchasers had to provide documents. Not unexpectedly, problems arose because the company could not persuade the societé de Tombac to buy its tobacco. The Ottoman company complained to the shah that tobacco could not be exported from Isfahan as it was being hoarded. The shah took rapid action, because the new company was contravening the contract he had entered into with the Ottoman company, which provided him with some money to pay off the British for the cancellation of their Concession. Chastised by his parent, Zill al-Sultan denied that he had had anything to do with it, and the shah's wrath fell on Amin al-Sultan and the merchants. The peasants too were displeased, as they disliked being told to reduce their tobacco crop, and suspected that the whole thing was a monopoly initiated by Zill al-Sultan.[83]

The Emergence of a Reform Movement

The formation of the company, however, produced new political language on the subject of its venture, and demonstrates how the merchants of Isfahan, though themselves pious, emphasised the religious basis of the company to secure it popular support. A leaflet distributed at the time stated that they had founded the company because people of Iran had to unite, and if they implemented the principles of their religion, there would be much progress. Government support was also important. Finally, the leaflet spoke of the *daulat va millat* (state and people) obliging the cultivators to grow less in the general interest.[84] Here we have an early reference to the term *daulat va millat* that was to become current at the time of the Constitutional Revolution, which represents an intermediary phase between the older references to *daulat va ru'aya* (state and subjects), and the term *millat*, meaning nation. The people were moving up from being subordinate to the state to being a partner with it, sharing in its authority, though they were not yet one of its integral elements.

The company survived and managed to do business, but the battle with the Ottoman company continued, with the Ottoman company trying to undercut the Iranians, whilst warning the shah that they would not be able to pay him anything.[85] In 1897 a meeting took place between Zill al-Sultan, the leading merchants of Isfahan, and the Ottoman company, where, after some discussion, all parties agreed to collaborate to their mutual benefit, and an agreement was signed to that effect.[86]

Meanwhile, problems had also developed with regard to the British Imperial Bank, which had been established in 1889, and received a concession from the Iranian government to provide banking facilities and issue notes. A branch in Isfahan was established in the same year. The bank undermined the position of the traditional bankers (*sarrafs*) who were instrumental in fomenting agitation against it in alliance with bazaaris and 'ulama, who saw it as a new and dangerous form of foreign influence in the country. In 1894 Aqa Najafi at first contemplated sending his *tullab* (students) to wreck it, but then opted to try to form a bank of his own.[87] He gave all the assistance in his power to the chief debtor of the Imperial Bank and wrote constant letters to the manager about other debtors, in an attempt to resist the Bank's claims. His own banking initiative was blocked by both the shah and Zill al-Sultan at the instigation of the British, the shah in particular having no desire to see further disorder such as that over the

Tobacco Concession.[88] However, Aqa Najafi persisted in his harassment of the bank, particularly when a dispute between the Chief Secretary (and bank debt collector) and one of the local *sarrafs* caused all the others to close. A meeting was held to discuss the matter in front of the deputy governor of the town, Rukn al-Mulk, which decided there was no case to answer. The Acting Manager, however, then felt obliged to respond to the presence of Aqa Najafi to state his case before him, thereby virtually admitting the right of the 'ulama to interfere in the civil administration of the city.[89] The British being now also anxious to get rid of the Secretary, he was obliged to leave. Thus Aqa Najafi and the merchants manipulated the disturbance to encroach on the rights of the government, and to embarrass the foreign power.

By 1895 one of the main problems for the people of Isfahan as elsewhere was the debased coinage, or so-called black money, in which the Imperial Bank would only deal on the most unfavourable terms. People saw a decline in their living standards, which they blamed on the foreign institution.[90] Aqa Najafi wrote to the 'ulama of Kerbala that Isfahan and its trade were in the hands of foreigners, and that banking was against the shari'a, which was being flouted by Christians.[91] He pursued Mulla Baqir Fasarki, known as the most pious of the 'ulama of Isfahan, to fight the 'degradation' of Islam and join him in saying all European goods were unclean, and thus bring the prices down by deterring their purchase.[92] 'It will be useful,' he is reported as saying, 'as the poor will gain and the people will be obliged to us.'

After an incident in which two Muslims were killed in Julfa, he wrote to Zill al-Sultan requesting the strengthening of the country (*taqviyyat-i millat*), and that the matter be remedied since the well-being of the people and the state (*salah-i millat va daulat*) required it.[93] He declared himself to have been a long time active in the well-being of people and state, and that he was trying to calm the people down.

On the assassination of Nasir al-Din Shah in 1896, Aqa Najafi kept to his house. Isfahan was quiet, largely due to the efforts of Zill al-Sultan. He summoned other members of the 'ulama to a conference, and obtained their adherence to his brother Muzaffar al-Din Shah. During the following twenty four hours, some of them rode through the town, quieting the people, breaking up meetings, and doing everything possible to prevent ferment and looting. Business resumed on the 5th June, shops and other concerns having shut on the 4th out of respect for the shah.[94]

Aqa Najafi continued to be active in the politics of Isfahan until his death in 1914, but he was to some extent superseded by the rise of his younger brother, Haj Aqa Nurullah, better educated and more intelligent. Aqa Nurullah was the founder of the Shirakat-i Islamiyya-yi Isfahan (the Islamic company of Isfahan) along with Rukn al-Mulk, and an Islamic hospital and school. He was active in Islamic unity and Islamic constitutionalism, his newspaper, *Jihad al-Akbar*, speaking out against the spread of foreign cultural, economic and political influence. In his view trade and industry had become a means of impoverishing the state because Iranian merchants had in reality become the hired labourers of foreigners. He believed strongly that Muslim weakness derived from economic weakness, and that local industry, especially textiles, must be encouraged.[95] Many years later, under Reza Shah, he led a column of merchants, clergy and peasants from Isfahan to Tehran to protest against a state monopoly of tobacco cultivation, an action which won the admiration of the young Khomeini.[96]

* * *

In conclusion, although the Qajar government, and in particular, Zill al-Sultan, was capable of using violent means to suppress popular discontent, it also engaged in a complex bargaining process, employing a variety of stratagems. These included divide and rule, for example attempting to separate the 'ulama from their following, and a judicious combination of threats and professed concern. The government also refrained from overreaction so as not to inflame the situation further and to create martyrs, who might be used to mobilise popular discontent. The shah was brought in as a last resort, to deploy his authority, in what sometimes reads like a well-rehearsed scenario. The government also knew how to give way on small issues and hold out on larger ones. Further, governors regularly engaged in consultation in the form of meetings and assemblies, and many problems were solved in this way.

The popular response to these tactics was primarily to play on government fear of disorder and insecurity, with consequent aspersions cast on its legitimacy as having in theory no authority in religion, other than adequate performance of its foremost duty: to protect Islam, its lands and its believers. It was also understood that the government, keeping only small military forces, feared disorder and its economic costs, and the people played on that fear. Against the small forces of the government, they could deploy weight of numbers, which made it all important for the governor to see that discontent did not spread and become widely organised. Governors who so failed tended to be blamed at court more than the populace. To mobilise just such numbers, the people, and more especially the 'ulama, called upon the examples of the heroic figures of the early years of Islam, and made scornful comparisons with those who had become models of cowardice, for example, the people of Kufa. The 'ulama also used legal arguments to threaten the governor, and some, indeed, took what opportunities were available to expand the sphere of influence of the shari'a at the expense of the customary law ('urf) used by the government.

In the last years of the period under study, 1889–96, the whole configuration of politics in Isfahan changed in a variety of ways and at a variety of levels, most of which are outside the scope of this book. The point to note here is that these changes were reaching into the bazaar, and into more traditional society. The catalyst was not so much the growth of the foreign presence as the growth in foreign trade, and most particularly the increasing predominance of foreign merchants and firms. Society was beginning to organise in different ways, to which the attempts to found new Iranian companies bear witness, as well as the collaboration of Zill al-Sultan in some popular initiatives. Papers such as *Qanun, Akhtar* and *Habl al-Matin*, played a part in influencing the ideas at popular level, as is evident in some of the terms used. This language shows the very beginnings of the emergence of a new political vision, with the calls for unity and collaboration, and most significantly the reformulation of the term *daulat va ru'aya* to *daulat va millat*, or even *millat va daulat*, implying a greater role for the people in the political affairs of the country. The arguments relating law to territorial jurisdiction to defeat foreigners with their own arguments are also the beginnings of the creation of a new Iranian identity. People and state were moving towards a new order, a movement which was to find expression, at least on the part of Isfahan, in the Constitutional Revolution.

Notes

1 Issawi, *Iran*, p. 13.
2 Morier, *Journey*, pp. 133–4, 142.
3 Macdonald Kinneir, *Memoir*, pp. 111–2.
4 Abbott, FO 251/42, p. 16. It will be noted that he does not mention carpets, and indeed Isfahan's formerly famous carpet trade did not revive until the end of the nineteenth century. See also Malcolm, *Persia*, II, p. 374.
5 Issawi, *Iran*, p. 28; Usscher, *Journey*, p. 590 puts it at 80,000 which is almost certainly too high.
6 A. Mounsey, *Journey through the Caucasus and the Interior of Persia*, London 1872, p. 97. A.R. de Gobineau made a similar estimate, see *Trois ans en Asie*, Paris 1932 edition, p. 229. He noted that there were few Europeans in Isfahan at this time, the mid-century.
7 Mirza Husain Khan Tahvildar, *Jugrafiyya-yi Isfahan*, ed. M. Sutuda, Tehran 1342, p. 65.
8 Ibid., p. 94.
9 Issawi, *Iran*, p. 139.
10 Curzon, *Persia*, pp. 41–4. Houtum Schindler put it at 82,000 in 1893, see. A.K.S. Lambton, 'Isfahan', *Encyclopaedia of Islam*, 2nd edition, IV, Leiden 1978, p. 104.
11 Issawi, *Iran*, p. 33, quoting L.A. Sobotsinskii, *Persiya*, 1913.
12 It was seriously behind with its taxes in 1835. See R. Farasati, *Farmanha va raqamha-yi daura-yi Qajar*, Tehran 1372, I, p. 175.
13 This account is taken from Mirza Muhammad Taqi, Lisan al-Mulk Sipihr, *Nasikh al-tavarikh*, Tehran 1337, III, pp. 103–9; Riza Quli Khan Hidayat, *Rauzat al-Safa*, ed. J. Kianfar, Tehran 1380, 15, pp. 8520–5; enclosures in Sheil to Palmerston, No.15, 15.12.1849, FO 60/146, and No.12, 26.1.1850 and No. 25, 23.2.1850, FO 60/150.The tax in question is mentioned as *kharaj*, see Sipihr, *Tavarikh*, III, p. 103.
14 For more on *lutis*, see Chapter 5.
15 The reference to barricades is very unusual, but it is not known if this event was influenced by some knowledge of the European revolts of 1848, or whether such organisation was established local practice.

16 See SAM 29500147 1,A4A334, Zill al-Sultan tel., 4 Jamadi I 1296/26 April 1879, where he says that in the past the bakers did not close and people did not cause disturbances.
17 This practice is known as *telegram-i huzuri*, i.e. a series of telegrams in which the senders were present in the telegraph office. The exchange, which took place between late April and early May 1879, is in the Sazman-i Asnad-i Melli, Tehran. The documents are not the original telegrams but have come from a register in which the text of each was recorded; they have not been filed in date order, and are not all dated. There are also problems with the given dates and the sequence of events, so this text is to some extent interpretative.
18 SAM 295001447 1,A4A334, Zill al-Sultan to Mustaufi al-Mamalik, 4 Jamadi I 1296/26 April 1879.
19 Mas'ud Mirza, Zill al-Sultan, *Khatirat-i Zill al-Sultan*, ed. H. Khadiv Jam, Intisharat-i Asatir 1368, II, p. 566. The recollections, written in 1907, are not always consistent with the telegrams and therefore cannot be accounted as accurate.
20 SAM 295001447 1,A4A334, Zill al-Sultan to Mustaufi al-Mamalik, 4 Jamadi I 1296/26 April 1879. Governors at this period, though sometimes themselves involved in grain hoarding, were also sensitive as to its distribution. The British Consul, passing through the province in the 1890s noted large stores of grain in the towns and villages, which the people were not allowed to touch, and caravans of donkeys bearing grain on the orders of Zill al-Sultan. The price of grain in Isfahan was often high, but on the other hand he appears to have kept much in store in case the harvest failed. No. 73, 28.11.1893, FO 248/572. In 1896, he employed the same measure of social control as in 1879, namely to keep the populace happy, he put 650,000 lbs of his own grain into the market, selling it at 5 krans the load less than the current price. No. 22, 15.6.1896, FO 248/634.
21 It will be recalled that this event took place not very long after the Reuter Concession crisis of 1872.
22 A separate telegram in the same series from the head of the telegraph office in Isfahan to Mustaufi al-Mamalik also reported a huge crowd gathering, and said that the people had brought Shaikh Muhammad Baqir from his house to the main mosque. SAM 295001447, 1,A4A334
23 SAM 295001444 1,A14A331, Imam Jum'a to Mustaufi al-Mamalik, 3 Jamadi I 1296/25 April 1879.
24 SAM 295001447 1,A4A334 Mustaufi al-Mamalik to the Imam Jum'a, 3 Jamadi I 1296/25 April 1879.
25 He does not reappear in the dialogue at this stage.
26 The Sipah Salar telegraphed the commander of the Khamseh regiment saying, 'I know that you have good officers, but soldiers must not go about the city without reason. All soldiers must be in their barracks at night. They must not think the city is a place of pleasure. They must not speak to women. There are to be no women in the barracks, as this is a specially sensitive time, and people are angry. Even in daytime the soldiers must not speak without permission, when in the city. Be sure they do not drink.' Undated in SAM 295001447 1,A4A334. See also 295001473 1,A14A320
27 SAM 295001447 1,A4A334 Mustaufi al-Mamalik and Sipah Salar to the 'ulama of Isfahan, clearly around early Jamadi I 1296/late April 1879, but date not noted.
28 Zill al-Sultan, *Khatirat*, II, p. 568.
29 SAM 295001447 1,A4A334, Mustaufi al-Mamalik to Zill al-Sultan, 4 Jamadi I 1296/26 April 1879.
30 Zill al-Sultan, *Khatirat*, II, p. 568.

31 SAM 295001447 1,A4A334, Zill al-Sultan to Mustaufi al-Mamalik, 7 Jamadi I 1296/29 April 1879; SAM 295001481, 1,A4,368 exchange dated 4 Jamadi II 1296/26 May 1879.
32 SAM 295001473, 1,A14A320, Sipah Salar to Zill al-Sultan, no day's date Jamadi I 1296/23 May–20 June 1879.
33 SAM 295001456, 1,A4A343, exchange dated 13–15 Jamadi I 1296/5–7 May 1879.
34 *Akhtar*, No. 10, 23.2.1881, No. 13, 16.3.1881, No. 18, 20.4.1881, No. 21, 11.5.1881, No.34, 10.8.1881.
35 No. 32, 25.2.1882, FO 60/444; W. Sparroy, *Persian Children of the Royal Family*, London 1902, p. 26.
36 He was also greatly in arrears with his taxes, see No. 269, 3.9.1890, FO 60/512.
37 No. 12, 18.1.1893, FO 60/542. Zill al-Sultan's view reflects a theory of kingship going back to the medieval period. See A.K.S. Lambton, 'Justice in the Medieval Persian Theory of Kingship', *Studia Islamica*, 17, 1962, p. 104.
38 On Aqa Najafi see S.M. Kitabi, *Rajal-i Isfahan dar 'ilm va 'irfan va adab va hunar*, Isfahan 1375, pp. 171–9; N. Mir 'Azimi, *Isfahan zadgah-i jamal va kamal*, Isfahan, 1379, pp. 404–8; M. Najafi, *Haj Aqa Nurullah Isfahani*, Tehran 1378 (biography of his brother); S.M. Mahdavi, *Tarikh-i ijtima'i-yi Isfahan dar qarn-i akhar*, Qum 1367, I, pp. 403, 415, 439, 440, 464–8, II, pp. 27–34.
39 Mahdavi, *Isfahan*, II, p. 415.
40 Kitabi, *Rajal-i Isfahan*, p. 175; No. 62, 17.10.1892, FO 248/548. See MTM Q 100750, Aqa Najafi to Zill al-Sultan, n.d., for an example of his intercession on behalf of the common people.
41 See for example, MTM Q100896, Aqa Najafi to Zill al-Sultan, n.d.
42 No. 149, 30.7.1889, and No. 161, 28.8.1889, FO 60/501. In 1893 he sent for the elders of the Jews and required them to justify their belief according to the Torah, and answer his questions. They replied that they were not learned men, and suggested he refer the questions to their leading rabbis in Baghdad and Jerusalem. Aqa Najafi was not placated. He gave them twenty-seven questions, and said if they did not provide satisfactory answers they must either convert to Islam or be killed. He was also again active at this time in persecuting the Babis. No. 63, 13.10.1893, FO 248/527.
43 No. 14, 10.3.1892, FO 248/548.
44 No. 35, 10.5.1893, FO 248/572.
45 No. 49, 15.2.1894, FO 60/557.
46 Encl. in No. 12, 24.2.1894, FO 248/596. Of missionary proselytising, at that time very assertive, Preece wrote that the missionaries were anxious to work up an incident over their not being allowed into Isfahan. Just at this slack time at home, such a question, getting into the papers, would and could be well used to ventilate the whole matter of missionary work in Persia and help them to attain their desired ends, not alone on the points under discussion, but it might also be used to induce Her Majesty's Government to obtain from the shah a declaration of religious liberty in Persia. No. 59, 4.10.1893, FO 248/572. Missionaries caused quite as many problems for Preece as for Zill al-Sultan.
47 No. 88, 11.4.1894, FO 60/557.
48 MTM Q 100970, Aqa Najafi to Zill al-Sultan, n.d.
49 MTM, Q 100754, Aqa Najafi to Zill al-Sultan, n.d.
50 MTM Q 100935, Aqa Najafi to Zill al-Sultan, n.d.
51 No. 6, 26.1.1896, FO 248/634.
52 Sent by telegram from the shah to Aqa Najafi, 11 Rajab 1307/3 March 1890, in I. Safa'i ed. *Asnad-i barguzida*, Tehran, 1350, p. 125.

53 MTM Q100895, Aqa Najafi to Zill al-Sultan, n.d.
54 MTM Q 100748, Aqa Najafi to Zill al-Sultan, n.d.
55 MTM Q 100795, Aqa Najafi to Zill al-Sultan, n.d.
56 MTM Q 100818, Aqa Najafi to Zill al-Sultan, n.d.
57 MTM Q100601–602, Aqa Najafi to Zill al-Sultan, 19 Shavval 1311/ 26 April 1894.
58 MTM Q 100612–113, Aqa Najafi to Zill al-Sultan, n.d.
59 No. 46, 27.6.1892, FO 248/548.
60 MAE, Ambassades/Teheran/62, No. 49, 5.11.91; I'timad al-Saltana, *Ruznama*, p. 769. See also Keddie, *Religion*, pp. 94–5.
61 I. Safa'i, *Asnad-i Siyasi*, Tehran 2535, pp. 22–3, tel 19 Rabi' II 1309/22 November 1891.
62 Ibid., pp. 25–6.
63 Ibid., p. 41. He meant government administration or common law duty.
64 Mirza Ahmad Khan Mirtip in conversation with the British Consul, No, 4, 29.1.1892, FO 248/548.
65 No. 7, 13.2.1892, FO 248/548.
66 No. 2754, decipher Zill al-Sultan to the shah, 5.2.1892, FO 248/553.
67 No. 27, 8.4.1892, FO 248/548.
68 No. 16, 10.3.1892, and No. 28, 9.4.1892, FO 248/548.
69 See Martin, *Islam*, p. 28.
70 The term used is *milli*, which at that time was just coming to convey the idea of national, as in *majlis-i shura-yi milli* the national consultative assembly, though few people understood the full meaning of nationalism as such.
71 Encl. in No. 47, 2.7.1892, FO 248/548.
72 F. Kashani Sabet, *Frontier Fictions*, Princeton 1999, especially p. 10.
73 No. 1, 3.1.1893, FO 248/572.
74 No 34, 10.5.1893, and No. 43,20.6.1893, FO 248/572.
75 No. 3, 7.1.1893, FO 248/572.
76 No. 5, 14.1.1893, and No. 10, 24.1.1893, FO 248/572.
77 No. 64, 13.10.1893, FO 248/572.
78 Decipher No. 16, 26.10.1893, FO 248/572.
79 Decipher No. 20, 2.11.1893, FO 248/572.
80 Issawi, *Iran*, p. 251.
81 No. 6, 26.1.1894, FO 248/596.
82 MFA, 1311 B23 F8 No. 10, 1311. For further details of the company see 1311 B23 F8 Nos.11, 12, 15, 16, 18, 19, 20 and 21. The documents are all dated 1311, except for No. 18, which is dated 1312, though it clearly belongs to the same period. The moving spirits were the Malik al-Tujjar of Isfahan, and Aqa Najafi, amongst others. It is also mentioned in No. 38, 8.2.1894, FO 60/557, and is referred to as the Ithna 'Ashiri (Twelver from Twelver Shi'ism) Company. Unsurprisingly, it was not viewed favourably by the British.
83 No. 5, 15.3.1895, FO 248/616.
84 MFA 1311 B. 23 F8 No. 15/3.
85 No. 5, 15.3.1895, FO 248/616; MFA 1314 B28 F2 No. 123, dated 7 Rabi' I 1313/ 28 August 1895.
86 MFA 1315 B31 F6, dated Rajab 1315/November–December 1897.
87 Encl. in No. 41, 11.2.1894, FO 60/557.
88 Encl. in No. 41, 11.2.1894, FO 50/557.
89 No. 170, 14.8.1894, and No. 178, 30.8.1894, FO 60/559.
90 *Habl al-Matin*, Year 6, No. 4 ,15 Rajab 1313/ 1 January 1896, No. 7, 29 Rajab 1313/15 January 1896.
91 No. 10, 19.2.1896, FO 248/634.
92 No. 8, 12.2.1896, FO 248/634.

93 MTM Q 100861, n.d.; and Q 100580, n.d. No. 8, 12.2.1896, FO 248/634.
94 No. 22, 15.6.1896, FO 248/634.
95 Najafi, *Nurullah*, pp. 12–16, 31–6.
96 V.A. Martin, *Creating an Islamic State*, London 2000, p. 30.

1. A group of entertainers. In the centre, wearing a huge turban, is Karim Shira'i, a well known buffoon of the period of Nasir al-Din Shah. (Courtesy of the Centre for the Great Islamic Encyclopaedia, Tehran)

2. The Imperial Guard. Their duty was to protect Nasir al-Din Shah and his court in Tehran. They were better dressed and paid than other soldiers. (Courtesy of the Centre for the Great Islamic Encyclopaedia, Tehran)

3. Aqa Anbar, a leading eunuch of the royal harem. He was most likely brought to Iran from Africa as a child slave. (Courtesy of the Centre for the Great Islamic Encyclopaedia, Tehran)

4. Veiled women in Isfahan. Although even their faces were covered, women engaged actively in political protest in the Qajar period. (Courtesy of the National Archives of Iran)

5. A group of *ta'ziyya* performers dressed as the opponents of the followers of Imam Husain at the battle of Kerbala. (Courtesy of the National Archives of Iran)

6. Mirza Sulaiman Khan, Rukn al-Mulk, deputy governor of Isfahan, with a group of his officials and servants. (Courtesy of the National Archives of Iran)

7. The soldiers of the military force of Zill al-Sultan, governor of Isfahan. They were amongst the best dressed and equipped in the country. In 1888 the Shah abolished this force, which he considered a threat to the throne. (Courtesy of the National Archives of Iran)

8. Portrait of a black slave, probably an Abyssinian, dated 1256/1840. In the manuscript he is holding, his face is compared to *lailat al-qadr* (the night of revelation). (In the possession of the author)

5

POPULAR DEMONSTRATIONS BY WOMEN IN NINETEENTH CENTURY IRAN

In the Iranian Revolution of 1979 one of the most notable features was that of political demonstrations by women in large groups.[1] At the time such separation of the sexes seemed to be an Islamised form of the organised mass demonstrations of a Marxist-Leninist kind which had been a feature of twentieth century politics. In addition, the demonstrations seemed to indicate a growing consciousness of women's role in the political arena, particularly as a result of new style modern organizations and societies. Yet, whilst it is true that twentieth century western methods of organisation had an influence on the Islamist movement of 1962–79, it is evident that separate women's political demonstrations were a much older characteristic of Iranian politics. There is in particular one well-known reference in the *Tarikh-i bidari-yi Iranian* (History of the Awakening of the Iranian People) to such a demonstration during the Constitutional Revolution of 1906, when a group of women attacked the shah's carriage whilst the 'ulama were in *bast* (sanctuary) in Shah 'Abd al-'Azim.[2] The Revolution was characterised by other demonstrations by women, either as a separate group or in collaboration with men.[3] More recently photographs have come to light showing women as an organized presence.[4] Afary has demonstrated how the roots of modern Iranian feminism were firmly established in the Constitutional Revolution, and has shown how women protesters were part of the new movement from its earliest beginnings.[5] This chapter raises the possibility that ordinary women were involved in open political activity much earlier, with motives that were probably mixed and not necessarily from a secular influence. In a word, women's demonstrations have a history going right back into the nineteenth century, and possibly before.[6]

It must, however, first be noted that it was very unusual for women to demonstrate as a distinct group before the twentieth century. It was not common in other countries of the Middle East or on the Sub-Continent, though examples can be found, for instance in Aleppo in 1751, when women occupied the minaret of the Great Mosque;[7] and in 1804 in Egypt, when women stoned soldiers from the top of barricades.[8] It was also not particularly a feature of the politics of Europe, though there are examples during the French Revolution.[9] Foreign observers in Iran commented that demonstrations in which women played a prominent part were characteristic of Iran.[10] There is therefore a question as to why these demonstrations occurred in Iran, and where and how they originated. After some introductory remarks on women in the nineteenth century, this Chapter will set out and examine the evidence on the demonstrations, bearing in mind that it is scanty, as with so much at the popular level in Iran before the twentieth century.[11]

The Position of Women in Qajar Iran

In Qajar Iran women were at a definite disadvantage compared to men. In a study of society in Tehran in 1269/1852-3, Ettehadieh notes that 1% of women at most owned houses, and the percentage who owned shops was even smaller.[12] Daughters received half their brother's share of inheritance, and a woman with children a quarter of her husband's estate, whilst one without children inherited an eighth.

The Islamic concept of *hijab* (decorum in dress) was strictly observed in the urban areas. In the street Iranian women were wrapped in dull looking veils, and though elite women were richly dressed indoors, out of doors they were attired similarly to those of other social groups.[13] Women's outdoor costume consisted of a dark blue mantle covering the head and shoulders, falling to their knees, and a white veil sewn onto the mantle at the forehead, but loose below. They wore very wide trousers (also dark blue), socks and slippers.[14] One of the principal ways of punishing women was to turn them into the public eye uncovered, as happened to the wives of the servants of the *karguzar* (foreign agent) of Bushire, when he failed to pay the arrears of customs dues.[15] The seclusion of women created problems in the treating of illness and, for example, impeded vaccination. In Bushire in 1884 it was proposed to overcome this problem by training Iranian women to carry out the vaccinations.[16]

Yet, despite the veiling to all but close relations, in marriage a bridegroom was often allowed a glimpse first.[17] The women of some parts of the country, especially Gilan, had more freedom of dress, as they rarely veiled their faces, and often tucked their garments thigh high when weeding and cutting the rice.[18] The tribal women of Fars were unveiled.[19]

In marriage women gained in respect if they had children, but if childless were looked upon as a burden.[20] According to Mounsey, looks alone kept the husband's affection, but Binning states that, contrary to European impressions of non-European men, husbands often consulted their wives and took their advice on all kinds of matters, and were not infrequently ruled by their wives.[21] Much of a woman's life was spent on the demanding

Persian cuisine, fostered by the Shi'i tendency towards the seclusion of women, combined with the new ingredients brought by international trade.[22] Many women, moreover, complained of unfair treatment as women, for example, a first wife being less well-treated than a second wife, of being thrown out of the house, but refused divorce; on the other hand, divorced men complained that their wives had taken their property.[23] Of course, it would depend on the family and to some extent also on the social milieu.

Women could use the legal system to their advantage and exercise agency in the process, not unusually winning cases. In the courts of law the *mujtahid* might well interpret the law in a way which worked for women.[24] Women were also determined in exercising agency, and in standing up for their rights. Magistrates' courts, which were held publicly, as a means of ensuring a check on their proceedings, were sometimes tumultuous. The women who attended could be the most vociferous, and the minor officials who were present to preserve order were not permitted to quell them with the blows they inflicted on the men.[25]

Although the shari'a was followed with regard to women's personal status, so was customary practice, particularly that of ensuring that a woman did not dishonour her family. Generally, officials took little notice of the ill-treatment or murder of a woman found in adultery, and her own family could connive in her demise.[26] In one incident a man and a woman were brought before a local so-called 'dervish prince' and tried for fornication. The man was killed and the woman put in a sack and beaten, but saved by a passerby.[27] In 1859 a pregnant woman was put to death for poisoning her husband, though the execution was considered contrary to the shari'a, which ordains that not only must a pregnant woman give birth, but also feed her child to the appropriate time of weaning.[28] Punishment for prostitution could be equally barbarous. In Rasht a woman suspected of prostitution with a Russian, was seized and taken to the local *mujtahid*, who inflicted one hundred blows on her with his own hands.[29] As was not uncommon at that time, the *mujtahid* then used the incident of female sexual transgression to incite the population against the foreign presence in Iran, in effect using her as a pawn in the politics of religion and state.[30]

Few people in Iran in the nineteenth century were educated, the literacy rate being about 5%, and the rate among women was lower, though possibly not as low as is sometimes suggested. The women of the poorer social groups, that is to say the majority, were uneducated. With regard to the better-off, Mounsey emphasises that women were mostly uneducated and had to rely on their looks to keep their husbands' affections, but Wills speaks of their being educated even in the middle classes (presumably among merchants and some members of the guilds). According to Watson, girls, presumably from the middle social groups, were allowed to attend a *mulla's* class up to the age of seven, after which their education became the responsibility of a learned woman. They could read, write, including composing poems, play music, and sew, but their education was necessarily narrow. Women of the families of the senior 'ulama were often educated to some extent: Bibi 'Alam Khurasani, for example, learned the Islamic sciences from her father, and *fiqh, usul* and *hadith* from her husband. Otherwise, children of the well-off were taught at home by tutors.[31]

Many women worked and were therefore integral actors in the local community. They could, for example, gain some property through engagement in small trades, such as that of pawnbroker.[32] A Jewish woman called Muravarid (the Pearl) was a vendor of jewels and shawls to women of the elite and thus had a certain influence in high places, which she was at one time able to exercise on behalf of the Jewish community of Hamadan.[33] Women were involved in the slave trade and one named Mulla Mariam assisted in landing slaves in Bushire in 1877.[34] It is possible she had contacts with the local harems. Much of the slave trade in Mohammareh in 1853 was managed by a female in the harem of the Shaikh, who had his entire confidence.[35] Sometimes a woman could keep a school for younger children, as in the example mentioned by Eastwick of two elderly Muslim women managing a school in Tehran.[36] Women could also be used as emissaries in a dispute, as when Saham al-Mulk, Governor of the Baharlu, and some of the Arab tribes, put down a rebellion headed by Riza Khan, and the latter's brother sent a woman to Saham al-Mulk imploring that a pardon be granted for the tribal rebels.[37] Employed in the carpet trade, in companies such as Ziegler's, where there were four women to a loom, they were paid very low wages, but could also be quite enterprising. Since they worked at home where the foreign merchants in particular could not enter without prior notice, they stole the designs, kept them hidden, and sold them to Iranian merchants.[38]

In the early part of the nineteenth century exceptionally high taxes were paid by female dancers and by 'votaries of pleasure' (presumably prostitutes).[39] They followed their professions under the immediate supervision of the governor, and their names and ages were carefully registered. If one died or married, another took her place. They were also divided into groups according to their merits and the regard in which they were held by their clients. Each group lived in a separate street, and their prices ranged from two tomans to small change (*pul-i siah*). Most women in work, however, were servants, and in the late nineteenth century received the lowly wage of three tomans a year, although the more senior ones were paid more.[40]

Wives usually went into service, unless they had children, or else they undertook the making, mending, and washing of clothes.[41] Other jobs included teacher of small children, midwife, and bathhouse attendant,[42] as well as spinning, carpet weaving, textile weaving and embroidery.[43] There is some evidence that women, but not necessarily those who worked, had increased wealth by the end of the nineteenth century.[44]

Women and Public Activity

The existing evidence does not permit us to say whether there was much change as between the eighteenth and early nineteenth century in terms of opportunities for women to come out of the house. Generally, women's movements were watched and controlled, and for security reasons they did not go out after dark.[45] Many religious ceremonies, for example *rauza khani* and *'Umar kushi*, took place in the house. However, trips to the bazaar, attendance at the mosque, and visits to family provided them with the chance to go into public space.[46] One observer in the early nineteenth century noted that old women of the lower social groups were the only ones seen in the city.[47] However in 1807, another remarked how the curiosity of the women in the house adjoining the one he lived in allowed him to see and talk to them, which their husbands did not mind.[48] In the mid-century, women were depicted as coming into public space regularly. Mounsey describes the bazaars as crowded with men, women and beasts, and also does not specify that the women were old.[49] Binning noted that the women of the urban lower social groups and the villages had little scruple in talking to a stranger, and many of the middle levels were not as shy as might have been expected.[50] The mother and sister of his landlord in Shiraz often came to his quarters to talk to him, and put aside their veils. When he walked on the roof of the house he lived in, the women in the neighbouring house came to stare at him, and were not particular about hiding their faces when no one else was observing, (though, of course, they were still in their own homes). In his observation women were free to go to friends, family, bathhouse, mosque and bazaar, and to receive visitors. He contrasts their behaviour with that of women of rank, who were always closely veiled and guarded by attendants.[51] Indeed, the behaviour of women in a notable household could, at least in theory be rigidly controlled. Gurney has drawn attention to one notable's attempt to ensure his household retained its good reputation during a period of his absence,[52] but it is not certain how far he was successful. Given some of the evidence above, it seems likely that the reality may not have matched his ideal. There were other public occasions when women came out of the house. For example in Rasht, at least, during a marriage procession, a dense crowd of female friends and relations lined the left side of the street.[53] Finally, we must bear in mind that there were differences as to time and place.

In the engagement of women in politics, which we are to study, there was an element of drama, and this extended beyond urban women. When Husain Khan Galidar was killed in an ambush, his widow sent her veil through the Dashti district calling on his tribe to avenge his death, which immediately attracted two thousand to three thousand volunteers.[54] In 1908 Sartip Muhammad 'Ali, former chief of the Kalkhur tribe, was abducted by a rival in Kermanshah on his way back from the mosque. The Sartip's womenfolk went at once to the mosque, and, throwing dust on their heads and rending their garments, appealed to the governor and all the chief *mujtahids* to have him restored.[55] The people of the town then generated a frenzy of religious outrage, and brought pressure on the *mujtahids* to complain, so that the governor had to take action. In reporting on women's petitions submitted to the shah in the 1880s, Schneider points out that they showed a considerable self-confidence, and that they constituted a surprisingly high proportion of the whole.[56]

Bread Riots and Political Demonstrations

Women were primarily responsible for managing food and sustenance, so they became most notably militant at the time of bread shortages. Political demonstrations by ordinary women in the urban areas were often ostensibly bread riots, and therefore so termed. However, they usually represented a deeper malaise resulting mostly from wider economic difficulties affecting the community as a whole. Sometimes the latter resulted from plague or famine, sometimes from a downturn in the local economy, and sometimes from mismanagement by the authorities, who could well exacerbate existing problems by hoarding grain. Thus revolts by the wider community would not unusually start with a women's protest or bread riot, and then spread to involve the whole bazaar network, including the merchants providing the wealth, the 'ulama the moral leadership and intercession with the state, the men from the poorer quarters the might, and the guilds organisation and facilitation.

The earliest references to women's riots date from the mid-nineteenth century, but the British diplomatic sources which provide the most detailed evidence are comparatively scarce before that time, so we cannot be sure that such women's riots did not take place in the earlier part of the nineteenth century, though they may not have been as frequent.

An early recorded example of women's riots took place in Tehran in 1849. At the hour of prayer a number of women from Isfahan created a disturbance in the main mosque of the city, and demanded that the Imam Jum'a intervene to prevent the sacking of Isfahan where there had been turbulence.[57] The women, having initiated the demonstration, were then joined by men, and the crowd grew to two thousand. They pulled the Imam Jum'a out of the pulpit with the intention of obliging him to go to the shah's palace to demand justice. The Imam Jum'a, who had no control over the situation, eventually escaped to his house and the crowd dispersed. This demonstration, not specifically related to bread, would seem to have been part of broader objections to government policy, and was clearly, like most of the other demonstrations, organised and premeditated.

Tehran was again the scene of a riot in 1861, when the shah returned from the hunt to be greeted by a large crowd, which included many women, and some men, amongst them members of the 'ulama.[58] Ostensibly, the crowd was not hostile to the shah personally, and whilst the women pleaded for assistance, members of the 'ulama reminded him of the precepts which enjoined beneficence. Another demonstration the next day included men, who criticised the shah in person, and led to the execution of the *kalantar* (mayor), Muhammad Khan, accompanied by orders that the price of bread be dropped.

A major demonstration involving women took place in Shiraz in 1865, when a crowd of tribal and city women went to the arsenal at the foot of the telegraph wire and complained that the Governor, Qavam al-Daula, cared nothing for the people except to take their gifts. They cited the insecurity of the city and the dearness of bread as the principal evidence of his inadequacies.[59] The governor sent an official with some *farashes* to drive away the women, at which the bazaars closed, evidently in support, and the area round Maidan-i Vakil (Vakil Square) became filled with women, men, *lutis* and country people. A senior government official went to the Maidan of the Arsenal to try to subdue the people, but they pelted him with stones and he fled. The people were only eventually quietened by the dismissal of the governor.

At the time of the famine of 1871, when bread was scarce and provisions expensive, the women of Tehran became so aggressive that the troops in the royal camp were put under arms.[60] Indeed the women who took part in all these demonstrations were notably assertive. Women were thus equally determined in Shiraz in 1878, when a crowd of them, again protesting at the price of bread, pulled the Beglerbegi off his horse.[61] One of the advantages women had was that, when protesting against powerful officials, their veils protected them from individual recognition, so that they could be more intimidating.[62] The mayor of Shiraz, Qavam al-Mulk, was the recipient of invective on the subject of bread in 1885, when two women suddenly positioned themselves in front of his horse, complaining of high prices. They insulted him, upon which they were removed to prison, causing the bazaars to close promptly, and a demonstration of women, children and men to follow. *Lutis* also involved were arrested, but there ensued two or three days when bread was plentiful.[63]

In 1893 the Governor of Shiraz, Sa'd al-Mulk, tried to abolish the right of taking sanctuary in holy places. A preacher in the Jami' Mosque was to announce the changes, but when he rose to speak, so did a group of women and other objectors, who abused the Imam Jum'a saying that first some arrangement should be made about the price of bread.[64] This would appear to have been the role of the women in expressing popular discontent at the abolition of sanctuary, particularly under an arbitrary regime. The meeting broke up to prevent a riot, but none of the other 'ulama accepted the new regulations.

There were also demonstrations in Isfahan over the price of bread in 1893. The people, chiefly women, crowded into the Shah Mosque and would not allow the prayer leader, Aqa Najafi, to say prayers, on the grounds that he was one of the causes of the raised prices. They prevented him from going to his own house, and obliged him to accompany them to see the Governor, Zill al-Sultan, of whom he then demanded a reduction in the price in no uncertain terms.⁶⁵ The price of bread again became high in Isfahan in April 1894, and there was grumbling among the women of the city at the cost of sugar, bread, mutton and lamp oil.⁶⁶ The Governor, Zill al-Sultan, felt unable to punish the women for their agitation (no doubt because it would provoke further disorders). However, a few women, who carried off a small amount of sugar from the confectioners ,were punished by being obliged to pay compensation. Later, on 24th April about forty women and two hundred children went to the mosque of Shaikh Muhammad 'Ali and verbally abused him. They then proceeded to the bazaars and began to remove items from the shops, and had to be driven away by the authorities. Fuel as well as bread could be the cause of an organised women's demonstration, as in Shiraz in 1894, when about forty women took sanctuary in the prince-governor's stables complaining of the lack of fuel.⁶⁷

Another type of disaster which could bring on a demonstration was disease. In Astarabad in 1895, a cholera epidemic produced considerable hardship. Blame, however, fell on the Russians, and on the sale of wine in the town, itself also associated with foreigners. Women took *bast* (santuary) in the Russian consulate as a means of protest, and the shops of Russian subjects were attacked.⁶⁸ This demonstration was said, with some reason, to have been specifically incited by the 'ulama. Similarly, in a period of grain shortage and government weakness in Ardebil a group of women, encouraged by *mujtahid*, came out with stones carried in *chadurs* (veils) tied round their waists. They attacked the castle where the governor was residing, so that he had to order his forces to fire on the crowd to disperse them.⁶⁹ However, it would be a mistake to see other women's actions, as some sources tend to do, as having been specifically instigated, rather than as part of a communal response, or as representing the preoccupations of the women themselves.

Even in Bushire, where riots were rare because of the British preoccupation with order, and the Iranian government's anxieties over the British presence, women's demonstrations occurred. In March 1897 the house of the Head of the (British run) Post Office in Bushire was stoned by a crowd of women, who had to be removed from the town, imprisoned or severely punished before the matter would settle.⁷⁰ No doubt there was an anti-foreign element in the women's protest.

Two demonstrations, however, stand out as being exceptionally unusual for their sophistication in terms of expression and organisation, which at certain points carry an element of choreography. One of them is the earliest nineteenth century example so far to come to light. A woman's demonstration formed part of a popular uprising in Isfahan in 1840 so serious that it brought the shah in person to the city. At this time Isfahan was dominated by *lutis*, which is perhaps a testimony to economic problems and unemployment. Certainly, there seem to have been struggles between different social groups with merchants being subjected to constant robbery by *lutis*. The latter were then protected by some of the principal *mujtahids*, especially Haj Sayyid Muhammad Baqir, and his son.[71] The disorder became so great that the shah marched to Isfahan with a force of thirty guns and fourteen corps of infantry, a most unusual event, which was to remain for some time in the popular memory. On his arrival in 27th February 1840, he and his court were for twelve days the guests of Sayyid Muhammad Baqir, which in reality constituted punishment by a major fine. Four hundred *lutis* were seized, executed or otherwise punished, and the *mujtahid*'s son was sent to Kerbala.[72] The shah, however, had some difficulty in persuading Muhammad Baqir himself and another *mujtahid*, Sayyid Ibrahim Karbasi, to go to Kerbala as well.[73] When Muhammad Baqir finally announced he was going to Kerbala, a crowd of seven to eight thousand came to his house and begged him not to leave, declaring themselves ready for martyrdom.[74] Two to three thousand women, having gathered together, went to the artillery quarters in the Maidan-i Shah (the main square), where they began to weep and wail. The shah came out onto the balcony of the Ali Qapu Palace, where he was residing, and asked what they wanted. They answered that as their husbands had not the courage to wait upon His Majesty, they had done so, and their prayer was that he would put all of them to death rather than permit the head of their religion to leave the city.[75] The shah replied that he could not possible prevent the sayyid fulfilling a religious duty, namely a pilgrimage to the tomb of his ancestors. A crowd of both men and women then went to the sayyid's house and would not allow him to leave it. The shah did not punish them. In the event the *mujtahid* prevailed and remained in Isfahan. After the shah left, to the evident annoyance of the more propertied section of the populace, he protected a well-known *luti* and vagabond who had taken refuge in his quarter, and when the latter was finally arrested, the *mujtahid* had him released on the grounds of repentance.[76] The shah had evidently curbed the worst of the disorder, but he could not eradicate it without resolving the underlying economic problems.

The second demonstration, a major event, took place in May 1893 in Shiraz. It brought about the fall of Qavam al-Mulk, *kalantar* (mayor) of Shiraz, about whom the people of the city went to the telegraph office to complain to the shah.[77] The people showed unanimity in refusing to accept the Qavam's promises of better living conditions, and in demanding he be sent away from Shiraz. This solidarity continued even under attack on the orders of the shah, and they were supported by the 'ulama who refused to go and advise the people to disperse, when asked to do so by the governor of Shiraz. Although the people were armed, and had been joined by riflemen, they showed no sign of violent hostility and did not use their arms.[78] During the demonstration the people occupied the telegraph office of Shiraz and telegraphed the shah concerning the price of bread, but nothing was touched.[79] But most remarkable of all was the role of the women in this demonstration. They led a procession, composed of an immense crowd, to the telegraph office to make the initial complaint.[80] On 15th May a band of women also collected all the Jews in Shiraz and, making them bring their copies of the Talmud, induced them to join the crowd, by whom they were cordially welcomed. That same day, the crowd now numbering fifteen thousand to twenty thousand men and women brought their holiest objects, the banner of Husain and the hand of 'Abbas. They remained beating their breasts and weeping, and saying 'Ya Husain' (Oh Husain!) until the removal of Qavam.

The Cultural Background to Women's Demonstrations

While it is difficult to produce any direct proof, it would seem possible that these demonstrations were in some way linked to *ta'ziyya* plays (Shi'i passion plays). These re-enact the drama of the seventh century battle of Kerbala when the Prophet's grandson, Husain, the third Imam of the Shi'a, was martyred in a struggle for justice against the army of the 'Umayad Caliph Mu'awiyya who had usurped his position. During the struggle a number of the Prophet's family were killed. Present at the scene of battle were his granddaughter, Zainab – the aunt of Husain, and Fatima, his daughter and the wife of his nephew, Qasim. Thus, in this passion play, women had a role in the actual field of struggle, although they did not themselves fight. They supported the men who went into battle, tried to prevent them from going to certain death, and wept at their departure, but accepted in the end that they must make any sacrifice necessary for the cause. Although women in the urban demonstrations were more assertive than the women at Kerbala, and were occasionally beaten, death and brutality were suffered by the men to whom they acted mainly as a support. There are therefore distinct parallels between the demonstrations and the *ta'ziyya* plays. This is not to argue that the demonstrations derive from the *ta'ziyya* plays but rather that they emerge from a common culture and are also a reflection of social, political and cultural trends in the nineteenth century and perhaps even earlier.

To understand this background further it is necessary to consider very briefly the history of the *ta'ziyya* plays.

Ta'ziyya plays emerge from a sense of community and collaboration being an expression of unity. It strengthens the feeling of community.[81] *Ta'ziyya* was also a means for the people of finding a common solace in the face of a political system that was arbitrary and oppressive. It enabled them to endure the often intolerable hardships of despotic government, and to find, from the examples of the tribulations of the Imams, the inner strength to withstand them and struggle against them as a community. *Ta'ziyya* flourished in the Qajar period when many *takiyyas* were built and people attended in their thousands.[82] Historians have dated the beginnings of *ta'ziyya* to the Safavid period, but at that time they were not what could properly be called plays, as references from the Safavid period speak of processions but not of play performances.⁸³ In the first decades of the seventeenth century Muharram ceremonial ritual developed in most urban centres, and by the mid-century there was some semblance of enactment, but without any spoken role.⁸⁴ Chelkowski argues that *ta'ziyya* as ritual theatre arose from a fusion in the mid-eighteenth century of two traditions of performance of the rites of 'Ashura, the one peripatetic and the other local.⁸⁵ As between the Zand period and the time of Fath 'Ali Shah there was a significant rise in both the number of performances of *ta'ziyya* and in the versions used, subsidiary stories being developed from the main narrative.⁸⁶ By the nineteenth century *ta'ziyyas* had acquired special structures for their enactment, called *takiyyas* and later also Husainiyyas.⁸⁷ The earliest permanent building was recorded by Masse in Astarabad in 1786.⁸⁸ From the late eighteenthth century foreign travellers such as Franklin, 1787, and Drouville, travelling 1812–13, provide descriptions of actual *ta'ziyya* plays, Drouville mentioning that parts were given in the battle of Kerbala, and that four thousand people became involved, but astonishingly none of them were wounded.⁸⁹ By 1840 *ta'ziyyas* were being written in poetry, and in the mid-1830s Kuzov saw a complete recreation of the death of Imam Husain in which all the details of the events were faithfully re-enacted.⁹⁰

Certainly by the early nineteenth century *ta'ziyyas* had female roles, although the female parts were always played by men or boys. The male actors were dressed in baggy black garments covering them from head to foot, with veils to hide their faces.⁹¹ Thus Franklin mentions the tragically fated marriage of the son of Imam Hasan with the daughter of Imam Husain, who was surrounded by the women of the family. When her husband goes into the field of battle, the young wife most eloquently expresses her unhappiness.⁹² At the end of a performance in Zanjan in 1862 Husain and all his family were killed on the orders of Yazid.⁹³ When 'Ali Akbar decided to go into battle, his mother fainted, but on recovering expressed the wish that her son be lion-hearted and prayed for his well-being.⁹⁴ *Ta'ziyya* was significant in demonstrating the heroism and courage of women, who expressed their feelings as mothers, sisters and wives, and their willingness to struggle in the service of their religion. In one *ta'ziyya* the mother of Qasim goes with great emotion to the Imam and asks if he would give permission for her son to partake in jihad.⁹⁵

Ta'ziyya, however, underwent its most pronounced development as a result of royal patronage, and that of the notables. It seems partly to have been a form of religious entertainment and partly a means of creating a bond of identification with the common people.⁹⁶ This movement developed from the time of Aqa Muhammad Qajar, and gradually encouraged the 'ulama to accept it, despite their doubts about its religious validity.⁹⁷ Early in the reign of Fath 'Ali Shah, one of the greatest *mujtahids* of the time, Mirza Abu'l Qasim known as Fazil-i Qumi (d.1231/1815) issued a *fatva* declaring that playing a part (*shabih khani*) was not forbidden but permissible.⁹⁸

Ouseley describes a *ta'ziyya* in the square of the shah's palace, and remarks that it had more valuable decoration than probably ever graced a European theatre performance, for the shah had lent a large quantity of his jewels for the production. Ouseley also mentions another *ta'ziyya* in which Husain resolved to go and rescue 'Abbas, his sister Zainab and daughter Sakina tried with their tears and entreaties and foreboding to dissuade him.[99]

Ta'ziyya spread further during the reign of Muhammad Shah. Haj Mirza Aqasi, his powerful Prime Minister, had his own *takiyya* (place of performance for *ta'ziyya*).[100] A *farman* (command) of Muhammad Shah's reign, later confirmed by Nasir al-Din Shah, commands that all of the landowners of Kushak village near Shiraz must pay for the village *ta'ziyya* as part of the village tax responsibilities.[101] By 1843 numerous *ta'ziyyas* with different scripts were performed in Tehran.[102]

The greatest patron of *ta'ziyya* was Nasir al-Din Shah, who inaugurated an official *takiyya*, known as the Takiyya-yi Daulat, in 1856, there having been, however, performances under court patronage earlier in his reign.[103] Following a visit to Europe in 1873, during which he attended a performance at the Albert Hall, London, he constructed a new government *takiyya*, an immense, circular building, with space for twenty to thirty thousand persons.[104] Women had a prominent role as, for example, in one *ta'ziyya* where there was a dialogue between Zainab and Husain in which they spoke of their sad destiny, and Zainab flung herself to the floor and poured dust on her head.[105] There were more than fifty *takiyyas* in Tehran alone in the reign of Nasir al-Din Shah. *Ta'ziyya* became very widespread and each town, large or small, had a *takiyya*.[106] Their founders were not only notables, but members of guilds, for example the goldsmiths, or communities from the provinces, e.g. Azarbaijan. The interior was sometimes gorgeous. The patron of each *takiyya* ensured, for the sake of his own reputation, that the interior be suitably maintained. The royal *takiyya* was financed by the shah but he bestowed upon the leading merchants in Tehran the honour of keeping up its decoration.

In Nasir al-Din Shah's reign, under the influence of the European theatrical tradition, *ta'ziyyas* in the royal *takiyya* divided between those of which the purport was mainly religious, and those from ancillary or other stories of religious origin which had an element of popular entertainment. I'timad al-Saltana mentions that, when he went to the *ta'ziyya* of Bilqais and Sulaiman (Bilqis and Solomon), the bride of Sulaiman, having been all dressed-up, appeared riding an elephant. At the point that they wanted to get her down, the elephant shied away and then bolted, still carrying the bride, to the merriment of the observers.[107]

Sometimes *ta'ziyyas* were performed just for women, for example in the house of Qamar al-Saltana, the wife of Sipah Salar, the audience, and exceptionally in *ta'ziyyas*, all the players were women.[108] Women's *ta'ziyyas* were closed to men, and those who held them gained the title of *mulla* (person of pious learning).[109]

Religious or not particularly so, *ta'ziyyas* provided new opportunities for women to go out and about, to contact other people and to witness different forms of expression. They were therefore important in drawing women out of their limited existence in the home and enlarging their experience. *Ta'ziyyas* thus had an enthusiastic female audience. Ouseley describes how the walls of the *takiyya* square in the palace in Tehran were covered in hundreds of women wearing white *chadurs* (veils).[110] At one performance in Zanjan, women sat on the right and men opposite.[111] In the government *takiyya* in Tehran the major part of the audience were women, who sat cross-legged on the floor in the centre, which was allocated as their particular space.[112] By the latter part of the nineteenth century the female characters had acquired their own *ta'ziyyas*, there being for example, the story of the death of Fatima-yi Zahra, and the martyrdom of the wife of Shimr (who had become an adherent of the family of Husain).[113]

* * *

The women's popular demonstrations described above varied in their purpose, but were mostly political by implication, specifically in being critical of government economic policy. They were not, on the whole, spontaneous or chance eruptions, but demonstrations that were organised by a community in which women were given a specific role.

The political culture of these demonstrations is peculiarly Iranian. With the more sophisticated demonstrations the women's role appears almost choreographed, and even with the simpler ones there is evidence of organisation, and I would not argue that this feature of Iranian culture would necessarily be new. The role of women in the *ta'ziyya* plays places them unusually on the battlefield of the political struggle itself, by contrast with the depiction of women as peaceful and resigned in the Christian tradition. The Shi'i women do not actually fight and die but have a strong role in support and communal empathy. Yet it cannot be said that these demonstrations are an extension of the *ta'ziyya*, but rather that the more premeditated ones are part of a development that gives political expression a new form.

The major demonstrations of 1840 and 1893, in particular, show that ordinary women had a valued role in politics as part of the community in the nineteenth century, yet they have come to light through largely chance mention in the more obscure contemporary documents of the British archives. As far as I have been able to investigate, Persian documents describing the same events from a later perspective fail to mention them. This is an example to support the case that women's role in history can easily be overlooked.

That there were such demonstrations in the earlier part of the nineteenth century shows a more traditional element, yet the slight evidence also raises the possibility, which needs further investigation, that women were becoming better-educated, better-off and better-organised by the final two decades of the period. This in turn raises the so far unanswerable question of the degree of influence of modern organisation, and Western forms of expression, on traditional Iranian culture. Further, it demonstrates that there were older roots to the role of women in both the constitutional and the Islamic revolutions.

Notes

1 I am most grateful for Dr 'Ali Bulookbashi, Dr Ziba Mir-Hosseini and Dr Sarah Ansari for the contribution their comments have made to this chapter.
2 Nazim al-Islam Kirmani, Mirza Muhammad, *Tarikh-i bidari-yi Iranian*, Tehran 1357–1978–9, I, p. 361.
3 See, for example, A. Kasravi, *Tarikh-i mashruta-yi Iran*, Tehran 2536, pp. 53, 57, 66, 101; J. Afary, *The Iranian Constitutional Revolution*, Columbia 1996, pp. 177–208.
4 A photograph taken during the disturbances of 1906 shows women participating in the political action as an organised group. M. Haqani, ' Nahzat-i mashrutiyyat bih ravayat-i tasvir', *Tarikh-i Mu'asir-i Iran*, 5, No. 18, p. 266.
5 Afary, *Revolution*, p. 177. She quotes Morgan Shuster as saying, in *The Strangling of Persia*: 'The veiled women of Iran who, with little or no experience, had overnight become teachers, newspaper writers, founders of women's clubs, (and) speakers on political subjects.
6 There is at least one example from the Safavid period. Interview with Dr M. Sefatgol, professor of Safavid History, Tehran University, 19.11.2002.
7 Marcus, *Middle East*, p. 100.
8 J. E.Tucker, *Women in Nineteenth-Century Egypt*, Cambridge 1985, pp. 141–2.
9 See D.G. Levy, H.B. Applewhite and M.D. Johnson, *Women in Revolutionary Paris*, Illinois 1980, p. 15.; D. Godineau, *The Women of Paris and the French Revolution*, trans. K. Streip, Berkeley 1988, pp. 98–9.
10 No. 18, 20.12.1849, FO 60/146.
11 Following the theme of the book, this chapter concentrates on women in urban society. However, they also appear to have had a role in conflict in country society, as happened at the slaughter of a government army, sent to suppress a revolt in Neyriz. The Neyriz women clambered onto surrounding rocks, and clapping their mouths with their hands, gave out cries of exultation. More government troops followed, this time with success. The men were killed and the women brought to Shiraz, where some were distributed to the soldiery and others were left to beg on the streets. Encl. in No.350 18.11.1853 and No.381 15.12.1853, FO 248/150. In the villages likewise, the women joined the men in battle. On his way to Hamadan, Alcock found that, due to the harsh conduct of Iranian officials, his party encountered villagers instantly armed, with the women being active in providing stakes and weapons for the men. T. Alcock, *Travels in Russia, Persia, Turkey and Greece in 1828–9*, London 1831, p. 77.
12 M. Ettehadieh, *Inja Tehran ast*, Tehran 1377, p. 261.
13 Encl. in No. 17, 5.2.1862, FO 60/266.
14 A. Mounsey, *Journey*, pp. 158–9.
15 Encl. in No. 135, 7.12.1887, FO 248/448.
16 Annual Medical Report, Bushire, p. 8, 17.4.1884, FO 248/300.
17 C.J. Wills, *Persia as It Is*, London 1886, p. 55.
18 Encl. p. 195, No. 16., 10.4.1860, FO 248/191.
19 Encl. p. 195, No. 18, 25.1.1882, FO 60/444. Women were not necessarily as decorous and modest as some sources would suggest. Wills describes being in

the house of a notable when two young ladies entered in 'becoming if slightly indelicate dress' with feet and legs bare, and skirts such as were seen in ballets. They asked him to examine their tongues and throat, and the eunuch could not control them. Then, together with the eunuch and a young black female servant, they partook of tea with shrieks of laughter, but all three women immediately rushed to cover their face when the master of the house appeared. C.J. Wills, *In the Land of the Lion and the Sun*, London 1883, p. 40. He further describes them as giving an occasional glimpse of their 'charms' to passers-by, Wills, *Persia*, p. 14. According to Mounsey, they were sometimes willing 'to gratify the curiosity of a European by lifting their veils', and further, on people's visits to the Shrine of Shah 'Abd al-'Azim to the south of Tehran, the road thither became a promenade, with the women keeping their attendants at a distance and uncovering 'charms' elsewhere kept hidden. Mounsey, *Journey*, p. 159. 'Ain al-Saltana, making the same journey, does not report being the recipient of such favours, but he noted on a rail journey to Shah 'Abd al-'Azim that the carriage was very crowded and that women outnumbered men two to one. *Ruznama-yi khatirat-i 'Ain al-Saltana*, eds I. Afshar and M. Salur, Tehran 1374, I, p. 351.

20 Mounsey, *Journey*, p. 160.
21 Binning, *Persia*, p. 393; see also K. Mu'tazed and N. Kasra, *Siyasat va haramsara (zan dar 'asr-i Qajar)*, Tehran 1379, p. 220 for marriage amongst the elite.
22 See S. Mahdavi, 'Women, Shi'ism and Cuisine in Iran' in S. Ansari and V. Martin, eds, *Women, Religion and Culture in Iran*, London 2001, pp. 10–26.
23 Ettehadieh, *Tehran*, p. 260.
24 See I. Schneider, 'Muhammad Baqir Shafti (1180–1260/1766–1844) und die Isfahaner Gerichtsbarkeit', *Der Islam*, 79, 2002, pp. 240–273 for discussion of an example. I am grateful for Dr Schneider for providing me with an abstract of the main points of this article in English.
25 J. Malcolm, *Persia*, II, p. 393.
26 Wills, *Land*, 276.
27 Robertson to Sheil, 20.8.1842, FO 248/101.
28 No. 35, 17.3.1859, FO 248/179.
29 Enclosure in No. 76, 7.7.1861, FO 60/257. For another example of the punishment of a prostitute see Kh. Bayani, *Panja sal tarikh-i Nasiri*, V, Tehran 1375, p. 367.
30 The 'ulama were, however, periodically vigilant about prostitution in any case. In Shiraz in 1894 Sayyid 'Ali Akbar at the head of about two hundred students and roughs entered a brothel by force in order to have the inmates arrested, but without success, as the women had been tipped off with the connivance of the police. No. 792, 16.10.1894, FO 248/602. In 1892 Sayyid Abu Talib of Isfahan stopped a woman in the street and asked why she was wearing galoshes, calling her all sorts of names. She answered that she was not what he imagined and called for assistance, at which a number of people appeared and he had to take flight. No. 3007, 3.10.1892, FO 248/553.
31 Watson, *Persia*, p. 19; Mounsey, *Journey*, 160; Wills, *Persia*, p. 67, M.H. Rajabi, *Mashashir-i zanan-i Irani va Parsigu*, Tehran 1374, p. 36. Rajabi mentions Rubaba Mara'shi, the wife of Sayyid 'Ali Shams al-Ma'ali, Nasir al-Din Shah's doctor, who started classes for women in her house in 1270/1853–4 and taught for thirteen years, despite some popular pressure to close, *Zanan*, p. 104. Afary points out that from the 1870s Muslim girls attended the American Presbyterian School in Tehran, but it did not attract girls from the community at large because of the religious implications, *Revolution*, p. 182. The question of the effect that such educated women would have had on the general community of women is a subject lacking evidence, and yet much in need of further research.

32 Encl. in 4.1.1845, FO 248/113
33 No. 17, 31.1.1866, FO 60/296. Compare E. Benbass and A. Rodrigue, *Sephardi Jewry*, Berkeley 2000, p. 38, which mentions that Jewish women traders had a significant role in purveying goods to the imperial harem.
34 No. 37, 23.3.1877, FO 248/329. The title of *mulla* (learned), was accorded occasionally not only to women, but to members of the religious minorities, for example, to a Jew.
35 Encl. in No. 131, 23.5.1853, FO 248/150.
36 E.B. Eastwick, *Journal of a Diplomat's Three Years' Residence in Persia*, London 1864, pp. 231–2. He also lived near the bathhouse and reports that, 'Swarms of muffled figures pass to a nearby bathhouse and ever and anon an unveiled face looks over into the Faringi's garden, and a girlish titter, or, maybe a word or two of not the most complimentary nature, is addressed to the walker in the garden.'
37 No. 575, 6.9.1893, Shiraz Agent FO 248/577.
38 No. 46, 23.2.1891, FO 60/522.
39 Scott Waring, *Sheeraz*, p. 80.
40 A. Mustaufi, *Sharh-i zindigani-yi man ya tarikh-i ijtima'i-yi Iran*, Tehran 1324, I, pp. 210–12 gives an indication of the lives of female servants. Ettehadieh found the female servants' wages to be 1 toman in cash per month and four sets of clothing each year, see *Tehran*, p. 262.
41 Watson, *History*, p. 27.
42 Ettehadieh, *Tehran*, p. 262.
43 Mu'tazed and Kasra, *Zan*, pp. 226–7.
44 Ettehadieh, *Tehran*, p. 263.
45 Mu'tazed and Kasra, *Zan*, pp. 218–9.
46 According to Picot, up to the time of Aqa Muhammad Qajar, in the late eighteenth century, women of all ranks were permitted to follow the army, but in the nineteenth century only women of the elite could do so. H. Picot, 'Report on the Persian Army', FO 881/7364, p. 25. Of course, the women of lower ranks would have been largely tribal.
47 M. Tancoigne, *A Narrative of a Journey into Persia and Residence in Tehran*, London 1820, p. 207.
48 Scott Waring, *Sheeraz*, p. 61. There are no more particulars as to the circumstances, and we must note that there would have been variations as between individual families.
49 Mounsey, *Journey*, p. 158.
50 Binning, *Persia*, p. 393.
51 Ibid., p. 393.
52 J. Gurney, 'A Qajar Household and Its Estates', *Iranian Studies*, 16, 1983, Nos. 3–4, pp. 137–176.
53 No. 46, 27.6.1861, FO 248/199.
54 Hennell to Sheil, No. 436, 9.9. 1844, FO248/113.
55 No. 46, 15.11.1908, FO 248/935.
56 Schneider, 'Jurisdiction', p. 7.
57 No. 18, 20.12.1849, FO 60/146.
58 MAE, Ambassade/Teheran/55, No. 5, 5.3.1861.
59 Encl. in No. 83, 11.8.1865, FO 60/290.
60 No. 108, 16.8.1871, FO 60/335
61 From 26 Zhi al-Hajja 1295/21. 12.1878, Sirjani, *Vaqayi'*, p. 103.
62 Sparroy, W., *Persian Children of the Royal Family*, London 1902, p. 238.
63 21 Shavval 1302/3.8.1885, Sirjani, *Vaqayi'*, pp. 243–4.
64 No. 555, 24.7.1893, FO 248/547. Inflation caused by fluctuations in the exchange rate between silver and copper, the debasement of the coinage and a

fall in the world price of silver affected the price of bread in the 1890s, causing much popular discontent. In September 1894 notices placarded around Shiraz threatened the governor with a further riot over the economic situation. No. 778, 20.9.1894, FO 248/602.
65 Decipher No. 16, 26.10.1893, FO 248/572.
66 Zill al-Sultan to Nasir al-Din Shah, No. 3403 and No. 3404, 26.4.1894, FO 248/599.
67 No. 808, 16.11.1894, FO 248/602.
68 Encl. in No. 25, 19.3.1895, FO 60/565.
69 R. Tapper, *Frontier Nomads of Iran*, Cambridge 1997, pp. 248–9.
70 MFA 16 Shawal 1314/ 20 March 1897, 1314 B29 F9, No. 102.
71 No. 42, 24.8.1840, FO 60/74.
72 Hennell to Sheil, No. 15, 20.4.1840, 11.5.1840, and 19.6.1840, FO 248/99.
73 Hennell to Sheil, 25.5.1840, FO 248/99.
74 Hennell to Sheil 18.6.1840, and 19.6.1840, FO 248/99.
75 If the role of the women here seems unusually assertive as compared to the men, it should be remembered that they were staying the shah's wrath in an attempt to avoid bloodshed. From that point of view it would fit with the *ta'ziyya* role for women in attempting to prevent the loss of life.
76 No. 42, 24.8.1840, FO 60/74.
77 No. 513, 19.5.1893, Shiraz Agent, FO 248/576.
78 No. 513, 19.5.1893, Shiraz Agent, FO 248/576.
79 No. 71, 13.5.1893, FO 248/578.
80 Sykes to Lascelles, 31.5.1893, FO 248/578.
81 E. Shahidi and A. Bulookbashi, *Pajhuhishi dar ta'ziyya va ta'ziyya khani az aghaz ta payan-i daura-yi Qajar dar Tehran*, Tehran 1380, p. 45.
82 S. Humayuni, *Ta'ziyya dar Iran*, Shiraz 1380, p. 70.
83 S.R. Peterson, 'The Ta'ziyeh and Related Arts' in P.J. Chelkowski, ed., *Ta'ziyeh, Ritual and drama in Iran*, New York, 1979, pp. 65–7; Humayuni, *Ta'ziyya*, p. 71.
84 J. Calmard, 'Le patronage des ta'ziyeh: elements pour une etude globale', in Chelkowsi, ed., *Ta'ziyeh*, p. 123. See also J. Calmard, 'Shi'i Rituals and Power II. The Consolidation of Safavid Shi'ism: Folklore and Popular Religion' in C. Melville, ed. *Safavid Persia*, London and New York, 1996, especially pp. 156–160.
85 P. Chelkowski, 'Ta'ziyya', Encyclopedia of Islam, second edition, Leiden 2000, X, pp. 406–8.
86 Shahidi and Bulookbashi, *Ta'ziyya*, p. 106.
87 Chelkowski, 'Ta'ziyya', p. 406.
88 Peterson, 'Ta'ziyeh', p. 65. There are suggestions of Russian influence in the development of *ta'ziyya* as theatre. Peterson notes that the earliest examples of theatres specifically developed for *ta'ziyyas* date from the first two decades of the nineteenth century in the Russian provinces, (ibid. p. 67). M. Mahjub considers that the change from processions to plays derived from Europe. He points out the early influence in north Iran, and sees a possible derivation in the Transcaucasus and other Muslim provinces of Russia. See 'The Effect of European Theatre and the Influence of Its Theatrical Methods upon Ta'ziyeh' in Chelkowski, ed, *Ta'ziyeh*, pp. 138–143. It is worth noting that European theatre had an influence on India at this time, financed by the Rajahs, R.K. Yajnik, *The Indian Theatre*, London 1933, pp. 84 ff.
89 Humayuni, *Ta'ziyya*, pp. 76–7.
90 Ibid., p. 77.
91 Chelkowski, 'Ta'ziyya', p. 407.
92 Shahidi and Bulookbashi, *Ta'ziyya*, pp. 78–80.
93 Humayuni, *Ta'ziyya*, pp. 79–80.
94 Ibid., p. 80.

95 Ibid., p. 923.
96 Shahidi and Bulookbashi, *Ta'ziyya*, p. 106.
97 Ibid., p. 160.
98 Humayuni, *Ta'ziyya*, pp. 61–2.
99 W. Ouseley, *Travels in Various Countries of the East, More Particularly Persia*, London 1823, III, pp. 165, 167.
100 Calmard, 'Patronage', p. 124.
101 Rajab 1259/July-August 1843 SAM No. 240023275 location 1AB2Ch716.
102 Shahidi and Bulookbashi, *Ta'ziyya*, p. 168.
103 Calmard, 'Patronage', p. 124. There is some indication that court *ta'ziyyas* had an element of entertainment apart from the religious content of the play. In 1855 Murray reported to Clarendon that he had attended 'a dramatic representation partly historical resembling the mysteries'. The play had 'certain ridiculous adjuncts including the appearance on the stage of a Frank ambassador (a standard character in *ta'ziyyas*) dressed up in an old cocked hat borrowed or bought from some of the foreign missions, and such other European clothes as can be found in Tehran. This ambassador, who is supposed to be interceding with Yezid for the family of Husain, is armed with a telescope with which he scans the spectators and the surrounding scene, and he is accompanied by his wife and a vast train bearing presents to the Musulman chief.' He goes on that the Iranian Government had thought to try and exclude the foreign missions from what 'the Sadr-i 'Azam has the effrontery to term 'the highest occasion of public worship in the Shi'ite creed, although he well knows that the dresses, the scenery, the music, the disguising of boys as women, the smoking, drinking sherbets in the building before and after the acts, together with other accessories are all so repugnant to the dogma and religious practices of Islam that none of the chief mullahs or ulemas will countenance the representations by their presence.' Murray to Clarendon, No. 52, 17.9.1855, FO 60/203.

Murray's observations on the foreign emissary in the play may be compared to those of Kuzov attending a *ta'ziyya* in Tabriz in the time of 'Abbas Mirza. He wrote that the foreign ambassador appeared in a representation that was exceptionally laughable, particularly with regard to dress, and was riding a black horse, although Iranians as a whole did not like black horses. Cited in Humayuni, *Ta'ziyya*, pp. 77–8.
104 Humayuni, *Ta'ziyya*, pp. 82–3; Peterson, 'Ta'ziyeh', p. 69.
105 Humayuni, *Ta'ziyya*, p. 113.
106 Chelkowski, 'Ta'ziyya', p. 407; http://www. Oracle/Transfer/Serjik/ahmadi/salehi135.doc, p. 4. I am grateful to Mr Mehran Afshari for this reference; A. Amin, 'Iran dar sal-i 1311 hijri qamari', trans. M. Gharavi, *Majala-yi barisi-ha-yi tarikhi*, Year 9, No. 4, 1353, pp. 90– 91.
107 I'timad al-Saltana, *Ruznama*, p. 517.
108 Shahidi and Bulookbashi, *Ta'ziyya*, pp. 109–110.
109 Ibid., p. 110.
110 Ouseley, *Travels*, III, pp. 165–6.
111 Humayuni, *Ta'ziyya*, pp. 78–9.
112 Humayuni, *Ta'ziyya*, p. 106.
113 Shahidi and Bulookbashi, *Ta'ziyya*, pp. 185, 289.

6

THE *LUTIS* – THE TURBULENT URBAN POOR

The name *luti* was given to people in a variety of occupations in urban centres for many centuries in Iran. It could indicate their cultural values, their economic standing, usually among the poorer social groups, and their political role. In a word, *lutis* could be the socially conscious leaders of the poor, whose heroic values inspired them, and they could be every sort of thug, rogue and thief. As will be discussed below, much has already been written on the subject of *lutis*, so this chapter will attempt to develop these views in the context of the south of Iran in the nineteenth century. It will finish by considering the implications of their culture in the political struggles of the period. *Lutis* will be considered primarily in their role as the unemployed, and the turbulent urban poor.

The Luti Culture and Its Origins

The *lutis* have a long history in the culture and politics of Iran, and there are some indications that their role declined from one of high ideals, associated with *futuvvat* or *javanmardi* (devout manliness), to one that was most commonly connected with disorder and thievery by the nineteenth century.[1] The followers of the *futuvvat*, which dates back at least to the twelfth century, and possibly even to the time of the caliphs, were originally dervishes, or mystics, who incorporated the precepts of their beliefs in works called the *futuvvatnama*, appearing not only in Iran but also in Cairo.[2] Their main aim was to abjure evil and purify the soul, their principal objectives being the attainment of the virtues of courage, generosity, loyalty, fidelity and purity.[3] They had their own ethos and customs, which could indeed be fanatical, for example requiring the killing of a female member of the family who was considered to have dishonoured it. Mostly bachelors, they were young men aspiring to a better life, living and eating together, and seeking recreation by the same means. They were also bound by a strong sense of group loyalty and identity (*'asabiya*).[4] Associated with this culture was the concept of *pahlavan* (hero) inspired by the stories of the warriors of Firdausi's *Shahnama*, recounted at their gatherings, lending to the Iranian followers of *futuvvat* a peculiarly Iranian literary dimension.

The audience took figures such as Rustam and Suhrab as their examples to be emulated and sought to recreate their heroism.[5]

Adherents of the *futuvvat* tended to be the people of the street and bazaar, the poorer social groups, but they also included the guilds, and sometimes they were joined by younger members of the highest classes. Sometimes *futuvvat* organisations included elders of the guilds, who were, in addition, the leaders of their particular quarters. In the Safavid period *futuvvat* became much more widespread among the common people, and their *futuvvatnama* provided guidance on how to live, with much of their advice attributed either to the Shi'a Imams or to the heroes of the *Shahnama*.[6] One of their duties was the propagation and teaching of the shari'a among the common people. Throughout the history of Iran, however, despite these high ideals, *lutis* were also associated with thievery, and while some *pahlavans* (heroes, champions) belonged to the military or to regular occupations, such as the guilds, others engaged in robbery, murder and sedition,[7] in which they resembled the half communal half criminal *zu'ar* of Mamluke cities.[8]

In addition to the groups already mentioned, the term *luti* was also used to describe entertainers, keepers of monkeys, bears and lions, jugglers, puppeteers, musicians and dancers, an association which on the surface seems curious and indeed was not an entirely happy one for the entertainers themselves.[9] Some such entertainers were known for their wit, and Scott Waring, for example, describes them as a kind of jester with free access to the prince and governor of Shiraz, whom they amused with stories, some indecent, which they related or invented about the inhabitants of Shiraz.[10] They are reported as having been allowed to take great liberties with the reputations of the most respectable characters.

The use of the same term to encompass both entertainers and the aspirants to *futuvvat* (devout manliness), law-abiding or otherwise, may originate in the use of a common culture and frame of reference in their self-expression and values. To some extent they belonged to the same underclass, for whom many of them provided diversion. The need to find a living through more than one occupation at this time would have meant that some entertainers had other, low paid jobs, and no doubt there were those among the low-paid who could earn a living through entertainment. However, they would also have been linked by the way they are perceived in terms of the Islamic emphasis on order (*nizam*). Islam frowns upon disorder as likely to encourage anarchy (*harj va marj*), which it dreads, and its upholders may seek to repress forms of expression which might even slightly undermine the Islamic system. The emphasis in Islam on decorum, for example in women's dress, emanates from this principle. Music and other forms of entertainment have been deplored by the 'ulama as likely to encourage unbecoming or immoral conduct, and to foster deviant thoughts. Both the entertainers and some at least of the urban poor have long been on the margins of this value system, lacking in the normal constraints, and liable to encourage indecency. Thus it may be that they came to be associated with each other. In addition, there is in both groups a tendency to non-conformism, and to express divergent and unorthodox views through a culture which, though ostensibly often pious, in reality is open to varying and individual interpretations, and is thus disapproved of by the 'ulama.[11] Its existence is a testimony to the willingness of Qajar government to balance these factors, and to tolerate a certain amount of turbulence, both as a safety valve for rebelliousness and discontent, and as a form of variety of expression, providing it did not go so far as to threaten the existing political system.

The question of the role of entertainers really belongs in another work, as this chapter is concerned with the political and economic role of the *lutis* as the urban poor in the nineteenth century (which is not to say that the entertainers could not be political, but the evidence as to their having had such a role is still very slight).

Lutis, thievery and poverty

European travellers passing through Iran in the nineteenth century, with sufficient means, and empathising on the whole with others also of sufficient means, had little doubt that *lutis* were thieves; and since some *lutis* deprived other people of their possessions in an unlawful way, that is what they might well be called. To Binning, they were determined, mischievous, depraved persons, who typically plundered a town when central control faltered, for example at the death of a shah. At that point they extorted money from law-abiding inhabitants by threatening destroy their property.[12] Brugsch remarked that the most feared section of most Iranian towns was that of the *lutis* or as he put it, idlers, who were organised in gangs and were involved in murky activities.[13] Ussher, passing through Shiraz in the 1860s, described them as 'thieves, pickpockets, idlers and scamps, who until recently had the respectable inhabitants of the town in terror'.[14] The thievery of the *lutis* was also noted by Mounsey, who said that they were ever ready to take advantage of disorder to pillage their neighbours, and consisted of rowdies, roughs and loafers, unscrupulous leaders of a lawless, riotous and anti-Qur'anic life.[15] However, making a comparison with European cities, he also noted that in reality they belonged to a class of society whose members had no obvious way of earning a livelihood, or at best a very precarious one, and who lived no one knew how.

The point about livelihood is a most significant one, for the poor in Qajar cities led an even more destitute and precarious existence than those in the cities of Europe. Most of our sources on *lutis* had not themselves endured such penury, and those not beguiled by the heroic aspects of *luti* culture did not always try to understand the thievery, which is not to say that there were not criminals amongst them. A comparison of the three cities of Shiraz, Isfahan and Bushire in the period under study indicates that the question of livelihood, or employment, was a serious one in explaining their way of life. In Isfahan *lutis* became particularly prominent and prevalent in the mid-nineteenth century, when trade was disrupted by the military ambitions of Muhammad Shah and the Herat war. In 1840 gangs of *lutis* virtually controlled Isfahan and Muhammad Shah himself had to come to put down the disturbances in the city.[16] However, although accounts such as the *Jugrafiyya-yi Isfahan* (The Geography of Isfahan) indicate that there were groups of *lutis* in the town later in the century, it was not until the 1890s that *lutis* again came to the fore politically in the Isfahan region. By that time the political configuration had changed, but major economic problems had returned in the form of inflation, debasement of the coinage, prevalence of foreign goods and unease about the financial situation of the country. Raymond has noted the appearance of similar gangs in groups of roughs in Cairo at times of economic hardship.

The role of the *luti* was different in Shiraz. Generally noted by both Iranians and foreigners for the turbulence of its inhabitants, Shiraz was regularly subject to disturbances, most of which involved *lutis*. As with Isfahan, the 1840s were a time of economic difficulty and householders were subject to attacks by *lutis*.[17] *Lutis* began playing up again in 1850 when the price of bread rose because of a plague of locusts, and *lutis* even went so far as to beat one of the prince-governor's own servants.[18] In 1865, when *lutis* claimed that the authorities controlled Shiraz by day, but they controlled it by night, the basic problem could be attributed to those authorities buying up grain, and selling it at a higher price to the distress of the poorer classes.[19] The economic difficulties and weakening of government authority saw an increase in the lawlessness of the roughs in the 1890s when they attacked the police and the governor's servants.[20] Since the population of Shiraz was partly tribal, it would seem reasonable to assume that the greater prevalence of disturbances generated by *lutis* thus arose from the fact that many poor tribesmen came into town in search of a livelihood and became *lutis*. The overall economic situation nevertheless played its part.

Bushire presents quite a different picture. In the earlier part of the century the people of the town are mentioned as protesting in various ways against the British presence, principally under the leadership of the *mujtahid*, Shaikh Hasan, (of the 'Usfur family), but there is no reference to *lutis*, though this may be a matter of terminology.[21] Nevertheless, the copious records on Bushire do not mention *lutis*, which is not to say that they did not exist, but rather that they did not have a prominent role in the politics and culture of the town. It may be that such an absence is due to the population being part Arab and also part Sunni, but more probably it may relate to the way the town had been managed from the beginning as a foreign dominated port. Certainly the British concern with order, and the even more emphatic determination of the Iranian government to control disorder so that the British had no pretext for encroaching on their territory, were factors to discourage *lutism*. Similarly, the growing prosperity of the town in the latter part of the nineteenth century, combined with the greater regularity with which it was administered, would also deter a *luti* culture.

Apart from the differences among *lutis* in terms of local origin, they also varied in age and social background. Most *lutis* in the nineteenth century, as earlier, were young and unmarried men. In such a precarious employment market they might or might not have had a job, usually a menial occupation such as gardener.[22] Jamalzadeh describes seeing them gathered outside the local *zurkhana* (lit. 'house of strength', a form of gymnasium) in Isfahan as 'a bunch of youths and novices and young toughs'.[23] An earlier description of the *lutis* of Isfahan sums them up as buffoons, mimics, drunkards, fornicators, rascals, rogues, thieves, gamblers and pigeon-fanciers, the source of quarrels, disputes, insolence and bloodshed.[24] Further, as in other societies, the respectable and the disreputable *luti* could well be one and the same person. For example, some of those who dyed textiles in Kashan earned additional income by living as thieves by night.[25] This ability to move between different identities is also illustrated by the fact that when the prince governor, Tahmasp Mirza, arrived in Shiraz in 1853, all who lacked food and clothing followed in his train, assigning to themselves the names of rifleman, servant, and so forth.[26] A *luti* who had killed the local official responsible for order (*darugha*) in Shiraz managed to present himself as sufficiently respectable to obtain employment with a British official in Isfahan.[27] Nayib Mihrab, a *luti* of Isfahan, had been an outrider of Rukn al-Mulk Shirazi but became a blacksmith.[28] From early times it would seem that the *luti* groups also attracted members of the notable classes seeking influence.[29] Most likely such recruits were young, but rich merchants, as well as princes, joined them.[30]

Luti Organisation and Networks

Despite its connection with a variety of activities, many of them nefarious, *lutism* was, like so much else in Qajar urban society, quite highly organised. To begin with, *lutis* were to be found in gangs, or groups, at the head of which was an elected leader entitled the *lutibashi*, and it was this quality of organisation in particular which enabled them to have an impact upon urban politics.[31] The leader of a *luti* gang was usually older and more experienced than the rest,[32] and could also belong to a higher social group. He was treated with respect and had a role in mediating conflict as between members of his own gang, and as between his group and others. According to Mounsey, in the 1850s the *lutibashi* of Shiraz laid by the money he had made, and invested it in lands and villages, which enabled him to lead a respected and comfortable later life as a pious Muslim.[33] Mounsey may be referring to a well known and ubiquitous *luti* leader of Shiraz named Haji Riza Qasi, who survived partly due to the protection of Nasir al-Mulk.[34] He was later arrested but allowed to go to Tehran for which he prepared an *istishhad-nama* (testimonial witnessed by a number of signatures) to the effect that he was an upright and respectable person.[35] In 1866 fifteen of the *lutis* of Tehran were treated as though they belonged to the notables of the city, and seemed to have endeavoured to raise the *luti* ethos.[36] They tried to follow the nobler precepts of *javanmardi* or *lutigari*, and made a point of being faithful to their promises and speaking the truth, honouring their debts and helping friends in need. Sometimes the *lutibashi* could actually be a member of the elite, as the term was used of the Imam Jum'a of Isfahan in the 1830s. It is, however, not clear whether this meant he actually headed a *luti* group or whether it meant that he exerted exception influence over large numbers of the *lutis* of the time by virtue of the contemporary political situation and of his own position.[37] In 1849 in Yazd a merchant named Muhammad 'Abdullah led a prominent *luti* group whose ostensible goal was the maintenance of law and order in the city.[38]

Luti groups were associated with different quarters of the city, and there was rivalry amongst them, though they could also engage in good-natured battles.[39] Ties of family, tribe, religion, local origin, and occupation no doubt gave the *lutis* of a particular quarter a degree of fellow feeling, and they considered themselves bound to help one another in time of need, whether for welfare or protection. A common meeting place for socialising and for discussion was one of the teahouses in the *luti*'s particular district. The *lutis* also identified themselves with their district with pride. They demonstrated this especially on religious holidays, whether for celebration or mourning, when they took part in street processions, and sought to eclipse those of other districts. Like the *zu'ar* of Mamluke cities, who murdered tax collectors and barricaded streets,[40] they defended their quarters against abuse. Battles between different quarters were not uncommon, sometimes motivated by revenge, as when the *lutis* of the Sang-i Siah quarter of Shiraz were set to avenge themselves on a *luti* from another quarter. Though the quarter elders were endeavouring to settle the dispute, it was still rampant some weeks later.[41] Jamalzadeh recounts how when the brother of the Imam of the Shah Mosque died, the *lutis* of a rival quarter were determined to use his funeral to gain revenge on 'the boys of Masjid-i Shah'.[42] Despite the governor giving orders that no one be allowed to take weapons, the rival leader, Yadullah Zurab, hid a number of sticks, clubs, swords and daggers in the coffins and catafalque that were part of the equipage of the cortège, and, at the appropriate moment, he attacked his opponents from Masjid-i Shah.

Lutis were associated not only with their particular district, but with the quarters entitled Haidari and Ni'mati into which most towns in Iran were divided. The origin of this arrangement is ancient and obscure,[43] but it seems to represent a custom that had naturally evolved, and which in some way helped to institutionalise, organise, moderate and ultimately control natural rivalries within a town so that they took an open and manageable form. *Lutis* were involved in a prolonged battle between the Haidari and Ni'mati quarters of Shiraz which occurred in various open places in the town in the disturbances of 1844. The struggle lasted from midday to sunset and was carried out with slings and stones until the Ni'matis were worsted.[44] In Isfahan these divisions were still a common form of identification in the mid-nineteenth century, but from the 1870s, under the strict governance of Zill al-Sultan, they died down.[45]

Another haunt of *lutis*, but also of more consistently respectable members of society were the *zurkhanas*. The culture of strength was a part of a perceived role of standing up to the state and protecting the community from oppression in time of need, and was thus linked to the tradition of a moral role for *lutism*. Physical prowess was thus an integral characteristic of the *lutis*, and under a leader entitled the *pish kisvat*, they took part in various types of exercise and wrestling.[46] The *zurkhana* (house of strength or type of gymnasium) was also a revered institution for strengthening the body, purifying the soul, and imbuing its members with the ethics of chivalry.[47] Jamalzadeh mentions that one of the *luti* leaders of Isfahan, Haj Ma'sum Juzani, a teapot mender, was the regular captain of the *zurkhana* of the Door of the Imam quarter of Isfahan.[48] The *zurkhanas* were also related to particular quarters, and linked to the composition of the religious processions in each quarter which took place on certain holy days.

Lutis and Non-Conformity

From the Islamic perspective *lutis* were also deviant in that gambling and drinking were activities they were happy to engage in.[49] In this they may be contrasted with the soldiery, who, however unruly, were more unusually involved in drunken disorderliness, which reinforces Fathi's point that in one incarnation at least the *lutis* were characterised by innate non-conformity and defiance of authority.[50] Certainly drunken rebelliousness was common amongst them in Shiraz, though it does not seem particularly to be associated with the *lutis* of Isfahan. This may be due to a greater availability of liquor in Shiraz, a wine growing area, and also to the fact that the influence of the 'ulama and the mosque networks appears not to have been so strong. Drunken *lutis* were thus a common occurrence in Shiraz, and were involved in disturbances in the street in 1845, and in 1848, when, for example, they held a party in a tavern, where a man was killed in a brawl.[51] The next year one of the *kadkhudas* (heads of quarters) was accused of allowing too much drinking and gambling in his area, and thereby encouraging *luti* disturbances.[52] He responded that the public purse derived a considerable revenue from the gambling and drinking houses, and if they were repressed a loss would accrue to the government. Fortunately popular intercession prevented him from being executed for this imprudent observation, and he was punished by beating instead. In the disturbances of 1865 following the death of the mayor Qavam al-Mulk, the *lutis* of the Maidan-i Shah attacked the Jewish quarter and carried off some wine and arak, which they proceeded to drink openly in the square. They then summoned some of the Jewish elders, and, saying, 'If you wish for safety, give us a sum that we may protect you from the plunder of the *lutis* of the other nine quarters of the town (Shiraz had ten quarters)'; they extorted cash and five jars of liquor from them.[53] After that time drunkenness among *lutis* becomes less prevalent, though it certainly continued, and drink was regularly consumed by the higher classes. A ruling of the shah in 1870 prohibiting the sale of intoxicating liquors in Iran may not have prevented their manufacture but may at least have had some effect on drunken disorderliness.[54]

The Role of Lutis in Popular Protest

It is a testimony to the significance of the role of *lutis* in disturbances that the government punished them more severely than other groups. In the 1840 turbulence in Isfahan many of them were put to death, and their leader, Haj Ghulam Husain, was tortured to death, his teeth being taken out and driven into his skull.[55] Shiraz in 1850 became quiet after one of the *lutis*, the son of Asad the swordmaker, had a dispute with one of the governor's attendants, for which he was given 1500 strokes and strangled.[56]

Lutis could play a significant role at times of political turbulence. In 1840, in what was arguably the political greatest crisis in Isfahan in the nineteenth century, *lutis* were described as dominating the city in their hundreds, to the point where Muhammad Shah himself had to come to settle the situation, a most unusual move.[57] The reference to hundreds of *lutis* is very uncommon, and suggests that on this occasion most *lutis* were overwhelmingly the unemployed poor rather than the usual rebels and thieves. After the death of Fath 'Ali Shah, the town had been under weak government as Muhammad Shah turned his attention elsewhere, and from 1839 in particular trade became dislocated by the estrangement between Iran and Britain, a downturn which came on top of the drop in trade in the south in this period. The economy was also affected by foreign imports so the shah had to issue an order that no sort of Russian cloth be brought in.[58] Further evidence of the disturbed state of the country is provided by the fact that there was disorder at Shiraz, Kashan, Isfahan and Kerman at the same time, and that these towns were deemed to have passed out of government control.[59] In Yazd, the population, with the local *mujtahid* at their head, had expelled the governor.[60] In Isfahan a form of class warfare began in which the poorer social groups robbed the wealthier ones, particularly its merchants and traders.[61] During the winter of 1839–40 the gates at the end of certain streets and at the divisions of the districts had always been kept closed. Some of the inhabitants of each district formed themselves into groups of security guards and kept watch the entire night, but, nevertheless, hardly a night passed without the event of a robbery or assassination.⁶² One of the problems facing these inhabitants was that the robbers were always protected by two *mujtahids*, the Imam Jum'a and Haji Sayyid Muhammad Baqir, the leading religious figure of Isfahan, and one of the most eminent *mujtahids* of his age.⁶³ Given that the sources on this event in one way or another represent the views of the government authorities, it is difficult to assess the *mujtahid*'s exact motives. At the time, influence among the poor to further political ambition was imputed to both of them.⁶⁴ It is evident from the difference in the shah's treatment of them, and the popular reaction, that they were regarded as having different roles and different motives. The 'feudal' (possibly endowed) property of the Imam Jum'a was removed, twelve of his Georgian slaves were seized and cauterised, and all his property, including four hundred muskets, taken on the shah's orders.⁶⁵ He afterwards died in prison. The evidence would seem thus to support the accusation that he was a *lutibashi* who plundered the people.

Sayyid Muhammad Baqir, however, received different treatment. To begin with, his punishment was much milder. On the shah's arrival, the *mujtahid* visited him and voluntarily offered to provide supplies for the whole court during their stay in Isfahan.⁶⁶ Whilst there was no doubt an element of duress in this offer it may also be seen as a means of mediating between the ruler and his people. The shah accepted it, but then ordered Muhammad Baqir to depart for Kerbala, such an enforced journey being a way of inflicting disgrace on the clergy, and of causing them to incur unplanned expense. At this point, the community of Isfahan began to complain in large numbers and various ways, seven thousand to eight thousand of them coming to Muhammad Baqir's house to offer their support.⁶⁷ A few thousand women demonstrated in the main square in front of the shah, begging him not to exile the *sayyid*, and, when he refused, they went to the *sayyid*'s house and implored him not to go.

Although the shah's visit to Isfahan did much to curb the so called power of the 'ulama and the *lutis*, it did not break it. Haji Sayyid Muhammad Baqir did not go to Kerbala. Further, the *darugha* (official in charge of law and order) was ordered to seize a man known as a notorious *luti* who had hidden under the *sayyid*'s protection during the shah's visit. The *sayyid* protested, and the *darugha* was forced to let the *luti* go.⁶⁸ But as for the rest of the *lutis*, the shah despatched them summarily. Hundreds were seized, and two hundred and seventy put to death, whilst a further four hundred were imprisoned. Their leader, Haj Ghulam Husain, was executed.⁶⁹

Without greater detail being available, the position of Sayyid Muhammad Baqir is difficult to assess, but he seems to have been struggling with a severe social and economic crisis at time of weak and ineffectual central control. His links with the *lutis* may have been an attempt to try and manage a deeply disturbed and financially stricken community in which some elements, however dubious, had to be used to maintain a form of organisation and control in the absence of state action.⁷⁰ He was known for acting not so much on the basis of the Qur'an and Hadith, but on his own sagacity, and is represented by Tunakabuni as a powerful and just man.[71] Seemingly he acted with unusual independence towards state jurisdiction. His leniency towards thieves may represent the view that there had to be some redistribution and balance of resources for the community to survive. They, in turn, drew authority from their connection with him.

The value of the *lutis* to the remainder of the populace is demonstrated by the disturbances in Shiraz in 1844–45. One group of *lutis* had been forced to flee the town because of the determination of the governor to punish them. A military detachment was sent to apprehend them but, despite their criminal activities which included robbery, drunkenness and murder, the populace of Shiraz rose up and threatened to expel the governor if he did not recall his troops.[72] When some of the *lutis* were later captured and imprisoned, their relations succeeded in obtaining the release of them all.[73] On another occasion, in 1848, Qavam al-Mulk had some of the principal *lutis* brought to his own house, and reprimanded them, but then gave them food to keep them out of trouble.[74] These incidents may, firstly, recall the youth of some *lutis*, but also suggest that they may have been in various ways a source of income to extended family networks among the poor. The encounter with Qavam demonstrates how, in a society little regulated by law, he needed *lutis* to enhance his own authority and influence, even though he was responsible for repressing them. On the other hand, the *lutis* could make bargains of their own, firstly to gain subsistence, and secondly be allowed to go on thieving from the more affluent, but within certain limits.

The *lutis* could be very assertive even though they knew they were also exposed to severe punishment. Thus in 1850 one of them beat one of the prince-governor's own servants, and another seized a *mirza* (clerk) of the Ilkhani of the Qashqa'i and beat him severely for having levied forage on a village belonging to him.[75] In such instances the *lutis* relied partly on the back-up of their fellows to protect them if necessary, and partly on the intercession of another, possibly a rival, member of a higher social group. Floor discusses how *lutis* were used by the notables and other members of the elite to extend their influence, and to combat their rivals in struggles for power and to settle family feuds. The same may be said for those in a lesser position of influence. In a quarrel between Husain Sultan and Haji Zaman, the *darugha* in Shiraz in 1850 the *lutis* took the part of the latter.[76] Their reason for doing so is not clear, but it could have been partly financial, and it would have placed him under an obligation to them. The impending arrival of a new governor in Shiraz, Firuz Mirza, who was known to be strict, opened up opportunities for the *lutis* to play up and bring pressure on the Mayor (*kalantar*), Qavam al-Mulk. He was trying to persuade them to leave town, as their activities could undermine his position,[77] particularly in view of his collaboration with them. Eventually he convinced them to flee, and thus connived at their departure.[78]

Lutis also played their part in popular protest to the elite, as in the food shortage of the mid-1860s in Shiraz, where *luti* harassment was in reality a symptom of simmering popular resentment. The Ilkhani (paramount chief) of the Qashqa'i and his son were attacked by a blacksmith in the bazaar of the shoemakers on an old score.[79] He collected a crowd who threatened the boy. The Ilkhani tried to explain that this was a question to be decided by the precepts of the shari'a, but the blacksmith treated him with great disrespect, using foul language. In the altercation that ensued between the attendants of the Ilkhani and the bazaaris, the *lutis* played a prominent part in driving out the former. The governor was not able to capture the offenders in response to the Ilkhani's complaints, and the following day a servant of the Ilbegi (another chief) of the Qashqa'i was robbed. Another fight ensued in which the *lutis* climbed on the roof of the Ilbegi's house and shouted abuse at him. An attempt by the local *kadkhuda* (quarter leader) to arrest them at the house of Mashhadi Riza, the singer, failed because his *farashes* (servants) refused to take effective action for fear of their lives. Frustrated in his attempts to punish the *lutis*, the governor beat ten *kadkhudas* for being ineffective. The bazaars subsequently closed, and the entire community mounted the roofs, as well as thronging the street, and stoned both the houses and the persons of the officials who approached them. The people quietened at the intervention of the Imam Jum'a and another leading *mujtahid*, and more particularly at a telegram from Tehran dismissing the Qavam al-Mulk, which was the principal aim of the populace, who blamed him for the high price of bread.

An incident in Isfahan, again in 1893 at the time of a rise in the price of bread, demonstrates how *lutis* could be used in a struggle for influence between rival members of the 'ulama. A disturbance on the eve of a Muslim ceremony between *lutis* of the Haidari and Ni'mati quarters at least partially had its origins in the rivalry between the Imam Jum'a and Aqa Najafi. A group of Haidari *sinazans* (breastbeaters) appeared in a Ni'mati area, seemingly at the invitation of the Imam Jum'a. The Ni'matis, at the instigation of Aqa Najafi, promptly made trouble for the Haidaris, and consequently for the Imam Jum'a.[80]

Such incidents were difficult for the police to control, particularly in times of economic crisis. In Shiraz in 1893, some roughs with evident links to one of the notables, 'Ain al-Mulk,[81] beat a police officer and wounded a soldier. The Beglerbegi's servants tried to bring them back to town from the countryside, whence they had fled. However, 'Ain al-Mulk's servants took the part of the *lutis* and obtained their release by force, indicating how common bonds could be formed in times of economic hardship.

In the same period there were disturbances in Yazd, where the removal of the governor Jalal al-Daula in 1893 led to the re-emergence of *lutis* with weekly shootings. The Vazir-i Yazdi, the official left in charge, was powerless to control them.[82] He seemingly made some attempt to reduce the lawlessness by taking many *lutis* into his service, an indication that a rise in unemployment was at least part of the problem. One of the Vazir's new servants was nevertheless very soon in a dispute with a peasant, whom he shot with a pistol. In one incident eight to ten *lutis* went to the *rauza khani* (religious ceremony) of a *sayyid* who was half a *luti* himself, but once there considered that he did not treat them with sufficient respect. They therefore waited till the crowd had gone, and then shot at him, afterwards barricading themselves into a house and shooting at everyone who came near. Men were sent to seize them to no avail, and eventually one of the 'ulama had to guarantee their freedom before they would leave. The expectations of the *lutis* and the role of the *sayyid*, demonstrates how *lutis* also belonged to a non-conformist and divergent religious culture, disapproved of, but necessarily tolerated. In 1893 murders, violation of women and robbery were reported as common, though the government attempts to suppress the disorder with executions was said to have had some effect.[83]

Attention has already been drawn to the link between *lutis* and the culture of heroism inspired by the courage of Imam Husain and his followers, and by the heroes of the tales of the *Shahnama*. Such *pahlavans* were powerful examples of the duty to protect people against oppression, and the stories of their deeds as recounted in the *Shahnama* were told at various kinds of assemblies and gatherings, encouraging listeners to take them as models and emulate their exploits.[84] Many gatherings took place in coffee houses, adorned with pictures of their saints and ideal examples in the popular style.[85] Brugsch noted, in the mid-nineteenth century, that along with their turbulence and villainy the *lutis* had their own special ethos, exemplifying valiant heroes depicted in paintings undergoing martyrdom.[86] Jamalzadeh describes their pictures as portraying the bravery of 'Abbas and 'Ali Akbar, and the seven exploits of Rustam, 'all with mustachios out to their earlobes, eyebrows like a curl of rope and shiny black eyes' such as to overawe timid mortals.[87]

But there was another side to the role of *lutis* in the community, and that concerned social justice and welfare, and the more equitable distribution of resources. Protection of women, children and the elderly and withstanding oppression and injustice, like Imam Husain and Kava the Blacksmith, were the duties of a conscientious *luti*.[88] He was supposed also not to care for material possessions, nor to deny any assistance to a friend. Nayib Mihrab from Isfahan had enormous authority and status in the bazaar, his most notable feat of honour having been to rescue a ribbon-seller from unjust punishment.[89] Yadullah Zurab was known to enemies as a lasso thrower, and to his friends and partisans as 'cherisher of the humble'. He also had a poetic talent, but, despite a spell as a horse-trader, maintained that he could not give up thievery as it was the habit of his of his forebears. Furthermore, he stated, he shared the proceeds with the poor.[90]

Lutis had other ways, apart from thievery, of stripping the better-off to their own advantage, or of reminding them of the privileges of their position. One of them was at entertainments at the houses of the well-to-do or the governor, where they subjected the guests to their wit and ridicule, in which they were allowed considerable latitude. At times it reached the point where their victims felt compelled for self-protection to make them a gift, thus persuading them to desist and ending their importunity.[91] A certain pressure was also exerted on the host to invite *lutis*, not just for the amusement of the guests, but also ensure that his good reputation should not be damaged by his failing to meet what were perceived as his social responsibilities.

Underlying many incidents involving *lutis* and the better-off was the notion that their conduct was to some extent justified by a lack of social justice, for which it compensated. The services of physicians in Iran at that time differed as between the well-to-do and the poor. For general patients they established their dispensaries at the heads of streets, and sick people were brought to the dispensary for treatment and the administration of medicine.[92] However, if any person of means fell ill, the physician was taken to him. The fact that the treatment of the poor and better-off differed, provided, on more than one occasion, a kind of unwritten justification for opportunistic *lutis*. In 1845 in Shiraz some of the *lutis* brought a horse to the door of a physician's dispensary, and claimed they represented a seriously afflicted invalid. The physician was sufficiently convinced to come, but after two or three streets, *lutis* made him dismount, and stripped him from head to foot, thereafter departing, firing their matchlocks.[93] Not long afterwards the *lutis* came upon a physician, mounted on a mule, coming from the house of Qavam al-Mulk. They made him dismount, saying, 'Son of a dog, how long will you ride and we go on foot?' Then they stripped him, and sent him on his way. In another incident involving the better-off, one night they raided the house of a woman pawnbroker who possessed some means, taking a ladder to the back of the house. When they entered her apartment, she tried to cry out, but was told, 'If you want to live, be quiet.' She covered herself with her bedclothes, and the *lutis* 'deliberately and without molestation or interference drew forth the articles of pledge belonging to the individuals (customers) and the woman's own property, leaving her with a coverlet.' The fact that she was not molested not only made them less liable to severe punishment, but also intimated to the woman herself that her occupation and possessions made her advantage and her position open to question.

* * *

Migeod and Floor see the term *luti* as referring to several distinct groups, for example, entertainers, the unemployed, the criminal, and both tried to create distinctions within it. Migeod seeks to differentiate between the use of the term *lutis* for criminals and the unemployed, and for entertainers. Floor, on the other hand, suggests separating them from the *aubash* (roughs) which he sees as a term to describe the lower class. He divided *lutis* into three groups, the artists, the adherents of the *zurkhana* and *javanmardi*, the criminals with strong bonds with the local authorities. This chapter, however, reintroduces complexity to what they have attempted to clarify. Simply, the sources examined demonstrate that the term *luti* meant different things at different times and places, and was also used by observers in different ways. Further, a *luti*, in the course of a brief period, could have a number of other identities in terms of both occupation and integrity. The picture that thus emerges is that, setting aside a few fellow travellers from the higher social classes, *lutis* were members of the poorer social groups of the urban areas who adhered to a certain culture of camaraderie, self-help, social obligation, valour, sometimes (though not always, piety) but were not particular as to honesty. Can we call them an underclass? There are similarities in terms of employment or the lack of it, of a common culture and of bonding, as well as elements of criminality. Society in Qajar Iran, however, was not so rationally organised, either socially or economically, as to make the term really appropriate. Looked at another way, should we jettison the term *luti* as providing only obfuscation in understanding the subject and refer to them as the urban poor or the urban unemployed? The matter is again not so simple, as many poor would not have considered themselves *lutis*, but simply the more poverty stricken members of a pious community, probably honest, but not necessarily so. Further, employment is a problematic term for such a society, where, although some people had the same occupation for most of their lives, others lived from hand to mouth or had one continuous inadequate source of income, and other occupations which they engaged in fitfully. So the terms 'employed' and 'unemployed' have to be used with circumspection. *Lutis* had, moreover, an identity which was peculiarly Iranian, for they were imbued with the long-standing values of the epics of the Persian tradition, familiar with the great deeds of its heroes, and inspired by the examples of the Imams. Whether orthodox or unorthodox, they were on the whole religious, which meant that they adhered to a certain ethic, and were able at times to assume authority. Thus the term *luti* is retained because it alone can convey accurately the relationships, culture and occupations of the more turbulent urban poor in Iran of the Qajar period.

What is the significance for urban protest of the *luti* culture? First of all, the *hamasi* (epic culture) gave them a means of assuming prestige and dignity at times of crisis in the struggle with the state. When oppression becomes intolerable any cut-purse or footpad could become Kava the Blacksmith or Rustam, possessed of virtues that riches cannot buy, so empowered with self-belief that he could withstand tyranny, and risk terrible death or disfigurement. Further, like the poor in Georgian England, they could inspire admiration for defiance of the authorities, in a system that was in one way or another deeply unjust.[94] The community in its turn relied on the *lutis*, most of whom were young men, to defend them and their interests in the times of famine and scarcity. One way of imposing the popular will on the authorities was to riot, and riots, given the costs both political and economic of disorder, were dreaded by the government. Here the youth and the physical strength of the *lutis* were vital elements in opposing such military forces as the government could muster. Rioting was also a stage in the negotiations ceaselessly engaged in between the community and the state. A not uncommon time to riot, especially when prices had risen, was 'Ashura, during the religious ceremonies commemorating the Shi'i martyrs, when feelings ran high, when ritual gave cohesion, and when particular participants, including *lutis*, adopted a religious and authoritative identity.[95] At such times, within limits, it was more difficult for the state to impose order and inflict its will, so that it was forced into conciliation.

It is of interest briefly to contrast Qajar Iran and Georgian England, for there are some similarities in the social conditions of the poor of the time. Both societies functioned with a lack. In Georgian England the influence of religion had receded, and with it both continual moral guidance well as the incentive of heaven and the disincentive of damnation. So the way was paved for the growth of a defiant popular culture at a time of great divisions between rich and poor and *laissez faire* policies. However, looked at from the point of view of Qajar Iran, there was always a law. In Iran, by contrast, religion had a very strong hold on all but the most unregenerate *lutis*. The gap was in the law, particularly in periods of economic crisis, for the shari'a extended little beyond civil matters, except in the form of principles and precepts, and government administration and customary law were not coded or regularised. So opportunities were created for the populace to take the law into its own hands or develop its own interpretation of what was rightful. In a largely self-policing community, where most people lived on both sides of the law,[96] the *lutis* were both a manifestation of lawlessness and a means of controlling its excess.

The *lutis* were also an instrument of social justice, as is reflected in their own self-image about their role in society, as the protectors of the weak and the benefactors of the poor. They could represent themselves as robbing the rich to give money, or some of it, to the poor, and could certainly imply to their victims that their fate was deserved for having much more substance than most. Of course, such claims could also be used to make nefarious activities seem righteous. Yet there is some evidence that the community itself accepted *luti* activity as a means of redistributing wealth in a society where taxation was arbitrary and erratic, and welfare provision by the state non-existent.

As Fathi has remarked, at times when the distribution of power was unresolved, *lutis* could find themselves in possession of considerable power, and thus influence the outcome of a particular struggle. There were ways in which *lutis* could manipulate these struggles to their own advantage. For example, they could procure lenient treatment for criminal activities, by bestowing their allegiance on whichever magnate could offer them the most advantageous terms; they could even use their very connection with him, and the embarrassment it caused him with the authorities, to extract more generous rewards. So they formed another and irregular channel of funding from the wealthier to the poorer sections of society.

Notes

1. A.K.S. Lambton, *Islamic Society in Persia*, Oxford 1954, pp. 18–19.
2. Raymond, 'Cairo', p. 111; M. Ravandi, *Tarikh-i ijtima'i-yi Iran*, Tehran 2nd edition 2536, III, p. 573; M. Afshari and M. Madayini, eds, *Futuvvat va asnaf*, Tehran 1381, p. 20.
3. Ravandi, *Ijtima'i*, III, p. 573. C. Cahen, 'Ayyar', pp. 159–161 and W.L. Hanaway Jr, 'Ayyar in Persian Souces', pp. 161–3, in E. Yarshater, ed., *Encyclopaedia Iranica*, London and New York, 1989, III.
4. Cahen, 'Ayyar', p. 159.
5. M. Afshari and M. Madayini, eds, *Haft Lashkar*, Tehran 1377, p. 27 of introduction.
6. Afshari and Madayini, *Futuvvat*, pp. 43–4. Their teachings were inspired by treatises referring to the prophets of the Old Testament, the Prophet himself, and the Imams of the Shi'a.
7. Ravandi, *Ijtima'i*, III, pp. 576–7, Afshari and Madayini, *Futuvvat*, pp. 30–31.
8. Lapidus, *Cities*, p. 155.
9. Tahvildar, *Isfahan*, p. 86; H.G. Migeod, 'Die Lutis: Ein Ferment des stadtisches Lebens in Persien', JESHO,II, 1959, quoted in W.M.Floor, 'The Lutis – a Social Phenomenon in Qajar Persia', *Die Welt des Islams*, XIII, Nos 1–2, 1971, pp. 103ff; J.E. Polak, *Safarnama-yi Polak*, 1865, trans. K. Jahandari, Tehran 1361, p. 38.
10. Scott Waring, *Sheeraz*, p. 55.
11. The aversion was to some extent mutual. Jamalzadeh mentions that the Haj Ma'sum Juzani, one of the *luti* leaders of Isfahan, who had twice been on the pilgrimage to Mecca, was very pious and saintly, but could not abide clerics, *Isfahan is Half the World*, trans. W.L. Heston, Princeton 1983, p. 183.
12. Binning, *Persia*, p. 273.
13. Brugsch, *Persien*, p. 182
14. Ussher, *Journey*, p. 511.
15. Mounsey, *Journey*, p. 218.
16. Encl. in Hennell to Sheil, 25.5.1840, FO 248/99.
17. Shiraz Agent, encl. in No. 578, 11.12.1844, FO 248/113. They even went so far as to bore a hole into the house of the British Newswriter.
18. Shiraz Agent, encl., in No. 61, 15.2.1850 and No. 224, 15.6.1850, FO 248/138.
19. No. 83, 11.8.1865, FO 60/290.
20. No. 498, 28.4.1893, FO 248/576.
21. See, for example, Hennell to McNeil, 30.12.1836, and encl. in No. 79, 21.11.38, FO 248/85.
22. A. Fathi, 'The Role of the Rebels in the Constitutional Movement in Iran', *International Journal of Middle Eastern Studies*, 10, 1979, No. 1, p. 58. His account suggests that by the early twentieth century *lutis* had become broadly more respectable. They worked in low prestige jobs such as hawker or gardener, but avoided work regarded as degrading, such as porter or masseur in the public baths. Fathi also mentions that they had special types of clothing including slippers (*giva*), a large silk handkerchief, a fine long chain to carry in their pockets, a small brass drinking cup and a knife. In the mid-nineteenth century the average Iranian of the poorer classes was pleased to dress in whatever came to hand.
23. Jamalzadeh, *Isfahan*, p. 170. He also mentions that they stood along both sides

of the lane, sprinkling rose water, offering greetings and compliments. At the *Zurkhana* ceremony the master recited the verses:
>   If I'd had news of your coming,
>   I'd have planted your path with fresh hyacinths.

24 Ravandi, *Ijtima'i*, III, p. 591.
25 A.R. Madani Kashani, *Tarikh-i ashrar-i Kashan*, ed. H. Pur Madani, Tehran 1378, p. 26.
26 Shiraz Agent, encl. in No. 321, 15.10.1853, FO 248/150.
27 Shiraz Agent, encl. in No. 90, 14.3.1850, FO 248/138.
28 Jamalzadeh, *Isfahan*, p. 185.
29 Cahen, 'Ayyar', p. 159.
30 Floor, 'Lutis', p. 112.
31 Mounsey, *Journey*, p. 218.
32 Fathi, 'Rebels', p. 58.
33 Mounsey, *Journey*, p. 218.
34 See Shiraz Agent, encl. in No. 315, 14.8.50 and No. 352, 16.9.50, FO 248/138.
35 Shiraz Agent, encl. in No. 383, 16.10.1850, FO 248/138.
36 Floor, 'Lutis', p. 111.
37 See Shiraz Agent, encl. in Hennell to Sheil, 9.6.1840, FO 248/99. The Imam Jum'a and his son-in-law, Haji Muhammad 'Ali, were considered at the time of the death of Fath 'Ali Shah as *lutibashis* who plundered the people, which would mean particularly those with property.
38 Floor, 'Lutis', p. 112.
39 Fathi, 'Rebels', p. 59.
40 Lapidus, *Cities*, p. 156.
41 Shiraz Agent, encl. in No. 90, 14.3.1850, and No. 143, 14.4.1850, FO 248/138.
42 Jamalzadeh, *Isfahan*, p. 186.
43 Anyone who moved from one of these quarters to the other had then to side with the new party. The shah was trying in vain to abolish these divisions. No. 1, 3.1.1845, FO 60/113.
44 Shiraz Agent, encl. in No. 578, 11.12.1844, FO 248/113. See No. 47, 19.7.1861, FO 248/199 for similar disturbances in Rasht, where a quarrel between members of the two quarters resulted in an attack on the *mujtahid*, Haji Mulla Rafi'. It was Muharram, and in an attempt to try and moderate the dispute, the governor ordered the processions of both quarters to present themselves at his house at the same time. This ruse had little effect, as Haji Mulla Rafi', who belonged in the Ni'mati quarter, was assaulted in the *takiyya* by the Haidaris. He received several blows and was nearly killed by a *sayyid*. The *lutis* of the Ni'mati quarter were then called to guard him. Various local notables hostile towards the *mujtahid* were also involved.
45 There was some recrudescence in the 1890s in Isfahan, as serious battles ensued on the eve of a sacred occasion in the Imam Jum'a's quarter between rival *lutis* of the Haidari and Ni'mati clans, and recruits were even invited to join the disturbances from the outlying villages. No. 56, 16.9.1893, FO 248/572. There was also a disturbance in Yazd in the general unrest of the 1890s, again involving rival gangs of *lutis*. No. 26, 20.7.1893, FO 248/572.
46 Fathi, 'Rebels', p. 58. See also Mounsey, *Journey*, p. 218.
47 A. Bulookbashi, *Qahvakhanaha-yi Iran*, Tehran 1375, pp. 129ff.
48 Jamalzadeh, *Isfahan*, pp. 183–4. Haj Ma'sum was a special disciple of the father of Jamalzadeh, the well-known constitutionalist cleric, Aqa Sayyid Jamal. When the latter came under threat from the brother of Aqa Najafi, and fellow clerics, he gathered some of the *lutis* who were his supporters, and equipped with swords and daggers, came to the support of Sayyid Jamal. While the *sayyid* was preaching, he was attacked by the clerics, but Haj Ma'sum and his partisans fell

on them, pulled off their turbans and tied them round their waists, and with blows and bludgeons, saw them out of the mosque.
49 Fathi, 'Rebels', p. 59.
50 Ibid, p. 59.
51 Shiraz Agent, encl. in No. 8, 4.1.1845, FO 248/113, and encl. in No. 45, 29.1.1848, FO 248/129. Brugsch comments that the famous Shiraz wine was not in fact from Shiraz but from an area nearby. The wine trade at that time was run by Jews for a levy of 4 ducats per day to the government. Brugsch, *Persien*, pp. 180–1.
52 Shiraz Agent, encl. in No. 140, 4.5.1849, FO 248/138.
53 Shiraz Agent, encl. in No. 83, 11.8.1865, FO 60/290. Alcoholic drink was made by the Jews and Armenians. A drunken disturbance in which a man was wounded was reported to the authorities in 1867. No. 24, 9.4.1867, FO 60/304.
54 No. 17, 25.9.1870, FO 248/262.
55 No. 18, 6.5.1840, FO 60/73, and No. 42, 24.8.1840, FO 60/74.
56 Shiraz Agent, encl. in No. 315, 14.8.1850, FO 248/138.
57 No. 15, 20.4.1840, FO 60/40. The most detailed account occurs in the British sources. It is also mentioned in Hidayat, *Rauzat al-safa*, 15, p. 8270; Sipihr, *Tavarikh*, II, pp. 99–100; Zill al-Sultan, *Khatirat*, II, p. 542; E. Flandin, *Safarnama-yi Eugene Flandan bih Iran*, trans. H. Nur Sadiqi, Intisharat-i Ishraqi 2536, p. 131ff; Polak, *Persien, das Land und seine Bewohner, Leipzig* 1865, p. 324.
58 Hennell to Sheil, 25.5.1840, FO 248/99. Part of the problem was that the Russians imported cloth dyed with indigo from Iran.
59 Encl. in No. 19, 12.5.1840, FO 60/73.
60 Encl. in Hennell to Sheil, 18.6.1840, FO 248/99. Following retribution by the authorities, he had taken refuge with Sayyid Muhammad Baqir, referred to as the chief *mujtahid* of Persia, from whose house he was dragged on the shah's orders and bastinadoed very severely. The beating of a *mujtahid* was not unknown, but it was unusual.
61 Sipihr, *Tavarikh*, II, pp. 99–100.
62 Encl. in No. 42, 24.8.1840, FO 60/74; encl. in Hennell to Sheil, 25.5.1840, FO 248/99.
63 See Mirza Muhammad Tunakabuni, *Qisas al-'ulama*, ed., M.H. Amini, Jamadi I 1396, pp. 135–168, translated by H. Dabashi in 'Lives of Prominent Nineteenth Century 'Ulama', in S.A. Arjomand, ed., *Authority and Political Culture in Shi'ism*, New York 1988, pp. 309–318. Haji Sayyid Muhammad Baqir is referred to as a unique in his time as a leader of the community, extremely pious, knowledgeable and possessed of great judicial perspicacity.
64 Encl. in Hennell to Sheil, No. 42, 24.8.1840, FO 248/99. In his recollections Zill al-Sultan describes Sayyid Muhammad Baqir as being hugely influential, *Khatirat*, II, p. 542; It was to Sayyid Muhammad Baqir that McNeill wrote in October 1838, in essence attempting to counter the attempts of the Iranian government to bring pressure on him to declare a jihad, by threatening British retaliation if he did. On receiving the letter the *mujtahid* ordered it to be read to a large assembly in his own house, and commented that the differences between the two governments did not concern the Shi'a faith, and thus if these differences led to war the people of Iran should not take part in the quarrel. See No. 53, 5.10.1838, FO 60/60.
65 Encl. in No. 18, 6.5.1840, FO 60/74; encl. in Hennell to Sheil 9.6.1840, FO 248/99, and No. 19, 12.5.1840, FO 60/73. (Georgian slaves were very costly.)
66 Encl. in No. 15, 20.4.1840, FO 60/73. It should not be automatically assumed that all the funding for his invitation would have come from him.
67 Hennell to Sheil, 18.6.1840, FO 248/99.
68 Shiraz Agent, encl. in No. 42, 24.8.1840, FO 60/74.

69 No. 19, 12.5.1840, FO 60/73, and encl. in Hennell to Sheil, 11.5.1840, FO 248/99.
70 Compare with magistrates in Georgian England, who sometimes released the criminal poor without penalties, in outright contradiction of the views of overseers and vestrymen. In so doing, they were putting into practice an undefined paternalism which perceived that mercy was from time to time required because so much dishonesty was rooted in poverty. T.Hitchcock, P. King and P. Sharpe, eds, *Chronicling Poverty. The Voices and Strategies of the English Poor 1640–1840*, Basingstoke 1997, p. 11.
71 Schneider, 'Muhammad Baqir Shafti', p. 252ff.
72 No. 1, 3.1.1845, FO 60/112.
73 Shiraz Agent, encl. in No. 169, 7.4.1845, FO 248/113.
74 Shiraz Agent, encl. in No. 45, 29.1.1848, FO 248/132.
75 Shiraz Agent, encl. in No. 61, 15.2.1850, FO 248/138.
76 Shiraz Agent, encl. in No. 61, 15.2 1850, FO 248/138.
77 Shiraz Agent, encl. in No. 224, 15.6.1850, FO 248/138.
78 Shiraz Agent, encl. in Hennell to Sheil 15.7.1850, FO 248/138.
79 Shiraz Agent, encl. in No. 83, 11.8.1865, FO 60/290. The preoccupations of the demonstration in Shiraz may be contrasted with those of one in the same period in Rasht. There the main problem was the foreign presence. The chief *mujtahid* of Rasht, Haji Mulla Rafi', led a popular protest against Christians, in which the role of the *lutis* was to attack by force the house of a Russian company. No. 31, 19.5.1861, FO 248/199.
80 No. 56, 19.9.1893, FO 248/572. It was customary for groups of men to pass through the streets in processions, mostly in Muharram, the Shi'i month of mourning, beating their chests and their backs, usually with chains, as a sign of piety and religious penance.
81 No. 498, 28.4.1893, FO 248/576.
82 Shiraz Agent, encl. in No. 54, 24.8.1892, FO 248/548.
83 No. 47, 20.7.1893 and No. 52, 18.8.1893, FO 248/572.
84 M. Afshari, 'Pahlavan', in *Danishnama-yi jahan-i Islam*, Tehran 1379, 5, pp. 827–9; and M.Afshari and M. Madayini, *Haft lashkar*, p. 27.
85 Bulookbashi, *Qahvakhanaha*, p. 97 ff. The tradition of such paintings was very old and related to the first appearance of coffee-houses. They represented the values of the common people, and included most particularly depictions of the battle of Kerbala and the events of 'Ashura. Such paintings reached their apogee in the last part of the Qajar period.

The coffee-houses were culturally linked to the *zurkhana* and had the same customers. They were two contiguous institutions which reinforced the religious and moral character of the community, both being filled with the ethos of bravery, chivalry, sacrifice and heroism. In the coffee-house the customers listened to recitations of poetry and the recounting of Rustam's battles with opponents such as Suhrab and Isfandiar, and Imam 'Ali's wars against demons. Most of those who recounted the stories were tradesmen. Ibid. English section p. 4.
86 Brugsch, *Persien*, p. 182. The culture of writing epics continued long after Firdausi, including into the nineteenth century. Interview with Mr A. Mir Ansari, Tehran 9.9.2002.
87 Jamalzadeh, *Isfahan*, p. 172.
88 A. Mustaufi, *Sharh-i zindigani-yi man*, Tehran 1324, I, pp. 408ff; Fathi, 'Rebels', p. 58; Floor, 'Lutis', p. 111.
89 Jamalzadeh, *Isfahan*, p. 185.
90 Ibid., pp. 186–8.
91 Scott Waring, *Sheeraz*, p. 55.

92 Such practice would appear to have been in line with the employment of physicians elsewhere in the Middle East. See Marcus, *Middle East*, p. 265.
93 Encl. No. 8, 4.1.1845, FO 248/113.
94 Compare the comment of the German traveller, Lichtenberg, on the underground in England in the eighteenth century. 'They take to stealing and are generally hanged between the ages of eighteen and twenty-six. A short life and a merry one is their motto, which they do not hesitate to proclaim in court.' Quoted in R. Porter, *English Society in the Eighteenth Century*, London 1990, p. 95.
95 Compare with eighteenth century England where food riots were conducted with rituals, songs and parades, all of which were fostered by local loyalties. D. Hay and N. Rogers, *Eighteenth Century English Society*, Oxford 1997, p. 137.
96 Scott Waring commented on the office of the *darugha* in Shiraz that, if he found anyone drinking wine or consorting with prostitutes, he compelled them to secure his connivance at no small expense. He had a large establishment under his supervision, used to patrol the streets and keep watch, which property owners subsidised at the rate of 2–3 pence per month. If a house owner was robbed, the head of watch (*kuchachi bashi*) was held accountable for the robbery and obliged to produce the stolen property or pay the amount of its value. However, this rarely happened as he was generally connected to all the thieves in the city and could answer for their obedience to his guidance. Robberies thus took place in areas not under the protection of the *kuchachi bashi*, and as it was commonly believed that he had a share of the plunder, they were all linked by a common interest. *Sheeraz*, pp. 67–8.

7

SARBAZ – THE UNRULY SOLDIERY

Through chance – that is, foreign interest in the Iranian military – the lives of one group of the ordinary people of Iran, its soldiers, are better documented than most.[1] The sources permit us to have an unusually detailed view of the pay, conditions, regulations and relations both with society and the state of the ordinary soldier. The term 'ordinary' will here be used to cover minor officers as well as other ranks, as the groups sometimes acted in collaboration. This chapter will firstly demonstrate what life was like for the ordinary soldier, in the belief that, although the army was obviously a special organisation, the experiences of soldiers were in many ways not so different from those of others at the poorer levels of society. Secondly, the chapter will seek to show the relationship of the soldiers with state and society, and consider the question of how far they were able to influence the political relations between the two.

Reform and Change in the Army

To start with, it is worth noting that to the uninitiated the Qajar army did not necessarily appear like a modern army, but in fact it was, in a rudimentary sense, though perennially in urgent need of reform. A glance at the composition of the Safavid army explains this assertion. The Safavid dynasty was initially sustained by the Qizilbash, a powerful confederation of Turkish tribes. Shah 'Abbas reduced the power of the Qizilbash in order to strengthen his own authority, and introduced instead another force of Armenian, Georgian and Circassian origin, who played a significant role in the civil and military administration.[2]

The difference between the Safavid and Qajar armies is due not so much to the long break between the two dynasties as to the influence of Europe, and above all to the reforms of the Crown Prince, 'Abbas Mirza, in the early nineteenth century, military success being seen as a victory over Russian encroachment on Iranian held territory. The army under Aqa Muhammad Qajar had consisted essentially of cavalry raised from the tribes and some additional levies.[3] 'Abbas Mirza brought modern order to the irregular troops at his disposal, assisted by a corps formed of Russian deserters.[4] He realised the crucial importance of the development of modern technology to success in war. At the same time Fath 'Ali Shah provided a rudimentary bureaucratic structure to supervise organisation and provision, under a minister of the army.[5] This minister was responsible for pensions, emoluments and sums for the maintenance of the army and registration of the soldiers. In 1807, a French mission under General Gardane was engaged to train 'Abbas Mirza's new force, the Nizam-i Jadid, along European lines. He established a corps of infantry and made some headway in training it, particularly in western drill.[6] The army was organised in regiments along European lines, and its officers acquired new titles to resemble their European counterparts (e.g. *sarhang* – colonel, *sartip* – general).[7] Gardane also ensured that the army achieved more effective use of firearms, as well as more solid fortifications.[8] The French were for a while succeeded by the British, who provided the army with the most substantial subsidy it was ever to receive, so that by 1813 the Nizam-i Jadid was composed of a disciplined infantry of twelve thousand men raised from the tribes of Azarbaijan.[9] In addition, there were irregular horse, tribal levies, and militia from the towns raised from time to time, which received irregular pay of 5–7 tomans a year plus grain. Under British auspices, Tabriz became a centre for the manufacture of gunpowder and gun carriages.[10] By 1820 the British had ceased to pay their subsidy and thereafter lack of funding prevented 'Abbas Mirza and all his Qajar successors from training and equipping the Iranian army to European standards,[11] although the attempts at reform continued intermittently.

'Abbas Mirza also attempted to impose conscription, following the Ottoman model, and devised a rudimentary scheme known as the *bunicha* system, which he introduced into Azarbaijan as part of his creation of the Nizam-i Jadid.[12] However, by the 1830s regularity in recruitment existed largely in name only, and traditional patterns of recruitment and appointment were still prevalent. Regiments were composed of men impressed from the district, estate or tribe of their colonel, and of officers who were his relatives.[13] In return for concessions of pasturage which allowed them exemption from taxation (according to the *tuyul* system of land tenure), the tribal chiefs each had to keep a certain number of cavalry mounted, corresponding to the number of their tents, at the disposal of the government.[14] Towns did not send contingents.[15] One feature which none of the reforms was able to change was organisation of the soldiery along non-tribal lines, as a result of which regiments continued to be related to tribes, and tribal solidarity was often stronger than military discipline.[16]

The dependence on Azarbaijan remained, and, contrary to feelings which prevailed elsewhere, military service was highly popular.[17] In 1847 when the regular infantry was reported, though without much confidence, as numbering fifty thousand, seventeen thousand were supposedly recruited from Azarbaijan.[18] The irregular infantry was estimated at 100,000 men, and indeed in some areas the whole population was armed, but only 8420 were in the actual pay of the government. The cavalry, recruited from the tribes, was nominally 31,349. The British, for a while, considered that the authority of the tribal chiefs had overall been much weakened,[19] but the longer term was to demonstrate their assessment as inaccurate. In reality the dependence on the tribes represented a bargain between the state and these combatant communities, for pay (or, in the absence of it, opportunity for pillage) provided poor tribesmen with a livelihood.[20] Thus the tribal levies of the Qajar armies were in the anomalous position of being sustained both by their tribes and by the state.

A further attempt to bring in conscription was made by Amir Kabir, as part of a comprehensive plan of reform of the state. The result was less than successful, but some residue of a countrywide and modest conscription system was to survive until 1925.[21] It operated by placing responsibility for providing recruits collectively on a village rather than on an individual, be it a tribal leader or landowner, and each village was supposed to support the families of the soldiers it provided for the state. Liability for military service was linked to revenue assessment.[22] In practice, the Qajars continued to rely largely on tribal levies serving under their own chiefs, above all from Azarbaijan, to provide their soldiery.

From what did the Qajar army derive its ethos? Essentially, it was from service to the shah, though, as will be demonstrated below, this not unnaturally had a clear correlation with availability and regularity of pay. There is not much evidence to suggest that soldiers thought a great deal about the shah as the Shadow of God and the Pole of the Universe or even as the dispenser of mundane justice, though for the period under study there was rarely question of his ultimate authority. Given that the colonel of the regiment was mostly a more senior member of the same tribe, control was exerted as much through tribal authority and distribution of benefits as through any other method. Since a certain tribal identity and loyalty bound each regiment together, their values were largely tribal – certainly more so than military. In a sense also, the shah probably fitted into this pattern of tribal loyalties as the paramount and most powerful chief. Whilst the majority of soldiers were doubtless practising Muslims there is no indication of the army being infused with any sense of religious purpose, though that could possibly have changed with the threat of invasion.[23] Thus early attempts to develop an identity based on loyalty to the state (that is to say, nationalism) by organising regiments through conscription rather than the tribe, failed. The army were loyal to the lands of Iran, however, when confronted with the Russian enemy.

For the remainder of the nineteenth century, and indeed, right up to the time of Reza Shah in the early twentieth century, pay, conditions and loyalties in the army were to change little. Promotion was achieved by bribery, and portions of pay, usually long in arrears, had to be given to the colonel when received.[24] Reporting on a military force sent to put down a rebellion, Sheil noted that its arms were good and the men hardy, but the clothing was poor. He considered the officers to be wholly incompetent, unacquainted with the most ordinary military duties, with command given to those who had little military experience. There was no discipline, or overall control: the arms were defective and clothing 'indescribable'. He added that expenditure on the army was impossible to guess as it was frequently disembodied and even at home for years. He noted that, although hopeless against troops of a disciplined army, its soldiers were good when opposed to troops of their own kind.[25]

In particular, the Iranian cavalry was admired by both the British and the Russians for its agility and mobility, and as a whole it was considered adequate in putting down tribal revolts.[26] The arms and horse of the cavalry in general belonged, on the whole, not to the state but to the individual, and they often constituted his entire property.[27] The soldiers overall were described by one observer as 'willing and obedient, sober and enduring' to the extent that, if cared for, they made excellent troops,[28] and by another observer as willing to endure fatigue to excess.[29] Wills commented that, at the end of the day, after a thirty to forty miles march the Iranian soldier sat down, smoked his pipe, mended his clothes, and hoped the local water would not be salty.[30]

By 1865 the soldiery were still mostly from Azerbaijan, and described as the most miserable people in the country.[31] The following year, the army was estimated, at least theoretically, to be around a hundred thousand. The shah's bodyguard consisted of two regiments of regular cavalry of eight hundred men each. The artillery was composed of five thousand men, and was reasonably well-organised.[32] In 1877 officers were still being described as ignorant of military drills, despite the establishment of a military college in Tehran.[33] There were also said to be too many officers. By 1886 the army was calculated as numbering 53,520 men liable for military service, but only 24,500 were actually serving (and that number may well be an exaggeration).[34] There was now a theoretical period of two years of service and one year at home, but the system was very lax, and it was estimated that half the regiments were at home and half on duty. A sum of £615,000 per year was supposed to be spent on the army, with the shah paying for rifles and cannon from his treasury. The soldiers were still largely recruited from Azerbaijan. Twenty thousand irregular cavalry (*savars*) existed, but they were not organised or drilled and there was no proper cadre of officers. The infantry was much the same. Each cavalryman supplied his own horse, forage and arms as before. However, the shah ordered that their weapons be kept in store. Discipline remained unsatisfactory, and usually, as previously, the soldiers obeyed their commanding officer because he was also their tribal chief.

The Problem of Pay

With regard to pay, the predicament of Iranian soldiers may be contrasted with their Ottoman counterparts, who disliked service in the army, but for whom the pay in proportion to the cost of the necessities of life was not insufficient, clothing tolerable and rations good.[35] By the 1830s pay in Iran was irregular or non-existent, and much was not passed on by the officers. Pay of the troops in 1841 was so greatly in arrears that there was little hope of it ever being recovered. Bills granted by the government for thousands of tomans were sold for hundreds.[36] After one garrison in Shiraz was ordered to leave for Bushire in 1841, the colonel announced there was not the means to go, and upon being pressed, took off his sword and threw it to the ground. Meanwhile, the troops about to march had taken to theft to supply themselves.[37] In reality, the army subsisted to a considerable degree on pillage, and it was to some extent incumbent on the shah to go to war once a year for this reason.[38]

Pay depended on taxes, but since taxes were always either in arrears or not returned in full, the government's methods of paying the army were highly irregular. Nominally, in 1847, the regular infantry received pay of seven and a half tomans per year, if on full service, but in fact the soldiers rarely received any money, as it was taken either by the shah himself or their officers.[39] By 1866, pay, when issued, was not unusually two to three years in arrears, and rarely in full.[40] Regiments could be given leave *en masse* for six to eight months, providing they relinquished their rights to arrears of pay. In 1877 their pay, despite inflation, was still seven tomans a year, plus a daily ration of food.

A certain amount of their earnings in the later nineteenth century were still taken by their officers. Soldiers in the shah's guard were normally paid about twelve tomans per year, for which they worked three to four months. They were also supposed to get a bonus of six months pay (seven tomans a year) but this was generally not received. Ordinary soldiers were meant to receive £3 per year (which would have been adequate if it had reached them) and two pence per day for bread. Fortunately, they paid no taxes, and, being mostly from the tribes, they were accustomed to living in the light tents provided by the government. At least it meant not being burdened with rent.[41] Throughout the century many soldiers supplemented their pay and tried to make some savings by working as day labourers, or butchers, or even, by 1886, money changers, suggesting a greater sophistication than in the past.[42]

Details of the earnings of an ordinary labourer are scarce, and would have varied from place to place, and season to season, but it may be useful to consider Watson's information that working hours lasted from sunrise to sunset, with Friday off. The labourer had a half-hour break at ten for breakfast, and one to two hours break and rest at lunch. He was paid between five and a half and eleven pence per day according to season. Wages were highest in autumn, and down in spring, whilst winter was a season of unemployment. About 50–75% was spent on food and clothing, the rest being either kept for winter or given to the wife.[43] Soldiers, by contrast, were given uniforms, albeit ragged, and could to some extent depend upon both the need and the obligation of the system to see that they did not actually starve while in service. However, in the seasonal nature of pay, poverty and insecurity, there must have been little to choose between the two occupations.

Recruitment, Benefits and Provisions

There was no systematic method of recruitment and no fixed age for entrance, though recruits were normally over fifteen. The very old and the very young were not supposed to be recruited, but since there were no particular limits of age or fitness, those responsible had the power to do what suited them.[44] They enlisted for life, but could leave on producing a substitute.[45] Otherwise, at the end of their service, they had no right to claim anything further from the government, and most ended their lives in a pitiful condition, indeed in destitution. Once they were worn out, they were discarded without any means of subsistence, as in the Ottoman army.[46]

There were no hospitals or provisions for the sick and wounded, and medical facilities remained primitive.[47] By 1874 the Azarbaijani soldiery in Bushire had acquired a Chief Medical Officer (Hakim Bashi), but it did not seem to make much difference to the soldiers' well-being. Of seven hundred men, two hundred had died in the past year from intermittent fever. They lived in cramped, poorly ventilated quarters, without any comfort, with about two out of every nine suffering from fever or dysentery, and all virtually uncared-for in terms of medical treatment and clothing.[48]

The clothing of the army was such that observers considered that they could hardly be recognised as soldiers.[49] As a painting of Muhammad Shah's coronation procession in 1835 demonstrates, their clothing in the mid-century was semi-European, symbolic in a sense of the state of the army itself.[50] They all had laced boots and European-cut coats (in various states of wear), but the rest was Iranian, especially their large trousers and lambs-wool hats. Their muskets were reported as being from the time of Waterloo. Soldiers in the capital were better clothed – in the provinces their uniforms were little more than rags.[51]

Order and Mutiny – Soldiers and the State

It will thus be clear that the lives of Qajar soldiers were not governed by rules and regulations, but by accepted practice, and by force, where they were considered to have transgressed it. There was no code of punishment, a matter left largely to the discretion of the commanding officer, for which reason a soldier's life was very brutal. Mutiny and other misconduct was normally punishable by either death or flogging, for example by strangulation or decapitation, by the bastinado or by the abscission of the ears, nose and hands.[52]

There was no such thing as a court martial, or martial law. Even Islamic justice made, as far as is known, no impression, and certainly for their military duties soldiers were not in any way subject to the shari'a or the authority of the 'ulama. Thus the large number of armed tribesmen, who, as soldiers, were the principal means of imposing law and order, were themselves one of the main sources of disorder.[53]

Mutiny was not uncommon, and dependence on the tribe, especially loyalty to the chief of the tribe, was the main fact in keeping soldiers from revolt or desertion.[54] Though in many ways patient with their appalling working conditions, if only because there was little alternative for most poor tribesmen and peasants, the soldiery from time to time challenged the authorities, often timing their protest at the beginning of a war or a revolt. Mutiny was nearly always related to pay. In the years of financial deficiencies and royal ambitions regarding Herat in the late 1830s, there were a number of mutinies which had their origin in lack of funding. Thus two regiments from Azarbaijan stationed in Bushire in 1838 deserted to go home, and had to be recalled by a contingent from one of the local tribes.[55] The shah ordered troops and money to be sent from Shiraz, but the population of Fars was proving recalcitrant over taxes, given the economic situation, and the governor of the province had an empty treasury, so no troops were sent. Discipline became harsher and deserters were beaten to death.[56] In 1847 the artillery surrounded the houses of the shah and Haji Mirza Agasi, and by incessant clamouring of the phrase 'Ya Allah' (Oh Allah!) were eventually able to extract from them a considerable sum.[57] The implication was that the shah was failing to give the soldiers their rights and thus not acting as a just ruler in the Islamic sense.[58] Even in the time of Amir Kabir there were complaints about pay, and soldiers from one regiment went to his house to complain vociferously about their conditions, shouting '*Ya Allah! Yah Allah!*' and '*Marg bar Amir!*' (Death to the Amir!).[59] The following day, still unpaid, they marched out of their barracks, headed by their drums, demanding vengeance.[60] The bazaars closed , and the situation, evidently emanating from general discontent, was only calmed by the intervention of the Imam Jum'a and other 'ulama. At the same time another regiment imitated this revolt by expelling all their officers from the camp and refusing to march unless arrears were paid. The adjutant general[61] and the treasurer general were put in confinement by the shah's regiments of guards until they were paid.

Similar disorders among the soldiers arose in 1856 when the Khalij Regiment, stationed in Kermanshah, protested at their lack of pay. Offenders were flogged and sent to the capital.[62] The patience of the soldiers over pay on the whole is illustrated by the fact that it took three years without pay before two regiments in Tehran mutinied in 1864.[63] They then barricaded themselves in the barracks, dismissed their officers, and in a demonstration of popular authority, appointed others in their place. The Tehran garrison at that time was reported rife with discontent and insubordination. One regiment on parade, when commanded by its Italian instructor to march double time, refused to obey the order, on the plea that marching wore out their shoes. During a further disturbance in 1868, the soldiers of one of the Azarbaijani regiments in Tehran, infuriated by the withholding of their pay, mutinied as a body, closed the barrack gates and refused to muster outside when summoned to do so.[64] They were particularly incensed that their remonstrations had been ignored. This mutiny did not have a positive outcome, for two regiments of infantry were sent to get the mutineers, and despite the fact that they piled their arms in the square before the attack, the regiment was disbanded and some of the soldiers severely flogged. Although the townspeople did not on this occasion become actively involved as well, the cause of the refractory regiment was viewed with sympathy and the punishment condemned.

Sometimes, however, the government took a *laissez faire* attitude to mutiny. When the escort of the Khan of Khelat deserted to Bampur, the governor of Kerman, despite orders from Tehran, did not take the trouble to find them.[65] Protest could also take mild forms. One day as the traveller von Thielmann passed before the local guardhouse, he noted that the sentry omitted to perform the necessary salute. When asked why, the man explained that he had not received his pay.[66] At times military protest became very bold indeed. In 1878, while the shah was on a pilgrimage to the Shrine of Shah 'Abd al-'Azim, his carriage was surrounded by about fifty soldiers from one of the Isfahan regiments on duty near the capital.[67] They first presented him with a petition and then closed round his carriage in a menacing manner, refusing to retreat when ordered. Two of the shah's attendants were knocked off their horses and one of the windows of his carriage broken by stones, so that the coachman had to drive on rapidly. The outcome is not known, except that the usual punishments were inflicted.

Another way of protesting, and criticising by implication the policies of the ruler, was to go into sanctuary. A mutiny took place in 1880, when one of the regiments in Tehran not having received their salary, took refuge in the Shrine of Shah 'Abd al-'Azim till they were paid.[68] In Bushire the soldiers were normally well controlled, at least in the latter part of the nineteenth century, mainly because of the British presence. However, in 1880, ninety two soldiers of the Garusi regiment garrisoning Bushire caused consternation to the Iranian government by taking refuge under the British flag.[69] The cause of the grievance was again pay, this time the soldiers being owed money by a government bailiff named Haidar Khan Zabit-i Tangestani. Since the soldiers were in sanctuary under a foreign flag, the Foreign Agent of Bushire (*karguzar*) had to deal with the matter. He informed the Sipah Salar (commander-in-chief) in Tehran, by telegram, that in an effort to win them over he had been to see them in informal dress, to which Sipah Salar responded:

> Till now I thought you were quite bright . . . what do you mean you went in informal dress? You are a *karguzar*, you have no formal dress.[70]

Orders were sent that, on emerging, the recalcitrant soldiers were to go to Shiraz, their leader, a captain, was to be questioned, and they were to be punished, 'but not so severely that they petition us'.[71]

By the 1890s the state of the troops was still being described as deplorable. They lacked food and clothing and 100,000 tomans that was supposed to be spent on them had, as usual, been misappropriated.[72] With the exception of a few picked troops, they had no uniform to speak of. Whereas earlier references indicate a degree of self sufficiency, or even of troops setting aside money for their families, the British noted in 1890 that troops drawn from the provinces received some assistance from their families. This, in addition to their work as labourers, was adequate for a diet of coarse bread. The sight of soldiers dying from fever caused by starvation, common at Astarabad, was not to be found at Tehran. The artillery were also still better off than the ordinary infantry.

In 1891 the garrisons of Tehran, having received no pay, went into a state of mutiny with some effect, as officers were given 25% of the amount due, and men 10%.[73] A new type of criticism was now creeping into expressions of discontent. For the first time resentment was not simply at the lack of pay, but at the level of the salaries of the royal family, and at the cost of appointing Europeans. The inflation generating restlessness in society in the 1890s also affected the soldiers in a way peculiar to them. Their ration allowance was calculated on the basis of the equivalent portion of grain. Although the price of grain went up, the ration allowance did not, and so the solider received increasingly less than he should have done, fuelling discontent.[74] This was, of course, at the time not only of the tobacco protest, but of the growing influence of the press, at least within Tehran and other towns. Further, there is some evidence by this stage of elements in the military being concerned with reform.[75]

In sum, soldiers did regularly protest over their pay and conditions. These protests signalled to the government the problems of potentially disloyal troops. The outcome of each protest is not always clear, but the tendency seemed to be that the ringleaders were punished, but the troops received a portion of what was owing to them. Mutiny, therefore, at a cost, had made some impression on the soldiers' lot.

Soldiers and Society

The disputes described above involved soldiers and the state. Soldiers interacted with society in both positive and negative ways. Generally, the presence of soldiers in any area was not particularly welcome, mainly because of the depredations they could cause as a result of their absence of pay. Unruly and unpaid soldiery could undoubtedly be hard on others in society, and the mere threat of the despatch of a regiment could quell protest, though not if a grievance was strong enough. A major fracas occurred in Shiraz between the soldiery and the people of the city in 1839, during which reportedly twenty people were killed on both sides.[76] In 1841 when Bushire was garrisoned by soldiers without much control, the inhabitants implored the governor of Fars to withdraw them, but in vain. According to one view they were deliberately behaving outrageously in order to be sent away from the heat of Bushire.[77] Robberies by the garrison in Shiraz in 1894 were frequent, and it was said that those robbed were usually punished by the authorities on the grounds that the soldiers had been falsely accused,[78] which was one way of making the inhabitants pay for their military. Such was society's fear of the depredations of the military in general that when a government order was issued for a large supply of baggage animals for an expedition against the Turkoman, the drivers of such animals, no doubt anticipating maltreatment of their beasts and minimal pay, threw off their loads and fled.[79] On another occasion, when it became known that the shah was planning an expedition to Mazandaran, the local muleteers refused to approach Tehran, lest their animals be seized for the shah's requirements.[80]

Thus in 1888, when a force of soldiers came to Lingah to settle a dispute, the inhabitants were reported to be much alarmed, echoing the views of the Russian peasantry, who did not consider soldiers welcome guests.[81] Disputes between the townspeople and the soldiery in Bushire were frequent.[82] In 1876 one of the night-guards was wounded by a soldier prowling the streets with intent to rob, and an Arab was hurt by another a state of drunkenness.[83] A woman was also wounded the following night. At this time they principally vented their fury at the absence of pay and rations through the sale of watermelons. A group of soldiers seized all of this fruit brought in to market, giving the owners any price they liked, and compelled purchasers to pay them an extortionate price for the produce. A second enterprise was to extract half a kran in tax on each load of watermelons. Their major (*yavar*) could not control them. Such activities drew the attention of the authorities, as they were intended to, and brought promises, at least, of pay and rations.

The mutiny of the ninety two men of the Garusi regiment, mentioned above, likewise embroiled other groups of society in a dispute over pay. The governor of Fars had given orders that the people of Tangestan must not give money to soldiers, but must, on the contrary, be sure to pay their taxes – from which, supposedly, the soldiers would receive their pay.[84] However, the soldiers deduced that they would not get their money from the government officials or their officers, and that they must therefore extract it at source, i.e. from the taxpayers of Tangestan. In that case, it was preferable to do so before the government tax collectors arrived, as otherwise the people would have no money to give them. There appears to have been an additional problem in that rival groups of soldiers were engaged in this practice.[85]

Soldiers could indeed be very violent, and their poverty was such that they could kill for one toman.[86] Upon complaints being made over the murder of an Armenian labourer by one of their number in Qumsha in

1876, he and three or four brothers, also soldiers, collected their fellows, and descended upon the officials of the town, including the governor, as a body to defend their comrades.[87] Another example of murder occurred when a man from Salam Abad was on his way to Bushire with two donkey loads of firewood was attacked. He was bullied and finally shot by soldiers.[88]

Though soldiers and many townspeople had a common bond in poverty and in dealing with an oppressive system, the soldiers' relations with society were on the whole poor. This may partly be explained by the fact that most soldiers came from the tribes, and thus belonged to a different social structure to most towns-people. But in truth the problem was not, as always, so much the conduct of the soldiery as the point that they had not been paid. In other words, the real cause of the difficulty was the poverty of Iran in the Qajar period.

Occasionally, harassment by soldiers was not against society, but instead might be said to represent its views. As one British Residency official in Bushire recounts:

> I was stopped and insulted last evening by some men who seemed to be ruffianly highwaymen in the street. They seized my hair though I was accompanied by Residency servants, a sowar and had a lantern. They have since stated that they are soldiers. This is not the first time they have shown they feel at liberty to molest British subjects.[89]

Soldiers and Social Protest

Despite the general trend of not having positive relations with society, soldiers sometimes sympathised with townspeople in opposing the government, and also the British presence, most particularly in periods of economic hardship. Thus in the 1830s and 1840s, when the British presence in Bushire was particularly unpopular and not yet well-established, they made common cause with local opinion by harassing the Residency servants, for example the water-carrier.[90] In 1842 they also harassed the assistant resident at the gate of the town and stoned the Residency water-carrier.[91]

The period of the tobacco protest demonstrated a serious rift in such loyalty as the army had to the shah. In Isfahan the feeling against the Tobacco Concession, and foreign involvement in the tobacco trade, was so great that even after it was abolished the people declined to resume smoking immediately.[92] The five hundred or so troops available for service to Zill al-Sultan at this time and recruited from Isfahan and its neighbourhood were reported as unreliable, which left the governor in no position to resist the protest movement.[93] In the riots of 1893 in Shiraz against Qavam al-Mulk over, amongst other matters, the price of bread, he summoned his Arab and Baharlu tribal levies to protect himself.[94] Nevertheless, the people were adamant that they did not want him as mayor (*kalantar*) of

Shiraz, and forced him to leave. A crowd gathered round the telegraph office, and the shah ordered them dispersed by force. On 18th May 1893 the Kazzaz and Khalij regular regiments and the artillerymen ordered to fire on the crowd, sided with them instead, saying as long as the people were loyal to the shah, they would not fight with them for the sake of Qavam al-Mulk. They further attacked the Arab and Baharlu forces of Qavam. As a result, the government was forced to conciliate the crowd, and promise the recall of their unpopular mayor to Tehran. This unusually strong collaboration between populace and soldiery took place against a background of gathering criticism of the government, as already mentioned, and most particularly because of the high price of bread due to inflation and the harvest being damaged by locusts.

In the same year in Isfahan similarly there were serious bread riots, and Zill al-Sultan caused his troops, numbering about 725, to be served out with rifles and twenty rounds of ammunition.[95] However, as the soldiers were just as much affected by the high cost of living, their sympathies were with the people of the town, and their loyalty could not be relied on, which forced Zill al-Sultan to negotiate with the discontented Isfahanis.[96] Thus an assembly was arranged at his palace, attended by five hundred representatives of different classes, and it was agreed that wheat should be sold at a reduced price of seventy krans per *kharvar* and bread retailed at sixty krans.[97]

* * *

The lives of the ordinary soldiers demonstrate the problems confronting the poorer levels of society in the nineteenth century in Iran – insecure, unstable, subject to rough and random justice, lacking food, clothing and ordinary comforts. In their case also they seem to have had little contact with their families for long periods of the year and sometimes never. The vision of Foucault, that lack of institutions brings liberty, is challenged by the lives of these Iranian soldiers. Anyone who cannot afford a prison can still effectively punish a man by beating him to death. The absence of prisons, let alone hospitals and other welfare bodies, exposed the soldiers to cold, starvation and swift death from disease, if they could not remain fit.

On the one hand the Qajars were largely dependent on the tribal khans, the very people who prevented the reform and cohesion of the state, to supply those forces which were supposed to give it security. Yet the rewards the state could offer the tribal officers and men in the army failed to change over the century, rendering the bargain increasingly obsolete. Disorganisation of the army reveals with particular clarity how the Qajar state was built on sand, especially when it is compared with the relative cohesion, regularisation and organisation of the towns. The nineteenth century, particularly the latter part, saw the development of prosperity through trade for certain sections of the urban community, especially the merchants. Thus urban society grew stronger than the forces of the state, a significant factor, albeit only one of many, that explains why a revolution came so early in a country that appeared backward in terms of modernisation. Further, it is clear that by the 1890s, with the influence of Europe in the form of trade, of the new press, and of new technology, ideas on reform were beginning to creep into the army, even at the level of the ordinary soldiers, in the towns. The collaboration of the soldiers with the populace against the regime is a feature not found in the early part of the century, when the military tended to rob the townspeople, whether in the name of the government or of themselves.

The relations with society varied. To some extent the townspeople, and more particularly those with a modicum of property, understood that the soldiers were present to protect them and keep order, as was demonstrated in the disturbances in Isfahan in 1840. On the other hand, soldiers were known to vent their discontent over their pay on the townspeople, either by deliberately harassing them to pressurise the government into paying them, or simply to extort money and food from them. In his study of Ottoman Cairo, where one in thirty five townspeople were in the military, Raymond concluded that the system allowed for some penetration between the subjects and part of the dominant class.[98] Though the military studied here are of a lower social group, it would seem, the connection of the soldiers with society in a civilian capacity did not appear to create any sort of bond, unless they were possibly from the same region. The Qajar army, unlike the Egyptian one, was tribalised, and this meant that the two groups, soldiers and townspeople, were separated by different lifestyles and different values, although they might have common elements in religion and its culture. Also ultimately, they had different sources of remuneration.

The accounts above also demonstrate that despite the harshness of the penalties imposed on them, the soldiers were capable of standing up to their masters, and had ways of bargaining with them. This might of course involve actually causing disorder or threatening it by harassment. But they also had a number of milder and more subtle strategies for negotiating over their pay. Further, they had the right of taking sanctuary, particularly in embarrassing circumstances, and implying to the population at large that the state was being unjust and was not rightful. It would seem that though the Islamic notion of the shah as the Shadow of God conferred on him a degree of authority, it was principally used to remind him of his deficiencies as an employer. It could not engender a unifying ethos in an army whose loyalties were largely tribal, especially given the absence of proper or regular pay. So the relations between individual and state did not change; rights and duties, such as they were, remained the same, and there was no advancement in building a proto-national identity through military reform.

In the end, though, perhaps what identified and bound them together most closely was the common experience of being soldiers. At the end of one battle between the townspeople of Bushire and the soldiers of the garrison over a baker who supplied the rations, one of the latter was killed. The other soldiers refused to allow him to be buried in Bushire, but determined to send his body all the way up through the mountain pass to Shiraz.[99]

Notes

1 I am grateful to Dr Stephanie Cronin for her comments on this chapter.
2 R. Savory, *Studies in the Safavid History of Iran*, London 1987, pp. 194–5. See also E. Farmer, G. Hambly, D. Kopf, B. Marshall and R. Taylor, *Comparative History of Civilisations*, Massachusetts 1977, I, p. 426.
3 J. Calmard, 'Les Reformes Militaires sous les Qajars (1795–1825)', in Y. Richard, ed., *Entre l'Iran et l'Occident*, Paris 1989, p. 20.
4 G. Drouville, *Voyage en Perse*, Paris 1925, II, p. 92, cited in V. Martin, 'Reform and Development in the Early Qajar Period', *Die Welt des Islams*, XXXVI, 1, 1996, p. 2.
5 Busse, *Qajar Rule*, pp. 117–8.
6 M. Atkin, *Russia and Iran 1780–1828*, Minneapolis 1980, p. 126.
7 These titles were not used before the Qajar period.
8 Calmard, 'Reformes', p. 23.
9 Malcolm, *Persia*, II, pp. 496–7.
10 Atkin, *Russia and Iran*, p. 135.
11 Busse, *Qajar Rule*, p. 122; Drouville, *Voyage*, p. 92.
12 S. Cronin, 'Conscription and Popular Resistance in Iran 1925–41', in E.J. Zurcher, ed., *Arming the State*, London 1999, pp. 145–6.
13 Enc. 11.11.1835 in No. 9, 20.1.1836, FO 60/40
14 MAE, Ambassade/Teheran/49, encl. in No. 4, 31.7.1848.
15 MAE, Ambassade/Teheran/58, No. 14, 10.3.1871.
16 Ibid., p. 128.
17 No. 73. 18.7.1847, FO 60/131.
18 No. 73, 28.7.1847, FO 60/131.
19 No. 73, 28.7.1847, FO 60/131
20 M.E. Yapp, 'The Modernisation of Middle Eastern Armies in the nineteenth Century: A Comparative View', in V.J. Parry and M.E. Yapp, eds, *War, Technology and Society in the Middle East*, Oxford 1975, p. 334.
21 Cronin, 'Conscription', p. 146. See also Calmard, 'Reformes', p. 28, and R. Tousi, 'The Persian Army 1880–1907', *Middle Eastern Studies*, Vol. 24 No. 2. 1988, pp. 209–10.
22 The means of calculation was to perform a survey of the number of ploughs required to keep an area under cultivation and to estimate one man per plough as available for military service. Ibid., p. 146; see also MAE, Ambassade/Teheran/58, No. 14, 10.3.1871. The community was supposed, in addition, to cultivate any land owned by the soldier while he was away, MAE, Ambassade/Teheran/60, No. 10, 1.9.1876.
23 By 1895 Christians were employed in the army, though it was noted as unusual. A Jahangir Khan Senaye, a Christian of Georgian origins, assumed the command of the Azarbaijan military with the title of Rais-i Nizam, conferred from Tehran, and aided by his secretaty, Mr Alberti. His principal mission seems to have been to manufacture powder of better quality. No. 1, 6.1.1885, FO 248/425.
24 Encl. 11.11.1835 in No. 9, 20.1.1836, FO 60/40.
25 No. 73, 28.7.1847, FO 60/131. A further estimate was given in 1847 that the expenditure on the army was one million tomans in theory, but in reality it was

not possible to raise such an amount, so at any one time about two-thirds of the army was on leave.
26 Brydges, *Dynasty*, p. 311. No. 32, 9.4.1836, FO 60/40.
27 Macdonald Kinnear, *Memoir*, p. 33.
28 Mounsey, *Journey*, p. 144. See also MAE, Ambassade/Teheran/49, encl. in No. 4, 31.7.1848.
29 Wills, *Persia*, p. 180. Later observers made similar comments, saying the Iranian army was composed of good soldiers, robust, healthy, cheerful and full of alacrity, as well as patient about hunger, cold and fatigue, see No. 197, 17.12.1877, FO 60/399.
30 Ibid., p. 180
31 Polak, *Safarnama*, p. 39.
32 Watson, *Persia*, p. 24.
33 No. 197, 17.12.1877, FO 60/399.
34 No. 73, 8.6.1886, FO 60/479.
35 No. 43, 6.6.1839, FO 60/66.
36 IO R/15/1/91, Shiraz Agent, 7.2.1841.
37 IO R/15/1/91, Shiraz Agent, 1.3.1841.
38 Macdonald Kinneir, *Memoir*, p. 34. It is possible that there was a decline, at least in the pay of the cavalry, from the early years of Fath 'Ali Shah's reign. Then the cavalry was reported as clothed and furnished with horses and arms at the expense of the shah. They received an allowance of barley and straw for their horses, and wheat, rice and butter for themselves. Their pay was then high in Iranian terms, and if their pay was kept back, they could complain effectively. They were paid either every three months or once a year, but their subsistence in the meantime was adequate, so they did not suffer much. Scott Waring, *Sheeraz*, pp. 81–2.
39 No. 73, 28.7.1847, FO 60/131.
40 Watson, *Persia*, p. 25.
41 Ibid.; Wills, *Persia*, p. 180.
42 No. 73, 8.6.1886, FO 60/479; Watson, *Persia*, pp. 25; Curzon, *Persia*, p. 606.
43 Watson, *Persia*, pp. 26–7.
44 Mounsey, *Journey*, p. 143; A.M. Piemontese, 'Artish-i Iran dar salha-yi 1874–5 miladi az did-i General Enrico Andreini', *Tarikh-i Mu'asir-i Iran*, 3, 1370, pp. 18–19.
45 According to Scott Waring, in the early years of the nineteenth century, when a body of men enlisted, their names and those of their fathers, and their ages, were set down in a muster roll. If they died their names were given to the officers who kept the roll. Thus a check was kept that the tribal chiefs did not try to keep a smaller number of men than their prescribed quota. Scott Waring, *Sheeraz*, p. 82. It is not clear if, and how far, this system changed throughout the nineteenth century.
46 No. 43, 6.6.1839, FO 60/66.
47 No. 73, 28.7.1847, FO 60/131.
48 No. 298, 5.3.1874, FO 248/300.
49 No. 73, 28.7.1847, FO 60/131. Things had not improved much by the end of the century, see Curzon, *Persia*, pp. 599, 603.
50 Mounsey, *Journey*, p. 141. Part of the manuscript depicting the army on the occasion of the coronation of Muhammad Shah in 1835 is published in Sotheby's catalogue, *Oriental Manuscripts and Miniatures*, London 1998, p. 74, No. 72.
51 Ibid., p. 144. MAE, Ambassade/Teheran/49, No. 4, 31.7.1848. See also M. von Thielmann, *Journey in the Caucasus, Persia and Turkey in Asia*, trans. C. Heneage, London 1875, p. 50. Thielmann conjectured that the uniforms were bought at bale price from contractors, and certainly for next to nothing.

52 Encl. No. 27, 25.2.1856., FO 60/208: No. 145, 12.12.1868, FO 60/313; No. 48, 5.4.1878, FO 60/409; Mounsey, *Journey*, p. 142.
53 See Yapp, 'Modernisation', p. 334 for the effect of the unpaid soldiers on the people of the countryside.
54 Mounsey, *Journey*, p. 144.
55 No. 77, 25.9.1838, FO 248/85.
56 Hennell to McNeill, 27.10.1838, FO 248/85.
57 No. 73, 28.7.1847, FO 60/131.
58 Records of other mutinies do not convey the style of language used, but as already indicated, the ethos of the army was, by virtue of its recruitment, more tribal than Islamic. Nevertheless, the use of the term 'Ya Allah' here would indicate that the country was in a state of oppression and that the actions of the ruler were not legitimate. The incident was also, however, particularly unusual as it involved the shah himself.
59 MAE, Ambassade/Teheran/50, 5.5.1849.
60 No. 18, 17.3.1849, FO 60/144.
61 Chief of staff, whose duty was to assemble troops for review and act as a master of ceremonies during military parades at the palace. Tousi, 'Army', p. 208.
62 Encl. in No. 27, 25.2.1856, FO 60/208.
63 No. 62, 26.7.1864, FO 60/283.
64 No. 145, 12.12.1868, FO 60/313; See also MAE, Ambassade/Teheran/57, 26.12.1868.
65 No. 104, 10.8.1871, FO 60/335.
66 Von Thielmann, *Journey*, p. 50.
67 No. 48, 5.4.1878, FO 60/409.
68 I'timad al-Saltana, *Ruznama*, p. 88.
69 SAM, No 295001685, 1A4A574, 19 Muharram 1296/12 January 1879.
70 SAM, No. 295001722, 1,A4A612, 21 Muharram 1296/14 January 1879.
71 SAM, No 295001685, 1A4A574, 19 Muharram 1296/12 January 1879.
72 No. 18, 25.4.1890, FO 248/505.
73 No. 2175a, 11.3.1891, FO 248/ 530.
74 Tousi, 'Army', pp. 212–3.
75 See No. 60, 23.9.1892, FO 248/548. In a conversation with Preece, a Mir Panj (general) serving under Zill al-Sultan complained of the poor state of the country, and the fact that only a tenth of the shah's budget was spent on it. As a result the soldiers had to work as labourers. He also criticised the 'ulama, then leading the tobacco protest, saying they would cause the British and Russians to interfere in the country, and should be confined to their priestly duties.
76 Encl. in No. 58, 15.8.1839, FO 60/67.
77 IO R/15/1/91, Shiraz Agent, 6.7.1841.
78 No. 713, Shiraz Agent, 28.5.1894, FO 248/601.
79 No. 65, 26.7.1864, FO 60/283.
80 No. 43, 17.4.1866, FO 60/296.
81 No. 21, 11.2.1888, FO 248/469. For the Russian peasant, soldiers were 'bears who come and go', see J. Keep, *Soldiers of the Tsar*, Oxford 1985, p. 191.
82 No. 666, 5.7.1876, FO 248/318.
83 No. 58, 15.8.1876, FO 248/318. Interestingly, reports of drunkenness among the soldiery were rare, especially compared to *lutis*.
84 SAM, No. 295001722, 1,A4A612, 21 Muharram 1297/14 January 1880.
85 SAM, No 295001685, 1A4A574, 19 Muharram 1296/12 January 1879.
86 Kh. Bayani, *Panjah sal tarikh-i Nasiri*, Tehran 1375, V, p. 367.
87 No. 62, 22.5.1876, FO 60/380
88 Head Munshi's report, 23.12.92, FO 248/544.
89 IO R/15/1/181, to Mahmud Yusef Khan, 1.11.1864, p. 47.

90 No. 455, 21.10.1843, FO 248/113.
91 No. 61, 16.9.1842, FO 60/90, and encl. in No. 92, 10.12.1842, FO 60/91.
92 No. 24, 17.1.1892, FO 248/548.
93 No. 4, 29.1.1892, FO 248/548.
94 No. 513, Shiraz Agent, 19.5.1893, FO 248/576.
95 No. 69, 28.10.1893, FO 248/572.
96 No. 70, 28.10.1893, FO 248/572. By this stage the dependence on Azarbaijan for recruits appears to have diminished, and certainly there were Isfahani regiments, including, it is likely, the troops mentioned here, who would thus have had more fellow feeling with the townspeople.
97 Decipher No. 20, 2.11.1893, FO 248/572.
98 A. Raymond, 'Soldiers in Trade: the Case of Ottoman Cairo', *British Society for Middle Eastern Studies Bulletin*, 18, 1991, p. 33.
99 No. 404, 28.8.1844, FO 248/113.

8

SLAVERY AND BLACK SLAVES IN IRAN IN THE NINETEENTH CENTURY

In his account of the peoples of the south coast of Iran, Sa'idi observes that the descendants of slaves are scattered along the region.[1] In every place there are a few people of black origin, the older ones at that time (1966) remembering their fears on landing. Once they were out of slavery, their lives were no different from those of the whites, and they were also busy with work and fishing, their lives shaped by the present. In this chapter on the nineteenth century in Iran, I will be focusing on black slaves. Firstly, the chapter will consider the overall context, and briefly explore the differences between the approach to slaves in the Americas in the slave-owning period, and that in the world of Islam. The Islamic approach to slavery and its implications will then be examined, as it is particularly important for understanding the treatment of black slaves. Next, the chapter will look at the nineteenth century Iranian practice in the context of the current debate on the treatment of black slaves, and will discuss the issue of race. This will include evidence on runaway slaves from the British public records as well as contemporary travellers' accounts of the status of slaves. Further some of the problems confronting the abolitionists in Iran and the British in the suppression of the slave trade will be explored. Finally, the chapter will consider some of the legal implications of the ownership of slaves and the suppression of the trade.

Slavery in Islam

Nineteenth century travellers to Iran commented on the difference of treatment between slaves in Iran as an Islamic country and that in the Americas, noting that the Islamic attitude was much more humane.[2] The believing slave in accordance with the Qur'an is the brother of the freeman in Islam and before God, and the superior of the free pagan, a point which is reiterated frequently in the *hadith*. Thus, although the slave is a possession, he is also a human being with a particular religious status and rights under the shari'a.[3] The assumption in Islam is that the natural state of human beings is freedom, but nevertheless the Qur'an does not forbid slavery, although commanding kindness to slaves and recommending manumission (formal release). As a result, with regard to the shari'a, slavery falls within the category of *umur-i mubah* (permissible affairs). In effect, this means that slavery is permitted, but is carefully regulated by a number of laws to ensure that the spiritual well-being and the physical well-being of the slave, as a Muslim, are carefully protected.

By contrast the Americas slave trade saw slaves as goods and chattels. In his recent work on Islam's black slaves, Segal points out that crucially the Western slave trade was allied to capitalism, since some of its immense profit was invested in industry. Thus slaves were perceived as units of labour in a production process that disregarded their souls.[4] Slaves in Islam were used in the service sector, mainly as soldiers, concubines, domestic servants and porters, and therefore were primarily a form of consumption rather than an element in production.[5] Polak observed that slaves in Iran were not set hard labour in the countryside, but were used in service.[6] In a society where the state was legitimised by the religion, the predominant influence was the Divine Will as reflected in the Qur'an, therefore slaves were people, not possessions. Thus one of the issues to consider in this chapter is whether the evidence in the available sources supports such a view.

To move on, then, to explore further the Islamic view of slavery. Is there any difference between Sunni practice in, for example the Ottoman Empire, and Shi'i practice, in Iran? Legal experts could no doubt find fine points, but my overall impression from reading both primary and secondary material is that slaves were better treated in Iran than in parts of the Arab world, perhaps because of custom, perhaps because the cost of transportation, and their difficulties in surviving the climate, gave them a higher value. In both sects, however, the theory and practice of slavery stems from Qur'anic injunctions and their interpretation in the shari'a. Whilst seeing the slave as a human being the Qur'an recognises the fundamental inequality of master and slave, and the predominant rights of the former. It also accepts the status of slaves as concubines. However, it enjoins kindness to slaves and commends the liberation of slaves as an act of piety that may also expiate sin. Masters are encouraged to allow the slave to purchase his or her own freedom and may even provide the means.[7]

The Supply and Sale of Slaves

Where did slaves in the Islamic lands come from? Islam prohibits the enslavement of free Muslims, and there is an implicit assumption in Islam that humankind should be free. In particular the enslavement of Muslims was prohibited, and although this point was not always adhered to in practice, on the whole the free subjects of the Ottoman Empire and Iran (whether Muslim or non-Muslim) were protected from enslavement. There were only two ways that a person could be enslaved: firstly, if they were born to a slave mother; secondly, and much more commonly, if they were captured, since the Qur'an permits the enslavement of infidels captured in war.

By the nineteenth century in Iran and the Ottoman Empire, these two sources of supply had long since ceased to be adequate for demand. Therefore, slaves were procured by purchase and importation. Up to this time many slaves had been imported from the Caucasus, the men for military or administrative service, the women to enter the harem as concubines. Black Africans were also imported, usually to act as eunuchs or as labourers, or, in the case of women, as domestic servants. By the nineteenth century the trade from the Caucasus had largely dried up, mainly because of Russian advances in that area, and consequent reconfiguring of the economy. Thus Iran and the Ottoman Empire became much more heavily dependent on Africa as a source for slaves and, as a result, black slaves grew in number. They were not captured in war by Muslims but weere seized by other Africans and sold to mainly Arab slave traders who, having transported them in appalling conditions to the Middle East, ensured their conversion to Islam, and sold them through a chain of recognised dealers along a number of established routes. For eunuchs, the main market was Baghdad.[8]

In Iran, whenever anyone wanted to sell a slave, they took him to a slave trader and put him in his charge. Most notably, a record was kept of the transaction, with the name of the slave and the circumstances of his slavery being written in the trader's book. At the time of the sale, the trader reported strong points and weak points to the prospective buyer, who then had the right to examine the slave. The rights of the buyer were much more limited in the case of examination of a female slave (*kaniz*), though they could always call on the assistance of a woman. It was not permitted to part a woman and child,[9] nor was it allowed to sell a Muslim slave to a non-Muslim.[10]

The black slaves were of two types, *habashis* coming from Abyssinia and *zangis* from Africa itself. *Habashis*, who were of a lighter complexion with features closer in type to those of Middle Eastern people, were twice the value of the *zangis*. They thus tended to be purchased largely by the well-to-do, and the women to be used more often as concubines.[11] They could also be the favoured companions of the young members of the family with whom they grew up. One British traveller, Wills, observed a young *habashi* slave playing with Jalal al-Daula, the son of Zill al-Sultan, and was told that he would one day be a great personage.[12] The *zangis* (also called *bombassis*, and *sidis*) were used in domestic service, particularly as cooks. Amongst the most valuable slaves were the eunuchs, who, because of the prohibition of mutilation in Islam, were normally castrated as children in Africa before they reached Islamic territory, at which point they were converted to Islam. Eunuchs were treated with great care because of their delicate constitution and their value. They could accumulate great wealth, which they generally left to the master or his children. However, they sometimes married as for example, Aqa Sulaiman, the Khaja Bashi, or chief eunuch of Zill al-Sultan, who had two wives and left his property to his widows. He is described as a successful gambler who kept a fine stable of horses.[13] Eunuchs could occupy positions of considerable responsibility at a variety of levels. For example in 1891 the principal eunuch of the governor of Shiraz is described as giving punishment to some of the more rebellious tribesmen.[14] A black eunuch, owned by Haji Ahmad Khan in Shiraz, was so highly praised that his renown reached the ears of the prince-governor, Shu'a' al-Saltana. When the governor tried to seize him by force, he and all the rest of the household had to take *bast* (sanctuary) to escape.[15]

It is not known how many African slaves were imported into Iran in the nineteenth century, except that they came in great numbers. In the early part of the century British estimates regularly put imports at between ten thousand to twenty thousand to the Persian Gulf as a whole, the main centre of the trade being Muscat.[16] With regard to Iran the British estimated the number to be 1080 in Bushire and other Iranian ports in 1842. None of the Iranian ports sent vessels directly to Zanzibar, except for Lingah, from which three or four boats sailed annually, each returning with about seventy slaves. The number of boats arriving in Kharg between August and October 1841 was noted as 117, carrying 1,217 slaves. According to a questionnaire of 1842, some three thousand slaves (two-thirds male and one third female) arrived in Bushire each year but only about 170–80 remained there, the rest moving on to Ottoman territory. About one quarter as many were sold at Bander Abbas and a small number at Lingah and Kangerun.[17] In 1847 it was estimated that importation on the Iranian coast amounted to 1150 negroes and 80 Abyssinians per year on average, though this did not include the comparatively small number who were brought back by pilgrims.[18] They were of all ages between four and sixty and many women and children were not bought but stolen.[19]

The Treatment of Slaves in Iran

What of the treatment of the slaves? Most of the sources make a clear distinction between transportation to Iran and elsewhere and treatment once arrived. The slaves for Iran came mainly from Berbera and Zanzibar in *buggalahs* sailed by the Joasemi Arabs of Ras al-Khyma on the Arabian coast. The accounts of the British officers patrolling the Persian Gulf and seeking slave ships testify to the appalling, cramped conditions in which they were held, with the added abomination that if the Arabs saw a cruiser coming they would throw the slaves into the sea to drown.[20] Indeed with regard to transportation, there appears to have been little difference in the degree of ill-treatment of slaves coming into the Islamic world from those going to the Americas.

The difference is marked, however, once they were settled in a household. Here we have to look at a difference in the sources as between travellers' accounts, which uniformly praise the treatment of slaves by Iranians, and the evidence taken from runaway slaves by the British in their attempt to curb and end the trade. Johnson remarked in 1818 that 'the state of the slave in a family of Mohammedans very commonly resembles that of an adopted child, allowing the individual to claim some share of the property of his master at his decease, and frequently before. A slave, if of competent ability, is early employed as an assistant and agent in traffic, and entrusted with his owner's property to a considerable amount, part of which is not unusually given him as a settlement when he is allowed to marry a freeborn woman.'[21] It may be noted however that this was not necessarily always a successful arrangement as at one point, when the Malik al-Tujjar, then governor of Bushire, became ill, his responsibilities were carried out by one of his slaves, who being inexperienced, lost control.[22]

Wills likewise praises the treatment of slaves in Iran:

> Slaves in Persia have what Americans call a good time. They are well-fed, well-clothed, given the lightest work, often given in marriage to the favourite son or taken as a concubine.

He added that slaves had certainty of comfort and were well-cared for till old age. Looked upon as confidential servants they were entrusted with large sums of money.[23]

Wills claims they were never sold, except on importation, and that he had never seen a Persian unkind to his slave. Indeed, travellers remarked on the loyalty of slaves to their masters, demonstrated, for example, by a black Swahili slave who joined his master in a tower in a struggle to the death in 1832–3.[24]

According to Polak, if a slave was ill-treated, the master could lose the right of slave ownership for ever, and had either to sell him on to another, or to set him free.[25] Nor did owners like to sell slaves, except in extremities, or when the slave was very ill-natured. In that case he would either be sold or set free without documentation, thus making it difficult for him to find work. Further, in the case of women with whom the owners had cohabited, there was the sense of a need to keep them to guard their own honour.[26] Manumission being commended by Islam, on joyous occasions in particular, one or two slaves were set free. Slaves could also be inherited by the children of the owner, or given as part of the dowry of a daughter.[27]

However, travellers' views beg a question about travellers' accounts as a source for this subject, for while European strangers could tell whether a slave was properly dressed and fed, they would not be witness to other forms of ill-treatment, and information on the living conditions of the slave would most likely come from the master. What, therefore, do the British sources on runaway slaves have to show to contradict or substantiate the travellers' views?[28]

After a treaty negotiated with the Iranian government in 1851, the British were legally allowed to give refuge to runaway slaves provided that they were what is called fresh imports – i.e. they were not born in Iran or had not come there before the Treaty had been agreed. Therefore there were a limited number of slaves whom the British had the right to help. This is one reason why the number of runaways was only around two dozen in the course of about forty years. And again, only about a quarter of these refugees claimed ill-treatment. There is one example of a black slave called Mahbub complaining of ill-treatment and abuse by his master in 1866.[29] In this case, his mother, who was African, complained that he had been kidnapped, supported by his brother-in-law, a Bakhtiari. In a deposition Mahbub stated that:

> My father, Anbar, was emancipated by the late Saif ibn Nebhan, the governor of Bander Abbas, and my mother Chekazi, by Allah Verdi Khan, governor of Beshakerd. We resided for a long time at Minow. Two years ago my father died. My mother went to Bassidore. I followed her there. Kerbalayee Taqi, son of Nabi Kebabi, kidnapped me and put me on a vessel bound for Bushire. At Bushire he sold me to Kerbalyee Ali Attar for 30 tomans. Shaikh Ali Damestani, one of the mujtahids of Bushire – having received information regarding my case, called Kerbalayee Ali Attar and told me that if any person came for me, he should let me go. I have now been with Kerbalayee Ali Attar for six months. He abuses and ill-treats me. I wish to go to my mother.[30]

In an example from 1893, a female slave named Halima was the subject of ill-treatment by women, in the first case when her master's wife sold her on without his knowledge, and in the second when the wife of a subsequent master, together with her sister and her mother, beat the slave.[31]

The most vivid description of ill-treatment comes from an Abyssinian women named Bahrazain, who took refuge with the British in 1892:

> A person named Haji Ibrahim kidnapped me and took me along with pilgrims to Abu Rashid. There he sold me and my sister, Nur Sabbah, to Haji Abdullah, who died there. Both my sister and I then hired a camel and went to Zubair, where two persons called Rahim and Yusif appeared: the latter took my sister as his wife and deceived me and brought me to Bushire. They sold me between the months of Muharram and Safar to Abdul Nabi through Aqa Reza Dallal. I work in the house of Abdul Nabi but am not properly looked after. I am beaten and get no clothes. I was originally free but have now been bought. I do not want my present master.[32]

The experiences of this woman shows how slaves were sold to and fro, not always kept as some travel accounts imply. Further it demonstrates the immense problems, particularly of a woman who did, through the death of her master, obtain freedom but, evidently having no written document of manumission, was seized once more into slavery.

On the other hand, there are also instances of slaves being offered freedom and the chance to go to Bombay, and thence to their home country, by the British, and refusing as they were well-treated. An example of one such is a Sacotra woman in 1853, who was married to one of the retainers of the Shaikh of Charrack. She was given the option of going to Bombay on a British ship and thence returning to her own country, but decided to remain in Iran as she was well-treated.[33] In another case not only did a slave named Zahra decide to remain with the man who claimed her in preference to freedom, but a fellow female slave expressed a wish to stay with Zahra and her master.[34] Nor did slaves necessarily only run away as a result of ill-treatment. One such was a female who escaped from Lingah to the British naval base at Bassidore, bearing valuables belonging to her master. She was nevertheless not returned.[35]

The Position of Slaves

It must also be realised that a slave who left his master would have no social position, that they would lose security and would be confined to the lowest levels of the labour market. Indeed one traveller commented that a master who wished to punish his slave set him free.[36] However, it must be born in mind that ordinary Iranian servants were not always well-treated, and that beatings were indeed common Qajar society. The courtier, I'timad al-Saltana, mentions them frequently.[37] Governors of provinces used beating as the most common form of punishment, and could themselves be publicly beaten for failing to remit taxes.[38] Soldiers regularly suffered such punishment as the bastinado, and abscission of nose, ears and hands.[39] Therefore, whilst the comments of some travellers on the conditions of slaves may present an idealistic picture, on the whole their portrayal of greater humanity in an Islamic land, in this case Iran, would seem to hold true. Two factors also noted by travellers provide some explanation for this treatment. The first is that the slave, from another land, having no family of his or her own, was dependent on the master and therefore more likely to be trustworthy and loyal.[40] Secondly, slaves were luxuries.[41] This point applies not just to the more valuable *habashis* (Abyssinians) owned by the notables and merchants, but to the *zangis* (Africans), who were often the property of more modest families. There were thus financial reasons why the slave should be well cared for, most particularly as African slaves lacked immunity to the diseases of the country and their life expectancy was therefore lower than that of other Iranians.[42] Polak mentions that the climate of Iran did not suit slaves, so they tended to die young, mostly of tuberculosis and scrofula (disease with glandular swellings), with few living beyond thirty. In any town, in his estimate, only about ten would live to be adults.[43] Slaves also acquired value through such training they might receive. In one case where the British interfered with the acquisition of a slave, both a merchant and a *mujtahid* of Bushire wrote to the governor complaining of British policy that:

> It would be a great loss to be deprived of the services of these slaves who have been bought several years before, taught Arabic, and at no small expense brought all the way across Arabia to Kuwait.[44]

Slaves could also have a variety of skilled or less skilled occupations, such as that of being a member of the personal guard of a notable. Thus 'Abd al-Nabi, the headman of the district of Jask, used a group of slaves to control the local people. The slaves removed some of the inhabitants' goods, and as a result people were afraid to bring things out to sell.[45] In 1825 Rahman bin Jabir, the well-known pirate, maintained his own fleet in Bushire, as well as a following of two thousand, most of them his own black slaves.[46] Slaves or former slaves could also find a role in combative sports. I'timad al-Saltana refers to a Ja'far Siah Pahlavan engaged in wrestling with Akbar Pahlavan in which neither of them could overcome the other on the occasion of comic games in front of the shah.[47] Indeed, black champions seem to have been a feature of the past as well, as demonstrated in Persian painting of the early fifteenth century,[48] and in the popular recollection of the heroes of the age of Shah 'Abbas, who included Qaimas Khan, the Ethiopian.[49]

Music also played a role in the lives and skills of slave. In one incident, a man named Ali, an inhabitant of Khesht, who was a singer and a domestic slave, found notoriety by running off with someone else's daughter.[50] The slaves of Bushire acquired the habit of collecting near the main gate and playing their drums (*tabl*). Significantly, the gathering included female as well as male slaves, and, though they probably wore the *hijab* which was obligatory for slave women as much as for their mistresses,[51] these mixed gatherings of singing and dancing may be perceived as an expression of their original African culture. Unsurprisingly, the 'ulama and other inhabitants objected to these musical occasions, but they continued despite attempts to stop them.[52] To this day on Kish Island there is a common dance of obviously African origin among the black inhabitants.[53]

Female slaves also received some training for their role in a household, as is indicated in the letter of a slave trader to a buyer referring to a female slave, which says, 'If you find her childish and stupid, put her for some days with another female slave to be disciplined.'[54]

Finally, though I have found only two records of a serious crime committed by a slave, both of whom connived in murder, one of his owner's wife,[55] we should note that they were not always quiescent. During a riot in Bushire, one of the ringleaders is mentioned as 'Sultan Haji Sandeh's slave'.[56] Likewise in a disturbance in Isfahan in 1879, a group of *lutis* led by Almas (Diamond), a negro slave of the Imam Jum'a, collected a large crowd of women and children, and complained against the authorities.[57]

Slaves and Racism

Another issue which has been raised with regard to the Iranian attitude to black slaves is that of racism. With regard to the religion, the Prophet said emphatically that no Arab has priority over a non-Arab, and the Qur'an makes no distinction between the souls of black and non-black.[58] However, Bernard Lewis has argued that there was a measure of stigma against blacks in Islam, there being three principal non-religious reasons. Firstly they had come into the Islamic world through conquest, and were therefore regarded as inferior; secondly, that to the Islamic world the population of Africa seemed less developed; and thirdly, the only black people that most Muslims encountered had the status of slaves.[59] The significance of this latter point is that in the past there were also European slaves in the Ottoman territories in particular. The Middle East is, further, not free of prejudices of an ethnic nature, and as Lewis argues, of racial prejudice and discrimination. He states that the limits of toleration of persons of African origin varied according to time and place, and that a myth of Islamic racial innocence has emerged in the West 'as a reproach to the shortcomings of the white man'.[60] Segal takes a more positive view, in particular placing greater emphasis on the role of religion in shaping all aspects of social relations.[61] He also contrasts the widespread hypocrisy in practice and nationalism in particular in the West and their effects on minorities, with the more generally enlightened practice of Islam. He highlights the common and religiously commended habit of manumission as having a significant role in countering racism. Most particularly he focuses on its aftermath of assimilation of blacks who were subject to no special discrimination in law; once freed they enjoyed the same legal rights as other members of the community.[62] There have been black slaves who rose to positions of great power in the Islamic world, such as has not occurred in the West. But even Segal brings an example of institutionalised racism from nineteenth century Morocco.[63]

What then of Iran? Whilst the positive factors in the Islamic attitude to blacks already mentioned hold true for Iran, Southgate has studied the negative images of blacks in certain medieval Iranian writings.[64] She points out that blacks were frequently shown as physically unattractive, intellectually inferior, remote from civilisation, sexually unbridled, and easily affected by music and wine. She mentions Harris's findings that a community of African descent living near Jiruft felt isolated and marginalised.[65] She concludes that there is some evidence for prejudice in the tenth to fourteenth century sources which she examined, but feels that it is difficult to draw firm conclusions as to its significance.

Before examining this topic with regard to Iran in the nineteenth century, it is perhaps necessary to define racism and distinguish it from other forms of human differentiation and discrimination. Nearly all peoples at all times have tended to be drawn to their own kind in terms of race and culture more, though not exclusively so, than to others, and to exercise prejudice and discrimination against those who are different. What distinguishes true racism from such differentiation is that it is systemised in relationships of domination and authority in heterogeneous societies. It is institutionalised, as happened in the Americas and in South Africa, in terms of ideological justification and administrative practice, drawing much of its justification from social Darwinism. Institutionalised means, primarily, that it is recognised and condoned in law. It means that it has the support of religious exegesis (albeit flawed), that it is reflected in the regulation of communal practice and customary attitudes, the clearest examples coming from Nazi Germany and South Africa, and finally, and, not least it is so incorporated into the social structure as to serve a distinct economic purpose. In sum, racism is the product of a secular Western need to define and discriminate in order to explore, know and control.

Institutionalised racism of this kind is not to be found in Iran at any period. So what was the nineteenth century Iranian attitude to black people in the context of the term 'racism'? That racial awareness existed is clearly evident from the sale prices of slaves. Non-black slaves fetched the highest prices, as elsewhere. Amongst black slaves there was the distinction already noted between Abyssinians, closer in physical appearance, religion and therefore culture to Iranians than sub-Saharan Africans, with the consequence that the former were more expensive. There is the evidence already adduced that blacks were comparatively well-treated in the household – but as concubines and servants. i.e. in menial or more low status positions – however, this point needs further exploration. There is the evidence that eunuchs in particular could rise to responsible positions, but as eunuchs, with the terrible price which that implies.

What do the sources say? References specifically to the topic of race are not common, but Mary Sheil, noting in 1856 that cruelty towards slaves in Iran was rare, said that slaves 'when restored to freedom take their station in society without reference to their colour of descent'.[66] The *Jughrafiyya-yi Isfahan* stated in 1294/1877 that there were many slaves in the city, some of whom had attained freedom, and others who were the children of slaves. Their progeny included children of African parents and those of mixed racial origins.[67] Similarly, slaves formed the third largest minority community in the population of Shiraz in the mid-nineteenth century.[68] No mention is made of any distinction in the treatment of the two, or of their being rejected by the social groups to which they belonged. Generally, the slaves were engaged in the same kind of occupations as poorer Iranians.[69]

The Suppression of the Slave Trade

Now what about suppression of the slave trade and the Iranian response? The first steps towards the suppression of the trade in Iran were taken between Sheil, the British Representative, and Haj Mirza Aqasi, the Grand

Vizier, in 1846. Haji Mirza Aqasi was in favour of suppression but pessimistic about putting it into practice.[70] The shah himself argued that suppression was contrary to Islam, basing his argument on the point that what Islam renders lawful cannot be forbidden.[71] 'If taking slaves is so bad why did the British do it themselves?' 'It was not forbidden according to the shariʻa,' says one comment on the margin of a despatch from Sheil in the Iranian archives, most likely expressing the shah's opinion.[72] Probably, his real purport was that the slave trade was so deeply embedded in the religion and culture of the country that an attempt to uproot it would provoke severe opposition and even disorder. To counter his arguments, Sheil obtained *fatvas* (judgements) from six of the ʻulama of Tehran, to the effect that the seller of men is the worst of men.[73] In any case in June 1848 the shah, at the end of his life and seemingly on the urging of Haji Mirza Aqasi,[74] suddenly agreed to the prohibition of the import of slaves by sea and issued a *farman* banning the slave trade in toto in Iranian ports.

But, though the Iranian government essentially agreed to suppression, and was willing to take the necessary measures to discourage it, it did not have the power to do so, especially as its control over tribes on the Iranian coast who were engaged in the trade was very weak.[75] A further problem was that the Iranian officials dealing with the traders were eminently bribable.

When Nasr al-Din Shah came to the throne, his government at first rejected any further agreements, and would only write to the governors of Fars and Khuzestan requesting they stop slaves coming in by sea and punish offenders.[76] However, the coming to power of Amir Kabir did bring a major shift in policy. An agreement reached between him and the British at the end of 1851, and made effective from 1st January 1852, granted the British the right of seizure and temporary detention of Iranian vessels engaged in the slave trade. Responsibility for the infliction of punishment remained with the Iranian authorities.[77] As part of this agreement the office of slave commissioner was established with an annuity of 150 rupees paid by the British.[78] Nasir al-Din Shah issued guidelines to Mirza Mahmud Khan, the newly appointed slave commissioner, on how the searches were to be carried out in collaboration with the British and what the penalties for disobedience were to be.[79] They included two hundred lashes plus a fine of twice the value of the slave for the first offence, the same for the second plus seizure of the ship for six months, and the same plus confiscation of the ship for the third. The problem was to ensure the enforcement of these careful specifications.

At the end of 1852, a further agreement permitted the British cruisers to enter the ports along the coast, such as Lingah and Kelat, to fine chiefs found participating in the trade.[80] Nevertheless, for a while there was little effective change, especially at the time of the Herat War. One of the main problems confronting the British was they could only seize slaves taken at sea, not those who had reached terra firma. Another was the reluctance of Iranian officials to challenge local social practice, particularly as it was justified in Islamic law.[81] A further problem was that the actual sea trade was in the hands of Arabs who were not Iranian subjects and the ships were therefore Arab. The Iranian government felt unable to act against Arab vessels, even though they were in Iranian waters, and most of the trade was carried out by Arabs.[82] Nevertheless, by 1859 the Iranian government had granted the British the right of search, (though it was not strictly in accordance with maritime law).[83] The new measure went some way towards inhibiting the trade, but the British continued to complain of lack of adequate progress. In the spring of 1861 the Iranian government sent Mirza Mahmud Khan, Ajudan-i Vizarat-i Umur-i Kharija, to find out what was happening with regard to the import of slaves. He returned to report that 380 slaves had been imported as opposed to the figure of 112 which the local authorities had given the British.[84]

By 1862 the British were dissatisfied with the results of the payment to the slave commissioner and began paying Iranian officials a small reward (50 krans) for each slave captured, which proved a success.[85] Suppression made some progress from this time, the main issue in most captures becoming whether a slave was newly imported or was already part of an Iranian household when he or she was discovered. In 1882 the Iranian government signed a convention to suppress the trade, and was a signatory to the major Brussels Convention of 1892, which signalled the end of the trade as a major activity.

The Problems of Emancipation

One of the problems faced by those actively engaged in the control of the trade was that some Iranians took their slaves with them on pilgrimages to Mecca which was however, increasingly a centre of the slave trade as the international campaign against suppression gained momentum. To pay for the voyage it had long been the habit of pilgrims to bring back slaves and sell them on the return journey.[86] When boats carrying such slaves were stopped the slaves were always presented by both traders and pilgrims as members of their families, who had accompanied them to Mecca in the first place. So it was not always easy for the British to prove whether they were established slaves, or 'fresh imports'. The most effective way was to test their language, but the slave trading system was to some extent able to overcome this by teaching the slaves some Persian or Arabic before they were sold on. If caught, slave traders still had ways of evading punishment, one being to say that it was a Muslim custom to liberate slaves on a voyage to Mecca as a religious duty, and they had bought the slaves for that purpose.[87] A further problem was that, despite the goodwill of the central government, the local authorities in Bushire and other ports and towns were involved in the trade or reluctant to challenge local notables, even at a late date.[88] In one such case it proved impossible to recover a group of six slaves landed in Bushire because those involved held influential positions in the town.[89] The British

Resident commented that, 'The sanctity of the Muslim andarun (women's quarters) is a good and sufficient plea in defence of the apathy and neglect of the authorities.'[90]

It may be noted that one of the dealers involved in the landing of this group of slaves was a woman known as Mulla Mariam,[91] it being unusual but not unknown for women to be involved in the slave trade in the Islamic world.[92]

On the other hand, so as not to undermine the effort of suppression, the British had to be careful to observe the rules of their agreements with the Iranian government. Thus when a runaway slave already in Bushire approached the captain of a British vessel and asked for protection, he felt compelled to refuse because it was contrary to the agreements mentioned above.[93] In 1862 there was a rare case of the British failing to follow the regulations. Two slaves, purchased within Iran, had taken refuge in the British Legation, and Alison, the British Minister, refused to return them to the dealer from whom they had fled, much to the annoyance of the Iranian government.[94]

With regard to the liberation of slaves, there was also a peculiarly Islamic difference between women and men. This is illustrated by two slaves, a woman and a man who found refuge in the British Residency in Bushire in December 1892 complaining of ill-treatment by their master. The man was manumitted but complications arose over the woman because the master claimed her as his wife.[95] This was a common tactic by dealers and purchasers of women slaves who were either caught with them at sea, or from whom they ran away. In this case the slave vigorously denied being the owner's wife in any sense.[96] The issue of what constituted a wife nevertheless posed problems. The British at that time saw only three ways of describing women connected to the master in a Muslim household: they were either wives, concubines or servants. The British used the term concubine to indicate some sort of dependent status which included intimate relations but no contract of marriage. A female slave could however have four types of situation in an Iranian household at this stage: wife, *sigha* (temporary wife), *madkhula* (one, possibly a servant, having intimate relations with the master but no formal status relating to such), and simple servant. Whilst *habashi* slaves might become *sigha*, it was apparently rare for Iranians to marry them, and the *zangis* seem only occasionally to have become *sigha*.[97] However, one way of escaping punishment for being found in the possession of a black female slave was to declare her to be a wife. From a case in early 1892, where the Iranian government argued that a slave had to be returned to her master on the grounds of being his wife, it is difficult to infer what her status was, though she seemed a recent importation.[98] The Resident observed that 'Some excuses of conjugal relations will always be forthcoming in the case of women so brought into the country.'[99]

The governor of Bushire responded that 'The right of British Officers is confined to capture at sea slaves that may have been imported for sale on shore, but neither he (himself) nor the British officer have any right to interfere with the families and people in respect of slaves whether kidnapped or obtained otherwise (on land).'

As soon as slaves entered anyone's house they became members of his family. Moreover, the majority of female slaves acquired conjugal relations, and no one had a right to interfere with people's domestic relations.[100] The governor of Bushire continued that in the religion of Islam it was not permitted for wives and concubines to stay in the abode of a foreigner.[101]

By the mid 1880s the advances in suppression of the slave trade at the international level and in importation into Iran were such that the trade was seriously in decline. The Anglo-Iranian Slave Convention of 1882 stipulated that pilgrims had to have a passport which stated how many negroes were accompanying them on their visit to Mecca. If they returned with more negroes than that passport stated, the extras would be assumed to be slaves.[102] Though in practice this did not always work, it acted as a disincentive. The Slave Convention also stated in Article III that the shah would punish all Iranian or foreign subjects engaged in the slave trade by sea, and would manumit or guarantee the safety of all slaves illegally imported, i.e. imported by sea, from then on. Previously, slaves could only be granted their freedom if they escaped or were found at sea, and if they were clearly fresh imports. By the 1890s, however, with the international support for ending the trade, the British began to stretch the interpretation of the term 'fresh imports' to include those who had been enslaved for some time elsewhere and then imported to Iran, e.g. from Basra. They also began to include those who had been illegally imported, but had not been able to escape from their owners for a year or more. As a result, although the slave trade declined, the number of slaves claiming protection and liberation rose, especially women.[103] Further, to the Iranians, the latitude permitted by the new treaty arrangements to the British to complain signified a level of interference that had become intolerable, and was in their eyes undermining Islam. The cases cited in the note above do not suggest that the British were using the slave trade to deliberately extend their influence, and though they had broadened their interpretation of the regulations, they continued to work within them. However, as part of a pattern in the growth of their influence from the later 1880s, they were becoming more highhanded.

All this created a problem for the government in terms of relations between state and society, and pressure was brought in particular on the governor of Bushire, Nizam al-Saltana, to do more to resist the demands of the British. The slave traders were caught short by the changes in the legal position as a result of Iran signing the Anglo Iranian Convention of 1882,[104] and the Brussels Convention of 1892, and were puzzled by the seizure of slaves speaking Arabic on Iranian soil. The traders had begun to convince the 'ulama that the campaign was undermining the precepts of Islam. The traders hoped to bring pressure on the 'ulama to telegraph Haji Mirza

Muhammad Hasan (Shirazi) of Samarra to tell the shah to order the release of slaves taken by order of the British, presumably on the model of the campaign against the Tobacco Concession, but with no success.

However, after a further case in 1893 the British Resident commented:

> The Ministry of Foreign Affairs Agent (Karguzar) admitted as much to me that one or two examples of refusal to surrender slaves who complained of mistreatment will do much to convince people here that they cannot breach the law with impunity and so will tend to check the importation of slaves by making it a more risky speculation than hitherto.[105] ... As it is, as the Foreign Agent has remarked, the people are beginning to open their eyes to the fact that the Treaty must be respected, and no cases of recent importation are known.[106]

The French also noted that slaves had become exceptional in the North, and had diminished in numbers since the agreement of 1882.[107]

It may be mentioned that, just occasionally, African women discovered on board ship by the British and claimed as wives turned out to be genuinely so, expressing a wish to remain with their masters, as with three cases in 1878, and a fourth where the slave expressed the wish to join the master, even though she had not met him.[108]

With regard to female slaves, in the mid-nineteenth century, if they were sent on to India, as was the practice, they would have less security than if they remained with their owner. In Bombay female former slaves were usually left after a short time '*to pick up their own livelihoods*'.[109] At this time some at least tried to return to their native lands,[110] this being clearly much harder in the mid-nineteenth century than towards the end, when no difficulty was perceived in sending one slave to Aden and thence onwards to her native Dongola.[111]

What became of slaves as a whole after they were liberated by the British? The government of India commissioned a survey of such slaves and discovered they made a variety of choices. The placement of emancipated slaves was a problem of the government of Bombay in particular. In 1889 alone the Bombay received 204 slaves in one capture and others in small groups.[112] Able-bodied slaves were employed as labour in the docks, but the Commissioner of Police advised that the Africans in the city formed an excitable turbulent element in the population. Slaves too young to earn a living were distributed among the missionary societies at a small charge per head, but their harsh unstable experience of life made the boys in particular difficult to control. Overall, the former slave population was becoming too high for Bombay to absorb, so other destinations had to be found for them. Fiji was suggested, but the government there was not enthusiastic, and the matter was not pursued.[113] East Africa was suggested but did not prove a popular destination with the former slaves, some of whom volunteered for service on British ships.[114] The most sought after destination was – Muscat, that former staging post on the slave route, but the slaves expressed satisfaction that they were now working for a living.[115]

* * *

Therefore, what was the state of the slave trade in Iran by the beginning of the twentieth century. Certainly it still continued, especially in remoter areas such as Seistan.[116] However, the agreements with the Iranian government over the right to search Iranian ships, and Arab ships in Iranian waters, gradually restricted the trade, until it was reduced to a trickle, and in 1893 as already mentioned the Resident reported that no cases of recent importation were known.[117] Although the support of the local authorities was not particularly efficient, the government policy was persistent, which greatly helped suppression. Further advances were made by the Convention of 1882 and that of 1892 above all. Of course, suppression was assisted by the international movement against slaving – it was banned, though again not fully in practice, in the Ottoman Empire in 1857. It was also assisted by the growth in the perceived value of free market labour. Since slaves in Iran, however, were employed almost entirely in the service sector (by contrast with Egypt), the suppression of the trade was really due to the changes in attitude within created by reformers, and by the disincentives created by the British policy of suppression. The ownership of another individual was implicitly banned in the amendment to the Iranian Constitution in October 1907, and finally abolished outright in 1928.

Notes

1 G. H. Sa'idi, *Ahl-i Hava*, Tehran, 1345, p. 5.
2 See, for example, J. Johnson, *A Journey from India to England through Persia, Georgia, Russia, Poland and Prussia, 1817*, London 1818, p. 12; J. Malcolm, *The History of Persia*, Vol. II, London 1839, p. 430; and C.J. Wills, *In the Land of the Lion and the Sun*, London 1883, p. 326.
3 R. Brunschvig, "Abd', *Encyclopaedia of Islam*, 2nd edition, Leiden 1960, pp. 26, 27; B. Lewis, *Race and Slavery in the Middle East*, Oxford 1990, p. 6.
4 R. Segal, *Islam's Black Slaves*, New York 2001, p. 4.
5 Although there is some evidence of slaves being used in agriculture in Seistan, they seem to have retained their shari'a rights, so they were not subjected to the kind of ill-treatment meted out in the West. (See H. G. Migeod, *Die persische Gesellschaft unter Nasiru'd-Din Shah (1848–1896)*, Berlin 1990, pp. 334–5, 341–3, which mentions they had their own self-governing villages.) I have found no reference to slaves being used in other production sectors, so there cannot have been many, if any at all. The fact that blacks live along the Iranian sea coast at present is not evidence in itself that their slave forebears were employed in the pearling trade.
6 J.E. Polak, *Safarnama-yi Polak*, (Persien, das Land und Seine Bewohner, Leipzig 1865), trans. K. Jahandari, Tehran 1361, p. 173.
7 Brunschvig, "Abd', pp. 25, 29–30; Lewis, *Slavery*, p. 6.
8 MAE, Ambassade/Tehran/62, No. 4, 5.1.1890.

9. M. Ravandi, *Tarikh-i ijtima'i-yi Iran*, Tehran 2536, III, p. 570. The shari'a also forbade the sale of female musicians and dancers.
10. By contrast with Egypt, where it seems to have been an accepted practice; see E. Burke, *Struggle and Survival in the Middle East*, London 1993, Chapter 4 on Shemsigul, who was parted from her baby and sold on in what was evidently regarded as a legal transaction. However, there is some evidence that children, rather than infants, could be sold very young in Iran through special merchants. See MAE Ambassade/Teheran/61, No. 4. 5.1.90.
11. Wills, *Persia*, p. 326; *Land*, p. 75.
12. Ibid., p. 76.
13. Ibid., p. 79.
14. No. 215, 16.11.1891, FO 248/533.
15. Sirjani, *Vaqayi'*, from 15.8.1901, p. 647.
16. J.B. Kelly, *Persian Gulf*, pp. 414–6.
17. C. Issawi, *Iran*, p. 125.
18. Hennell to Wellesley 8.5.1847, FO 248/129.
19. IO R/15/1/168, Jenkins to Jones, No. 130, 5.11.1858. This despatch mentions a 'most heartrending appeal' of one female slave to Jenkins to be sent 'to the port of Berbera, which is her country, from which she was forcibly stolen by a Joasemi Arab and brought to Ras al-Khyma'. She had been with her husband and young children at Berbera when she was kidnapped, and begged for her return to her native land. The British arranged for her dispatch to Bombay and then to Aden (but such a case was unusual). See also Jones to Jenkins No. 396, 6.11.1858 and Anderson to Jones, No. 476, 11.2.1859 in IO R/15/1/168.
20. IO R/15/1/168, No. 90, 2.7.1859.
21. Johnson, *Journey*, p. 12.
22. No. 58, 15.8.1876, FO 248/318.
23. Wills, *Land*, pp. 326–7.
24. Busse, *Qajar Rule*, p. 211.
25. Polak, *Safarnama*, pp. 173–4.
26. Idem, Malcolm, *Persia*, II, p. 425.
27. B.A. Mirza'i, 'The African Presence in Iran: Identity and Its Reconstruction in the 19th and 20th Centuries', *Outre-mers: Revue d'Histoire*, 2002 No. 2, pp. 229–246. There is an example of a slave been given as part of a dowry in a marriage contract (*'aqdnama*) from the Qajar period in the Ethnographic Museum, Sa'dabad Palace, Tehran.
28. The travellers emphasise that slaves were employed for domestic use in the towns. Although they passed through much of Iran they were obviously not familiar with all of Iran's vast countryside. The question of how many slaves there were in the rural areas (outside of the households of landlords and khans) is a problem, and there is some evidence for the nineteenth century of slave labour on a large scale in the countryside in the southwest. In particular evidence remains of groups of black slaves being brought to specific areas possibly for a particular building or other project in earlier times. Bastani Parizi notes their presence in Kerman province in such names as Kuhistan-i siyahan (Mountains of the Blacks), and Qal'a-yi Zangian (Castle of the Blacks), Zangiabad (Village Built by the Blacks). M.I. Bastani Parizi, *Tarikh-i Kerman*, Tehran 1361, pp. 307, 346.
29. Pelly to Alison, No. 6, 18.6.1866, FO 248/232.
30. Pelly to Alison, No. 6, 18.6.1866, FO 248/232. The attitude of the *mujtahid* may be noted in a case where the ownership was clearly not fully legal, but the master had bought the slave in good faith. The Iranian authorities at Bushire, however, supported the view of the original seller, stating that, 'In no religion or creed has one party authority over another's slaves.'

31 No. 39, 22.4.1893, FO 248/566.
32 Talbot to Lascelles, encl. in No. 34, 13.2.1892, FO 248/543.
33 No. 29, 12.12.1853, FO 248/157.
34 Encl. 1 in No.3, 14.1.1878, FO 248/342.
35 No. 957, 27.3.1863, FO 248/242.
36 Wills, *Land*, p. 326.
37 There are numerous examples, but for more details see M. Kia 'Inside the Court of Naser od-Din Shah Qajar, 1881–1896', *Middle Eastern Studies*, Vol. 37, No. 1, 2001, pp. 101–141.
38 Encl. in Hennell to Sheil, Shiraz Agent, No. 169, 7.4.1845, FO 248/113.
39 A. Mounsey, *Journey*, p. 142.
40 Johnson, *Journey*, p. 12–13
41 Wills, *Land*, p. 74
42 On the problems of regaining the initial outlay of the price of the slave, see Polak, *Safarnama*, pp. 173–4.
43 Polak, *Safarnama*, p. 174.
44 No. 66, 13.8.1892, FO 248/543. In another example, four eunuchs had also been trained in cooking, table service and the charge of money, Shiraz Agent. No. 76, 9.10.92, in No. 88, 15.10.92, FO 248/544.
45 No. 126 tel., 30.12.1886, FO 248/436.
46 J.S. Buckingham, *Travels*, p. 356.
47 I'timad al-Saltana, *Ruznama*, p. 430.
48 See R. Hillenbrand, ed., *Persian Painting*, London, 2000, p. 44, Pl. 7, Zangi champion, *Sharafnama*, c. 1405.
49 Jamalzadeh, *Isfahan*, p. 172.
50 Ross to Kennedy, 5.12.1890, FO 248/502.
51 In the streets slave women wore the same *hijab* and *chadur* of Iranian women, so it was impossible to distinguish who they were out-of-doors. Polak, *Safarnama*, p. 175.
52 Encl. 8 in No. 69, 19.10.1869, FO 60/320; I. Safa'i, *Yik sad sanad-i tarikhi az dauran-i Qajariyya*, Tehran, n.d., 2nd edition, pp. 151–2.
53 I. Afshar Sistani, *Jazira-yi Kish va Darya-yi Pars*, Tehran 1370, p. 237. Song, music and dance in parts of south Iran still retain the influence of Africa, Mirza'i, 'African Presence', p. 243. It may be noted that the descendants of black slaves in Gujarat, India, have also retained their music and dance, though not their language. A. Whitehead, *The Lost Africans of India*, BBC News, South Asia, 27.11.2000.
54 Encl. in No. 65, 17.3.1877, FO 248/329.
55 S. Sirjani, *Vaqayi'*, from 4.12.1902, p. 690–1, and 14.1.1903, p. 693.
56 I.O. R/15/1/182, No. 107, 18.6.1870.
57 Zill al-Sultan, *Khatirat*, II, p. 568.
58 Segal, *Slaves*, p. 46: Lewis, *Slavery*, p. 17.
59 Lewis, *Slavery*, p. 17.
60 Lewis, *Slavery*, p. 100.
61 Segal, *Slaves*, p. 5.
62 Ibid., p. 9.
63 Ibid., p. 65.-
64 M. Southgate, 'The Negative Image of Black Slaves in Some Medieval Iranian Writings', *Iranian Studies*, XVII, No. 1, 1984, pp. 3–36.
65 Ibid., p. 9.
66 Sheil, M., *Glimpses of Life and Manners in Persia*, London 1856, pp. 243–5.
67 Tahvildar, *Isfahan*, p. 122. Mirza'i argues that marriage between a black man and a white woman was not acceptable ('African Presence', p. 237), but I have found no evidence to support this for the nineteenth century, and it is also

contradicted by the recollections of my acquaintance. It may of course have varied from place to place. Ses Sa'idi, *Ahl-i hava*, p. 6 for the southern coast.
68 H. Brugsch, *Persien* II, p. 181. He comments that the largest minority was the Armenians, being about one thousand people, then came the Jews, who constituted a few hundred, with the slave community coming third.
69 According to Mirza'i, the black population of Bander Abbas in 1898 was about 300 and lived in a black quarter, working as minstrels, stone-breakers, and wood-cutters. 'African Presence', p. 240.
70 Kelly, *Persian Gulf*, p. 593; see also IO R/15/1/123, Hennell to Sheil, No. 318, 11.8.1850.
71 In the correspondence on the subject in the Ministry of Foreign Affairs archives there are occasional comments in the margin, the source of which is not clear, but from the forcible turn of expression it is likely that they directly reflect the shah's view. For example on one of Sheil's despatches there is the following comment: It is against my religion. It is clear in the verses in the Qur'an (here there is a quote which refers to Qur'an, V, Nos.49, 50, 52). It is no joke to me. The British government is going to have to accept it. MFA 1263 B6 F6 No.4.
72 MFA 1263 B6 F5 No.1.
73 Sheil to Palmerston, 27.4. 1847, FO 84/692. It would seem that these 'ulama regarded slavery as *makruh* (reprehensible) – though not forbidden, by contrast with other 'ulama, to whom it seems to have been merely permissible. I am indebted to Robert Gleave for this reference.
74 M. Mahmud, *Tarikh-i ravabit-i siyasi Iran va Inglis dar qarn-i nuzdahum-i miladi*, Tehran 1367, II, pp. 532–3. I am grateful for this reference and other points from the Persian sources to Dr L. Dehqan and Dr M. Dehqan Nejhad of Isfahan University.
75 For problems see IO R/15/1/123, Hennell to Sheil, No. 234, 24.6.1850 and No. 318, 11.8.1850.
76 Safar 1265 (Dec.–Jan. 1848–9) in MFA 1263 B4 F12 No.4
77 Rabi' al-avval 1268 (Dec.–Jan 1851–2), MFA 1263 B6 F12 No. 4; No. 65, 18.3.1877, FO 248/329.
78 No. 387, 3.4.1875, FO 248/310.
79 Rabi' al-avval 1268 (Dec.–Jan. 1851–2), MFA 1263 B6 F40 No.1.
80 IO R/15/1/171, Sheil to Kemball, 10.12.1852, mentioned in Jones to Anderson, No. 310 p. 16, 15.9.1858.
81 See, for example, encl. in Talbot to Lascelles, No. 34, 13.2.92, FO 248/543.
82 IO R/15/1/177, No. 404, 17.11.58.
83 IO R/15/1/177, No. 112, 15.1.59, Anderson to Jones No. 5440, 23.12.1859, No. 183, 18.2.1859.
84 MFA 1263 B6 F15 N8.
85 IO R/15/1/177, No. 12, 14.4.1861, and No. 2, 16.1.1862.
86 Hennell to Wellesley, 6.5.1847, FO 248/129.
87 No. 31, 23.3.1878, FO 248/342.
88 See No. 55, 6.6.1894, FO 248/591, for an example,
89 No. 39, 31.3.1877, No. 37, 23.3.1877, FO 248/329.
90 No. 39, 31.3.1877, FO 248/329.
91 No. 37, 23.3.1877, FO 248/329.
92 E. Toledano, *State and Society in Mid-Nineteenth Century Egypt*, Princeton 1982, p. 59.
93 No. 774, 17.7.1871, FO 248/271.
94 24 Shavval 1278 (24 Apr. 1861) MFA 1278 B9 F20 No.12.
95 No. 3134, 10.2.1893, FO 248/574.
96 Decipher No. 32, 8.12.1892, FO 248/544.
97 Wills, *Persia*, p. 75; No. 41, 13.3.1878, FO 248/342.

98 Talbot to Lascelles, No. 34, 13.2.1892, FO 248/543.
99 Talbot to Lascelles, No. 34, 13.2.1892, FO 248/543.
100 According to Nizam al-Saltana, when governor of Bushire, all the female slaves of those parts had had intimate relations with their masters, and were in the position of being 'their true wives'. Nizam al-Saltana, II, p. 462. Nizam al-Saltana may have had a point, as according to some interpretations of the Qur'an a master could lawfully enjoy a slave, but not prostitute her, see Brunschvig, "Abd', p. 25. According to Malcolm, women slaves could be sold, 'but this right is seldom exercised, it being at variance with the jealous sense of honour felt by almost all Muslims with regard to females with whom they have cohabited.' See *Persia*, II, p. 425.
101 Nizam al-Saltana *Khatirat*, II, p. 462.
102 FO 84/1615, 3.5.1882. The treaty was signed 2nd March 1882.
103 See, for examples, Talbot to Lascelles, 13.2.1892, FO 248/543; No. 66, 13.8.1892, FO 248/543; No. 76, 15.10.92, FO 248/544; No 54, 2.12.1892, FO 248/544; No. 11, 21.1.1893, FO 248/566; No.3134, 10.2.1893, 248/574; No. 64, 24.8.1895, FO 248/610.
104 No. 66, 13.8.1892, FO 248/543; No. 76, 15.10.1892, FO 248/544.
105 No. 39, 22.4.1893, FO 248/566.
106 No. 39, 22.4.1893, FO 248/566.
107 MAE, Ambassade/Teheran/61, No.4, 5.1.1890.
108 Encl.1 in No.3, 14.1.1878, FO 248/342.
109 No. 71, 20.4.1878, FO 248/342, underlined in the original.
110 IO R/15/1/168, No. 130, 5.11.1850.
111 No. 2 decipher, 14.2.1893, FO 248/566. See also encl. in No. 39, 22.4.1893, FO 248/566 for another example.
112 IO/R/15/1/200, No. 880, 2.2.1889.
113 IO/R/15/1/200, No. 2233, 19.8.1889.
114 IO/R/15/1/200 note in No. 379, 8.8.1899.
115 IO/R/15/1/200, note in No. 379, 8.8.1899.
116 Issawi, *Iran*, p. 126. The use of slavery was greater in this area and in Baluchistan, both in domestic service and in agriculture, but travellers report that they were well treated. Liberated slaves in these parts seem to have mixed with the local population and formed a distinct social group, engaged in fishing, sailing and agriculture. E.A. Floyer, *Unexplored Baluchistan*, London 1882, p. 64; A.W. Hughes, *The Country of Baloochistan*, London 1877, p. 45; R. Hughes-Buller, *Baluchistan Gazetteer Series, Vol. VII, Makran*, Bombay 1906, p. 105; Migeod, *Gesellschaft*, p. 334.
117 No. 39, 22.4.93, FO 248/566.

9

SLAVES II: HAJI BASHIR KHAN – LOVE IN A COMPLICATED CLIMATE

Haji Bashir Khan was the black slave of the Malik al-Tujjar of Bushire, who was one of the wealthiest merchants in Iran. In 1889 he ran away with the daughter of the British Residency News-writer and married her without her father's consent. In what became a *cause célèbre*, he was perceived as challenging the prestige of the British Empire, and disturbing the peace of the Iranian state. This chapter explores the implications of his case, including its Islamic dimensions, and the challenge he mounted in view of his position as the slave of a wealthy merchant.

Haji Bashir Khan and the Malik al-Tujjar

It is not clear when Haji Bashir Khan was born. In 1896, in the *Safarnama* (account of a journey) of Sadid al-Saltana he is described as being about sixty years old,[1] so he must have been born about 1836. He is mentioned as one of the *khanazadan-i khanavada* of the Malik al-Tujjar. This expression was used to describe slaves born into an Iranian household but having no connection by blood to the master's family. In the copious British correspondence on Haji Bashir Khan there is no suggestion that he was in any sense a relation of his master. It may be assumed that either one or both of his parents were slaves, but we cannot be certain which, and if the former, who or what the other person was. It is also not known whether his slave origins were *habashi* (Abyssinian) or *zangi* (African) though normally, when a slave was of *habashi* parentage, the sources tend to mention it, as *habashi* slaves were so valuable. It is known that he had a brother, named Ghulam 'Ali, who was also a slave of the Malik al-Tujjar.[2]

Known for his forthright and forcible opinions, Haji Bashir Khan was generally regarded as superior in intelligence to many of the learned men of Bushire.[3] Whilst the title Khan did not have great significance, government officials, for example, preferring Mirza,[4] Haji indicates a man of standing, with the wealth to cover the costs that a pilgrimage to Mecca entails, though sometimes servants and slaves were taken by their masters. Haji Bashir Khan was, as we shall see, a person of considerable substance. Sadid al-Saltana estimated that he was at one time worth 50,000 tomans,[5] and the British sources refer to his possession of property, including houses inside and outside the town, and substantial sums of money.[6]

How did a slave come to be so wealthy? The children of slaves in Iran were well-cared for, and often brought up with the children of the owner, as Muslims, ranking only below relations in the household. They also had the status of favoured confidants of the children they grew up with.[7] Because of the mutual dependence of slave and master, in most households the person most trusted was a slave, and, as said, slaves often rose to influential positions and acquired great wealth. The master's authority over the life of the slave, and its legal security, meant that the master could train a gifted slave from childhood and use him in the loyal management of his affairs. In a country where infant mortality was high, and even the wealthy often only had one or two male children, the bonds of slavery replaced the ties of blood in establishing a connection of trust. On the other hand, the master's family was the slave's family, in a land of extended families, and though those slaves who amassed considerably wealth could buy their freedom if they wished, they rarely did so.[8] The Malik al-Tujjar, who had a number of slaves, gave them responsibility for various affairs. For example, Haji Bashir Khan acted for the Malik in 1887 in Lingah,[9] and another slave carried out some of the Malik's duties as governor when he was ill in 1876.[10]

In order to fully understand the behaviour of Haji Bashir Khan, it is also necessary to consider the position of his master. The Malik al-Tujjar belonged to a family of enterprising merchants, which came to Bushire from Kazerun in 1210/1795–6,[11] at the time it began to develop under the influence of the British. The first member of the family to receive the title was Haj 'Abd al-Muhammad in 1260/1844. He died in 1273/1856–7 without issue and was succeeded by his brother Haj Muhammad 'Ali Malik al-Tujjar, who passed away in Bushire in 1295/1878, also without issue. The title, with all its accumulated wealth, then passed to his great-nephew, Haj Muhammad Mahdi, who was born in Calcutta in 1277/1860–1, where he lived until 1870, and was Malik al-Tujjar of Bushire from 1299/1882 to his death in 1890. He was thus the owner of Bashir at the time of his elopement.

By the end of the nineteenth century the family was immensely rich, and had for some time been demonstrating political aspirations. Haj Muhammad 'Ali Malik al-Tujjar had been politically active and had for a while been in charge of import trade in the south, becoming temporary governor of Bushire in 1876.[12] He was also involved in the Chinese opium trade, all of which led to his wealth doubling to the point where Haj Muhammad Mahdi is said to have inherited c. 300,000 tomans from him. Now one of the richest merchants in Iran, Haj Muhammad Mahdi travelled a great deal, on pilgrimages and abroad, and acted as agent for other companies as well as his own. He also developed political aspirations, becoming governor of the Persian Gulf ports, including Bushire and Lingah, in 1885, and had a role in the appointment and dismissal of governments there. However, his political activities took their toll on his wealth, which reportedly dwindled in a very short time. Sa'adat comments, 'If his actions were not to his own benefit, to the government of Iran his money was useful'.[13] In 1886 he was removed as governor of Bushire, but then appointed Admiral of the southern ports by Amin al-Sultan. During his period of office, he went to Bander Abbas in the Iranian naval ship, the *Persepolis*. On this expedition, he won much acclaim for asserting Iranian sovereignty over several of the Persian Gulf Islands. One of these had been held by a British Indian subject, a merchant named Ibrahim bin Muhammad, which brought upon him the suspicion and opprobrium of the British. They were further antagonised by his making what they called false accusations against the Residency Agent in Lingah in 1887.[14] Haj Muhammad Mahdi, however, also engaged in philanthropy, providing the ground for the Sa'adat School, the first modern style school in Bushire, which included maths, geography, history and English in its curriculum.[15] One of the Maliks built a house for one of the leading 'ulama, Haj Sayyid Muhammad 'Ali Bihbihani, and was the founder of the Masjid-i Nau.[16] The Malik family were, in addition, involved in the network of merchant councils established in Iran in the latter part of the nineteenth century.[17] The Bushire Council met in the governor's house with the participation of the Malik al-Tujjar and dealt with merchant affairs. The Malik al-Tujjar also represented the interests of the trading community to the Prime Minister or even the shah himself.

Haj Muhammad Mahdi, having failed both politically and financially, became a British subject, and returned to India.[18] He was succeeded by his son, Haj Kazim. Born in Calcutta, he lived in Bombay, and was originally reluctant to give up his status as a British Indian subject to assume the responsibilities of the Malik al-Tujjar.[19] However, on being denied his British Indian status because of assuming the responsibilities of the Malik al-Tujjar, he soon became involved in the politics of Bushire. He took a leading role in a popular uprising against Muhammad Riza Qavam al-Mulk in 1894, when the latter was governor of Bushire, during which the people complained to the government via the telegraph office.[20] He engaged in rivalries with local officials, and in 1896 endeavoured to take on an authoritative role in the crushing of a local Khan.[21] In 1897, however, he was forced to take *bast* (sanctuary) in the British Consulate as a result of government financial demands on him,[22] and thereafter forsook Bushire for Tehran.

Marriage between a Slave and a Free Woman

Such was the family into whose household Bashir was born. But there is little trace of him before the events of 1889, though his elopement had a history. For some years Bashir had been a close connection of the British Residency Newswriter,[23] Aqa Muhammad Rahim, and his wife had likewise become a close friend of Aqa Muhammad Rahim's daughter. However, because of circumstances unknown, which Rahim considered scandalous, Rahim tried to end the connection, as a result of which his daughter became estranged from her family. At this point Bashir seems to have developed the plan of running away with Rahim's daughter,[24] possibly cementing an existing connection which was disturbing her father and pre-empting his action. In any case, there seems to have been a prearranged plan as the girl (as she is referred to throughout in the British sources) ran away with a quantity of jewellery, clothing and 36,000 krans evidently seen as a dowry. A marriage seems to have taken place as a local *sayyid* said that on 13th April 1889 Bashir had asked him to perform the ceremony, but described the girl as his domestic servant and the daughter of Rahim Baghban, a petty trader. The *sayyid* confirmed the marriage as having been performed on 24th April, so presumably the elopement took place on that day.[25]

When Rahim heard that his daughter had gone, he went to Bashir's house to demand her return. Bashir evidently being out, he removed her by force, despite a struggle with some of Bashir's slaves,[26] in which one of them was wounded. In the following days both Bashir and Rahim fought strenuously to obtain the support of the 'ulama for their points of view, demonstrating the force of a shari'a ruling in this, particularly, a family matter.

Rahim pronounced his daughter to be of weak mind,[27] and got a ruling from a *mujtahid* (Sayyid Hasan Rashti) that a girl of weak mind cannot marry without her father's or guardian's consent, which implies that a girl not of weak mind can do so. Bashir, in the meantime, was reportedly endeavouring to bribe various senior members of the 'ulama to give an opinion in his favour, but without success. He then resorted to petitioning the deputy governor requesting that he ask the British to make Rahim give up his daughter. He complained that during the abduction Rahim had wounded his other wife, and had severely beaten two female servants, as well as wounding a slave.

Rahim now realised the weakness in his original argument over his daughter's mental state, and referred the matter to various *mujtahids* as to whether the marriage of his daughter, without his consent, to a slave, without the consent of the master, was valid. Reportedly they all said the marriage was null and void, except one who said that no *mujtahid* in Bushire was competent to decide. However, a telegram arrived from Tehran saying that Bashir's marriage was indeed valid.

From the point of view of the local authorities, the case was immensely complicated by the fact that the British had decided that Bashir's actions were really directed at them. In their view, his elopement was a plot to undermine their prestige, instigated by the Malik al-Tujjar, who had already demonstrated his animosity by what the British considered to be intrigues against them when governor of the Persian Gulf ports in 1887.[28] They believed that he was attacking their position by undermining their information gathering system, for which Rahim, as newswriter, was partly responsible. The unfortunate position of the local authorities was exacerbated by the fact that the shah was away in London, and there was therefore a lack of support and guidance from Tehran.[29]

The Governor of Bushire, Sa'd al-Mulk, evidently initially under British influence, at first decided to settle the matter by summoning a *majlis* (informal council) and having Bashir banished to Iraq, whilst also recovering the jewellery. However, Malik al-Tujjar and his relation, Haji Aqa Muhammad Mu'in al-Tujjar, now stepped in. Although Malik al-Tujjar, then in India, disclaimed all knowledge of the elopement, he was reportedly collaborating with Mu'in al-Tujjar, who was endeavouring to protect Bashir. They were said to have offered the governor 20,000 krans to settle the matter in Bashir's favour.[30] The governor of Bushire now began to speak of a possible role for Bashir as the governor of Bander Abbas, or of his leasing the customs. He opined that Bashir had offended the *'urf* law, by which he meant that he had transgressed local custom by contacting a woman without her father's consent (in other words the *'urf* law favoured Rahim).[31] But he also said that his worst problem was dealing with the religious part of the case, the rest being easy.

The British and the Implications for Their Prestige

Rahim's view, heavily backed by the British busily defending their prestige, argued that no Muslim has a right to entice an unmarried women from her father's house and marry her without his consent, whether she be willing or not.[32] Bashir's party, on the other hand, argued that the girl was an accomplice (i.e. she had left her father's house of her own volition) and there was therefore a contract, to which the response was that her departure was a deliberate insult to Rahim (and the British). The British were confident that their view was in conformity with Muslim practice.[33] In a similar incident, which took place in Khesht, where a slave ran off with a woman without the father's permission, he was forced to give her up, and Haji Shaikh 'Abd al-'Ali, Imam Jum'a, declared the marriage illegal as it had been performed without the father's consent. The woman was therefore divorced and, having been remarried, had several children.[34] The British argued that normally such an act was perceived as assailing the principles surrounding the Muslim home and an invasion of domestic authority, for which Bashir would have been dealt with severely by the governor.[35]

Aware that if the disturbance was not settled before the return of the shah, his position would become even more vulnerable, the beleaguered governor of Bushire offered to send Bashir away for a few months, but begged that there should be no corporal punishment. The British were demanding 5000 tomans compensation for Rahim, punishment and exile. The governor and Mu'in al-Tujjar, at the request of Malik al-Tujjar, held a *majlis* (assembly), once again demonstrating the role of consultation in Iranian politics of the time, to discuss releasing Bashir. At the meeting it was agreed that Mu'in al-Tujjar would stand surety for Bashir as regards to his person and property as well as for the claims of Bashir. Punishment was commuted to a fine, and Bashir was to go to the 'Atabat.[36] Bashir therefore mortgaged his houses both inside and outside town, to Mu'in al-Tujjar, and pawned jewellery to provide added security in case the properties did not fetch 5000 tomans.[37]

When released from Charburj, the seat of government, Bashir found much of his furniture missing, including an ice-making machine and a piano, as it had been taken away by Rahim along with his daughter. Blaming his wife and servants, he lashed out at them, so that they fled.[38] The governor, evidently afraid of every sort of disturbance, took a bond from them that they would not return, and obtained written confirmation from Bashir that he had received no money from him. Therefore, on 26th July 1889, Bashir embarked on a mail steamer bound for Basra on his way to Kerbala, and was seen off by a crowd of supporters.[39]

By March of 1890 Rahim's claim for compensation for the jewellery had still not been met, despite representations by the British, and the Iranian authorities were not being co-operative.[40] No doubt they realised the Rahim's claim was not a popular case, which illustrates the ways in which Iranian authorities took account of local opinion in the way they followed up claims. Since British claims never met with much sympathy, it formed a means by which popular opinion could bring pressure on the authorities against British influence. The underlying threat, of course, was that of the much dreaded disorder.

The Iranian Government and the Problem of Order

For the same reason – potential disorder – the Iranian authorities did not want Bashir back. The governor of Bushire warned Amin al-Sultan in April 1890 that his return was not advisable, particularly as the substantial landed property he owned in Bushire gave him influence there.[41] Bashir's brother Ghulam 'Ali, also still a slave of Malik al-Tujjar, and possibly at the instigation of the latter, who was then in India, accused Rahim of using foreign protection to oppress his opponent.[42]

Bashir wanted Rahim to prove his claim according to the shari'a. Sa'd al-Mulk had been right in recognising that the most difficult part of the case was the religious aspect, for the 'ulama of Bushire and the 'Atabat now became involved in the issue to an exceptional degree, as both sides sought legitimacy for their arguments. Bashir persuaded Shaikh Zain al-'Abidin Mazanderani, an eminent *mujtahid* of Kerbala, to send a telegram in June 1890 to Amin a-Sultan to say Bashir had taken refuge in the Shrine in Kerbala, and that all assistance should be given to him in the return of his wife and the property which had been seized.[43]

However, sometime towards the end of 1890 Rahim had his daughter married to a Muhammad Khalil. In March 1891 the governor of Bushire complained to the Resident that it was most incorrect to disregard the orders of the 'ulama of Iraq.[44] He further referred to the consummation of the marriage, which he designated as 'too shameful to mention', and predicted that there would be a commotion, particularly as it would provoke the 'ulama. The governor wisely accepted that the step taken by Aqa Muhammad Rahim had not been deliberately intended to create disorder, though otherwise it would have been sufficient for him to have been convicted of the same. He strongly advised the British to hold Rahim in check and to make sure that the matter did not become more widely known, which might possible quieten the 'ulama. The British, who probably had not given thought to the distinction between the signing of the contract and the consummation of the marriage under Muslim practice at that point, failed to understand that they were seen as undermining the authority and prestige of the 'ulama. Making the most superficial analysis of the matter, they believed the governor was preparing the way for a disturbance worked up by the government, as there had largely been indifference at the time of the marriage. However, as the matter had in the meantime been placed under the direct responsibility of the central government, the authorities in Bushire did not want to discuss it further.

The 'Ulama and the Question of Legality

The 'ulama of Bushire declined to remain quiet. They both ordered the closure of the bazaar, and also refused to carry out their shari'a duties, including prayer leadership, thereby implying that the government was unjust and acting illegally. Of course, Mu'in al-Tujjar[45] was not inactive, visiting Haji Shaikh Muhammad, the Imam Jum'a, Haji Sayyid Mahdi and Aqa Sulaiman to muster their support, and possibly being the source of threats to arrest Rahim's new son-in-law. Each side now began discrediting the credentials of the other's support from the 'ulama. Rahim produced a communication from Haji Sayyid Husain Rashti in Kerbala claiming that the telegram sent by Aqa Shaikh Zain al-'Abidin to the leading 'ulama of Bushire had been falsely attributed to him, and suggesting that the 'ulama of Bushire communicate directly with Shaikh Zain al-'Abidin by letter so that the facts might be known.[46] In this telegram Bashir is for the first time referred to as black, demonstrating how little significant his colour was.

In what he called 'the marriage outrage case', the Resident in Bushire sent a telegram to the British Representative in Tehran informing him that efforts were being made to incite ill-feeling and requesting that he have strict orders sent to the governor.[47] However, the other side was also bent on stiffening resolve. The governor told a Residency emissary that a telegram had arrived from the 'ulama of Kerbala and Najaf saying that if Rahim had married his daughter to someone else, it constituted adultery, and

Khalil should be executed as he was liable for it.[48] His copy of the telegram was certified by the signatures of Sayyid Ja'far, Mirza Abu'l Qasim, Mirza Habibullah Rashti and Shaikh Zain al-'Abidin Mazandarani. Further, the Imam Jum'a and other 'ulama of Bushire had denounced the present marital status of Rahim's daughter as contrary to the shari'a, and required that she be separated from Khalil forthwith. The 'ulama further informed that governor that if he could not do it, they would take the matter to Tehran. The Resident responded that the matter was being deliberately stirred up and the governor must settle it, at which the governor protested at his high-handed tone. Reasons or other evidence for British suspicions that the governor himself was involved were not forthcoming. He explained to Amin al-Sultan that on Friday 26th March 1891 he had been with most of the important merchants to the Jami' Mosque and had endeavoured to conciliate some of the leading 'ulama about Aqa Muhammad Rahim's daughter.[49] However, Haji Sayyid Mahdi and the other 'ulama were not convinced and still refused to resume their duties in their mosques.

Problems for the Local Authorities

The governor was disturbed by the relentless British perception that he was merely trying to assist Bashir, and their refusal to understand the nature of the popular discontent. It was in reality not simply about the shari'a but about foreign interference reaching down to the level of ordinary Islamic practice, and thus undermining Islam and thereby also the state. The true preoccupation of both local and central authorities was for security of the state, as the incident was taking place on a frontier, and Rahim, having foreign support, was refusing to submit to Iranian government decisions.[50]

The Bashir case brought about the removal of Sa'd al-Mulk and his replacement by Nizam al-Saltana as governor of Bushire. In a sense this appeared to make way for compromise, as the Resident informed the British Representative that he quite understood 'the necessity to close the case here by some concession on Muhammad Rahim's part'.[51] The central government was also ordering the local authorities to settle, though the governor replied that he could do so if the Residency stopped interfering.[52] He then went on to suggest that Rahim stand out for the validity of the second marriage but drop his property claims. There were also indications that the town was tired of the matter, and one of the 'ulama who had remained in his house in protest was ignored, and had to be 'begged by the people to resume his duties'.

Mu'in al-Tujjar was also working towards a compromise. His version involved getting the 'ulama of the 'Atabat to order both parties to divorce the girl.[53] Optimistically he believed this would lead to admission of the validity of the first marriage, enabling Bashir, in accordance with the shari'a, to make a declaration that the divorce was contrary to his inclination, and claim in another court that it be annulled. Then he would keep the girl. A *majlis* was duly convened outside the town, with the result that the Imam Jum'a and other leading 'ulama drafted a proposition to be sent to the 'ulama of the 'Atabat that they issue orders that both men divorce the girl.

The British party, however, had found a sympathetic *mujtahid* in Kerbala, 'duly licensed to perform marriages. That person ought to make out a good case for his friend'.[54] With regard to the opposing arguments, the Resident was concerned that the new governor might want 'a double divorce exparte' (presumably Mu'in's plan) to which he could not agree.

To try to resolve the matter, in May 1891 Aqa Muhammad Rahim set out from Baghdad with the intention of moving the case from Kerbala to Kazimain, and the Resident telegraphed the British representative in Tehran asking him to have the Iranian consul at Baghdad expedite a settlement by having Bashir attend the court case, a request which was followed up by the Iranian Government. It was thereby hoped to have the problem resolved 'according to the law'.[55]

By August 1891 the affair had still not died down. The issue of several *fatvas* by the 'ulama on the case had given it renewed significance. The governor of Bushire (once again Sa'd al-Mulk) asked the Iranian Government to have the matter settled by the leading *mujtahid* of Samarra (possibly Mirza Hasan Shirazi), because any order he issued would be accepted by the public, and the interference of others would insult the 'ulama and increase the problems making it so difficult to settle.[56] However, the leading *mujtahid* of Samarra refused to decide the case, presumably because its intense politicisation would make any judgement open to misinterpretation. The British, meantime, having found a friendly *mujtahid* in Kazimain, were determined to have the matter settled there,[57] and, knowing what they believed to be Shi'i doctrine, clearly held the view that the *fatva* of one *mujtahid* was as good as another.

By June 1892 Bashir had obtained decisions from Haji Mirza Muhammad Hasan Hujjat al-Islam and Haji Zain al-'Abidin in the 'Atabat in Mesopotamia, that Rahim's daughter was his legal wife, and should be restored to him.[58] If her present husband had any claim he should refer it to the courts of the above mentioned 'ulama in the 'Atabat. Further, the girl was sound of mind when the marriage ceremony was performed and she was not in any way forced into it by Bashir. In addition, Haji Zain al-'Abidin said the decision of Aqa Sayyid Husain (evidently the *mujtahid* sympathetic to the British side) in favour of Aqa Muhammad Rahim could not be recognised as he was unknown, and not ranked amongst the 'ulama. The governor of Bushire (once more Nizam al-Saltana, evidently responding to local pressure), telegraphed the Minister of Foreign Affairs, Amin al-Mulk, saying that Bashir had obtained decisions in his favour from the most respected 'ulama in favour of the right and legality of his marriage. Rahim should therefore hand over his daughter and stop trying to complicate the matter and save time.

The British, their prestige at stake, pointed out that there was a suspicious absence of dated evidence from the copies of Bashir's decisions, which had been certified by the 'ulama friends of Mu'in al-Tujjar. They argued that Rahim had a valid decision in his own favour, and that both parties should be present at court.[59]

Resolution of the Case?

There the correspondence on the subject ends. It is likely that the force of circumstances rather than the rulings of the 'ulama decided the case, and Rahim lost his jewellery, and Bashir never regained his wife. In Sadid al-Saltana's *Safarnama* he is mentioned as having two sons, Aqa 'Ali Reza and Aqa 'Abd al-Rasul, and as being the close associate of Mu'in al-Tujjar. No mention is made of a wife, nor is he referred to as being still a slave, so he may, after such costly and turbulent events, have obtained his manumission from his new master. He was much reduced in circumstances since the affair between him and the family of Al-i Safar,[60] but nevertheless still leased property worth 500 tomans a year, and owned what was considered the most beautiful garden in Bushire. Aqa Muhammad Rahim died in 1905, at which point there was a dispute among his heirs.[61]

* * *

In conclusion, the story of Haji Bashir Khan indicates in more detail the rights of a slave, including marriage to a free-born woman, and, since the issue was never raised as a problem, presumably in most circumstances, the right to such a marriage without his master's consent. He also had the right to own property and slaves on his own account, which he was able to dispose of as he wished, though ultimate responsibility for him and all he possessed lay with his master. As a well-educated and wealthy person, Bashir also had the status of a minor notable in the society of Bushire.

It would seem that his elopement with another man's daughter without her father's consent was contrary to the local custom or *'urf* law, where the conduct of a woman, and her effective protection, reflects much on the prestige and status of the male members of the family and on the family honour as a whole. However, as to whether such a marriage was contrary to the shari'a was altogether a more complicated and uncertain matter. Whilst the fact that the arguments of the British were in conformity with both local practice and the views of some 'ulama may have created distortion in the opinion of the time, it is clear that a case could be made under the shari'a for a woman to marry without her father's consent.

On the question of race, the want of references to Bashir's colour are an indication of its lack of significance in that society, and no distinction was made with regard to race since he was by culture and religion an Iranian.

The fact it played no role in the matter is further evidence to support the view that race was not significant in nineteenth century Iranian society.

Haji Bashir Khan was a black slave who challenged the prestige of the British Empire, disturbed the peace of Iran, and caused consternation and disagreement amongst the leading Shi'i 'ulama. Whilst his story owes much to his own courage, determination and force of character, it cannot be fully understood without consideration of the position of his master, the Malik al-Tujjar. Like his relation, the Mu'in al-Tujjar, the Malik belonged to a rising group of immensely wealthy and influential merchants, who profited not only from the British protection of trade in the Persian Gulf, and the connection with India, but from technological change and advance in communication, such as the advent of steam, the opening of the Suez canal, and the development of the Karun River. Their wealth grew independently of the Iranian state, and was not easily reached by its taxation system, giving them a position of growing influence and freedom of action. They had connections with one another throughout the country, with the 'ulama through their piety and religious donations, and with the less well-to-do or many poorer members of the bazaar through their trade. They could manage their own affairs by consultation, though regularly acted in collaboration with the local authorities. By the end of the nineteenth century they were growing increasingly assertive, and it is from this background of challenge that Bashir comes. Haj Muhammad Mahdi Malik al-Tujjar challenged the British, and Mu'in al-Tujjar was to be one of the prime movers in the constitutional movement leading to the Revolution of 1906.

Whilst the British in this story lived up to their reputation for interfering and hectoring, it is to be noted that in the end they too had to compromise. The property they claimed for Rahim was not returned, an event that was not atypical. Sometimes, in cases such as these, the various rights were not clear, or the amount too insignificant to pursue, but sometimes also, as in this case, popular feeling was so strong that it was not possible to follow it because of the danger of provoking disorder. This is something that was disliked quite as much by the British as by the Iranian government, because of its implications for commercial and strategic influence. Therefore the British had to negotiate and compromise not just with the Iranian government but with Iranian society.

Notes

1 Sadid al-Saltana, *Safarnama-yi Sadid al-Saltana*, ed. A. Iqtidari, Tehran 1362, p. 22.
2 No. 15.4.1890, FO 248/489.
3 Idem.
4 Polak, *Safarnama*, p. 36.
5 Sadid al-Saltana, *Safarnama*, p. 22.
6 See, for example, Ross to Kennedy, encl. in 19.8.1889, FO 248/484.
7 Polak, *Safarnama*, p. 174; Malcolm, *Persia*, p. 430; Wills, *Persia*, p. 76.

8 Wills, *Persia*, p. 77.
9 No. 137, 2.7.1887, FO 248/448.
10 No. 58, 15.8.1876, FO 248/319. The legal status of a slave put in charge of his master's business was '*ma'zhun*' (Arabic 'authorised') Brunschvig, "Abd', p. 29.
11 On the family of Malik al-Tujjar see Sadid al-Saltana, *Safarnama*, pp. 23, 384–5; R. Dashti, *Tarikh-i iqtisadi ijtima'i-yi Bushihr*, Tehran 1380, pp. 168ff.
12 No. 58, 15.8.1876, FO 248/319.
13 Shaikh Muhammad Husain Sa'adat, *Tarikh-i Bushihr*, Tehran. 1340, University of Tehran Library, Ms. Adabiyyat 95 Hikmat, p. 173.
14 Ross to Kennedy, encl. in 19.5.1889, FO 248/484. For a fuller account of his proceedings, see Davies, *Fars*, p. 462.
15 19 Sur 1299/1881–2, AM, 1PA1SV04, 2970202838.
16 Dashti, *Bushihr*, p. 107.
17 Dashti, *Bushihr*, p. 103.
18 Ross to Kennedy, 9.4.1888, FO 248/469.
19 No. 18.10.1891, FO 248/524.
20 Dashti, *Bushihr*, p. 136; Sa'adat, *Bushihr*, p. 191–2.
21 10 Rabi' II 1314/19.9.1896, MFA 1314 B29 F9 No. 79.
22 *Habl al-Matin*, Year 4, No. 28, 5 Muharram 1315/6 June 1897.
23 His duties were to gather information on local events and write a regular report for the Resident.
24 Ross to Kennedy, encl. in 19.5.1889, FO 248/484.
25 Legal marriage was open to slaves, male and female, and it was permissible for Muslim slaves to marry free Muslims. The general rule appears to be that the slave would need the master's permission, but, as this case illustrates, such a view was not absolute. See Brunschvig, "Abd', p. 25, 27.
26 In which we have an example of a slave himself owning slaves, though they would all ultimately have belonged to the master. Brunschvig, "Abd', p. 27, 28.
27 And therefore not responsible for her own actions under Islamic law.
28 Tel. No. 17.5.1889, FO 248/484; Ross to Kennedy, encl. in 19.5.1889, FO 248/484.
29 Ross to Kennedy, encl. in 19.5.1889, FO 248/484.
30 Ross to Kennedy, encl. in 19.5.1889, FO 248/484.
31 In other words the '*urf* law favoured Rahim, and was potentially in conflict with the shari'a, which could be said to favour Bashir.
32 Ross to Kennedy, 18.6.1889, FO 248/484.
33 Ross wrote angrily to Kennedy that if Bashir had offered such an insult to one of the governor's own dependents, he would have received a prompt and exemplary punishment. Ross to Kennedy, 19.5.1889, FO 248/484.
34 Ross to Kennedy, 5.12.1890, FO 248/502.
35 Ross to Kennedy, encl. in 19.5.1889, FO 248/484.
36 Ross to Kennedy, encl. in 19. 8.1889, FO 248/484.
37 The master was supposedly not responsible for the debts of an 'authorised' slave, but if the worst came to the worst, he could sell the slave to pay them, Brunschvig, "Abd', p. 29. In the event, the Malik al-Tujjar in India seems to have left the matter to his relation, the Mu'in.
38 Ross to Kennedy, encl. in 27.7.1889 and 5.8.1889, FO 248/484.
39 Ross to Kennedy, encl. in 27.7.1889, and tel. 26.7.1889, FO 248/484.
40 Ross to Kennedy, encl. in 29.3.1890, FO 248/502.
41 No. 1296, 15.4.1890, FO 248/489.
42 No. 1297, 15.4.1890, FO 248/489.
43 Amin al-Sultan to Drummond Wolff, No. 1528 rec'd 18.6.1890 FO 248/509.
44 Ross to Kennedy, encl. in 8.3.1891, FO 248/523.
45 Haj Muhammad Mahdi Malik al-Tujjar died early in 1890 and was succeeded by

his son, Haj Muhammad Kazim, who immediately fell out with Mu'in al-Tujjar over jointly owned properties in India, Mu'in demanding that the matter should go to a *majlis*. Dashti, *Bushihr*, p. 172; No.2019–2020, 25.1.1891,FO 248/530. Mu'in al-Tujjar, however, continued to champion the cause of Bashir, presumably from both personal and clan loyalty.

46 Ross to Kennedy, encl. in 18.3.1891, FO 248/523.
47 No. 16, tel. 17.3.1891, FO 248/523.
48 Ross to Kennedy, encl. in 18.3.1891, FO 248/523.
49 No. 2176, 1.4.1891, FO 248/530.
50 No. 2176, 1.4.1891, FO 248/530.
51 Talbot to Kennedy, 13.4.1891 and encl. in No. 37, 1.5.1891, FO 248/523.
52 Encl. in No. 37, 1.5.1891, FO 248/523.
53 Encl. in No. 37, 1.5.1891, FO 248/523.
54 Talbot to Kennedy, 30.4.1891., FO 248/523.
55 Encl. in No. 37, 1.5.1891, FO 248/523; No. 2272, 25.5.1891, FO 248/530.
56 Sa'd al-Mulk to Amin al-Sultan, No. 2451, 7.8.1891, FO 248/531.
57 No. 2561, 5.10.91., FO 248/531.
58 No. 19, 16.7.1892, FO 248/553.
59 No. 19, 16.7.1892, FO 248/553.
60 Sadid al-Saltana, *Safarnama*, p. 22. A probable reference to the dispute with Aqa Muhammad Rahim, who belonged to the Al-i Safar merchant family. See Dashti, *Bushihr*, p. 186.
61 MFA 1322–12–9, 1492 150.

CONCLUSION

Iranian society in the Qajar period was shaped by the values of Islam, encapsulated not only in the shari'a but in the customs and culture of the country in such a way as to reflect the precepts of the religion, even though it might be referred to by allusion rather than by specific statement. In negotiating with each other, state and society implied a recognised Islamic value system understood by both sides. This system was implicit in both customary practice and the *'urf* (customary) law, which is not to say that all *'urf* or custom or culture was necessarily Islamic in origin. Nevertheless, what was non-Islamic was still by default incorporated into the Islamic system under the Qur'anic principle that what Qur'an allows, God has not forbidden, and it is therefore permissible.

The most fundamental principle of the understanding between religion and state was justice, and the aspect of justice implied in the term *'adl* most consistently explored here is that of equalising or balancing. It carries the notion of a structure of checks and balances whereby the state ensures that the community is united and stable, and that ideally it benefits both spiritual and economic welfare as far as possible from all the means that it has. The different groups of society have to be managed in such a way that the interests of each are recognised, and that they meet their obligations and receive their rights. It is implicit for example in the donations of alms, so that some provision should be made for the poor and disadvantaged, just as much as it is implicit in the meting out of punishment to those who are seen as undermining the well-being of the community. Underlying these principles is the belief that the greatest evil is anarchy in which all oppress one another, and Islam and believers cannot thrive.

On this basis state and society in the Qajar period negotiated with each other, and the fact that they understood the value system which encompassed all parts and levels of society enabled them to maintain a cohesion that was important to the survival of the independence of the country: in fact it was more important than military force. Negotiation was carried out on the basis of acknowledged rights and obligations. It was the duty of the shah to protect Shi'i Islam and the community of believers, their lives, wealth and honour, from which he derived what was in practice the most significant of his titles, Shahanshah Islam Panah, the Guardian of Islam. A further duty was to ensure just rule, by which was meant rule such that his subjects, the recipients of his kindness, could peaceably go about their business, and disorder was kept at bay. He had also to ensure that there was no outright infringement of the shari'a, though in reality in the Qajar period there was a pragmatic aspect to this dimension of rule in that some activities, such as wine drinking, were tolerated as long as they did not intrude on the observance of religious practice, or were likely to cause disorder. It was also the duty of the shah to ensure that his subjects received what was their due in terms both of the shari'a and of customary law, and to ensure that their grievances were redressed. In more practical terms he had also to collect taxes, and make appropriate appointments to offices.

It was the shah's right to expect that the subjects should observe their duties, and that they respect his authority and judgement. Correspondingly, the subjects also had rights, to expect that the shah should conduct himself with justice, that he should maintain the proper balance, that he should rule in accordance with the shari'a, if not in every letter, at least in recognised principle. Specifically, their grievances should be attended to and redressed (*ihqaq-i huquq*), according to their rights as recognised by the shari'a. The duties of the subjects were to be obedient to the shah, on the understanding that he would attend to their petitions and complaints, to pray for his well-being, and go peaceably about their business. Where the shah failed to meet his obligations, the condition of the community moved from one of justice to oppression (*zulm*), where the shari'a could not operate, where the shah lost his authority and therefore his legitimacy, and his right to rule was therefore open to challenge.

In the course of their struggle with the state, the people deployed a variety of terms to imply its failure to regulate the affairs of the community effectively and fairly. Thus Aqa Sayyid 'Asadullah departed from Isfahan for Tehran in 1850, to demand peace, order, and a *qanun-i 'adil* (a just law), one that was in conformity with the principles of the shari'a and regulated with balance the affairs of the community. The closure of the bazaar in the same city in 1879, was justified to the governor by the 'ulama as their shari'a duty, which is to say that a state of government contrary to the shari'a existed, which compelled them to boycott the state. At that same point the people of Isfahan came out, designating the city to be in a state of *zulm* thereby openly implying that the government was unjust and extortionate, and should be overthrown as illegitimate. Only a very determined and confident rebellion could go as far as that. The Shah duly responded that as seditious subjects, they deserved to perish, and called the 'ulama to account for failing in their duty of admonishment. They were also accused of failing to assist the government in granting the people their rights (*risidigi bih huquq-i mardum*), that is to say, to resolve the crisis by ensuring that the needs of all parties were both met and balanced.

Such was the basis of understanding between state and people on the nature of government in the Qajar Iran, and they did not necessarily confront each other when a disagreement arose, or when the understanding appeared to have broken down. Rather they engaged in a process of bargaining, which involved all levels of society. The way in which they bargained depended upon their means. A merchant, such as Mu'in al-Tujjar, would deploy his wealth to induce government officials to listen to him, and persuade the bazaaris, probably already financially dependent on him, to mobilise to support him. He would make grants to religious institutions, and donations to a respected *mujtahid*, so that religious pronouncements might be issued in his favour. Likewise a member of the 'ulama, such as Aqa Najafi, could use the authority vested in him as one learned in religion and the law to make pronouncements from the pulpit, and guide his flock to his favoured policy, assuming that they perceived it as in their interest.

Humbler members of society, guildsmen and labourers, poorer women, soldiers and the unemployed, had the option of organising. To compensate for their lack of status, and where their grievances were not acknowledged, they united in protest against perceived injustices, whether arbitrary administration of the law, or financial deprivation. A kind of unspoken dialogue, enacted in a series of manoeuvres, developed between the protestors and the government, by which the protestors sought firstly to legitimise their campaign, and secondly to undermine the authority of the state or its representative. One manoeuvre was for a whole community to run away, as the people of Kharg Island did in 1843, or those of Neyriz in 1894, leaving the government with no subjects, and so no taxes, and no good order, and ultimately, so the line of reasoning went, no state – the fate of an unjust government.

Unity was brought about through networks: of family, of quarters, of a common guild, or through all the guilds, of dependence on a particular *mulla* or merchant, of commercial connections, of clan and tribal relations, or of common bonds in one locality or village. The bazaar was made up many such networks, but for protest against the state to be achieved on a major scale, most, if not all of them, had to be involved. The closure of the bazaar of Bushire in protest against Shaikh Nasir in 1838 indicated to him that his government had not achieved a just balance over the levying of dues. The attack by bazaaris in that same year against the Residency *sarraf*, who was engaged in the wine trade was, on the one hand, a way of signalling to the foreign power that too much interference might require greater resources to control than it was willing to commit. It was on the other hand, a warning to the government that it might pay the price of insurrection if it did not uphold its duty as an Islamic government of protecting religion. It indicated to the Iranian government that failure to resist foreign involvement in the country made it liable to the accusation of failure to protect Islam, its paramount duty.

Another tactic was to take *bast* (sanctuary) *en masse*, for which there are nineteenth century precedents to the great *bast* of the Constitutional

Revolution. The Garusi Regiment in Bushire in 1880 contrived to make the Iranian government look foolish and inept by taking sanctuary under a foreign flag, and so managed to extract some of the payments due to them. The 'ulama, in contention with the state, had the paradigms of the struggles of the early Shi'a against oppressive rule to draw upon in mobilising support against the state. In Isfahan in 1879 the populace were reminded of how the people of Kufa risked all in their battle against oppression, implying that they lacked the courage and character to resist the tyrant of their own times, so indicating that the current regime was not behaving as a righteous government should: an implied threat to the government. The use of holy relics, the banner of Husain and the hand of 'Abbas, and the cries of 'Ya Husain' and 'Ya 'Ali' in Shiraz in 1893 again sought to undermine government authority by challenging its legitimacy and suggested that the city was in a state of *zulm* (injustice, oppression).

A governor faced with protest, like Zill al-Sultan in 1879, had to be very careful not to over-react and make the protest worse. The ability to contain protest, and to ensure it did not escalate into a major disturbance and disorder, was an important skill of an effective governor. Punishment was effective, and part of the system of control, but over-punishment had repercussions for the state. When Farhad Mirza punished 'Ali Akbar Qavam al-Mulk in 1841 he quickly restored such a powerful subject to his position. Rukn al-Daula in 1892 was not so wise. His removal of Muhammad Riza Qavam al-Mulk, which disturbed the tribes of Fars, indicates a failure to understand the system of checks and balances in the government of that province, and to regulate society in such a way as to establish equivalence, which resulted in serious disorder. Despite the provocation given him with the murder of the deputy governor in 1849, Sipahdar, governor of Isfahan, did not retaliate against the insurgent populace, but against a select few, and used the best available means, the mediation of the 'ulama, to settle the situation.

A need to maintain social justice and an equitable balance of resources was a concern of both religion and state. A governor who understood how to secure a sufficiently fair distribution of wealth (and it was never very fair) could quell anger and dissatisfaction where another had failed, like the government of Isfahan after the crisis of 1850. By the same token, a *mujtahid* who sensed that unemployment and lack of social justice was behind criminal actions, could assist and protect and in other ways support the poor against the retribution of the state, as did Sayyid Muhammad Baqir in Isfahan in 1840. Helping the individuals benefited the community by enabling it to endure in a time of scarcity, though when it came to famine, only proper control of the grain supply could be of any use at all.

Of course, the community was not always at one, and there are a number of incidents in the foregoing account of different social groups being at odds with one another. The most notable example is that of Isfahan in 1840, when, in what was clearly a period of economic crisis, the property of wealthier social groups came under attack from the poor. Differences between social groups were manipulated by 'Ali Akbar Qavam al-Mulk in the 1840s as he reinforced his position and extended his control in Shiraz. Sometimes, also, there were conflicts of interest between members of the same group, as with the merchants of Bushire at the time of the first Herat war, some of whom benefited from their connections with the British, and some of whom did not.

Lutis, in particular, had a role to play in conflicts between urban groups, and social justice was an important element in their culture. One of the roles of the *lutis* was to protect the weak, the poor, and the disadvantaged by ensuring that they benefited from a more equitable distribution of resources. They also prided themselves on standing up for the vulnerable against oppression by the officials of the state. Supposedly the proceeds of their more nefarious deeds were to be given in charity to the poor. Whatever the reality of individual claims, the community would not have tolerated *lutis*, and especially engaged them in their struggle against the state, if they had not been part of the common culture of justice, in the sense of maintaining an equilibrium through a variety of functions. Correspondingly, the knowledge of that fact conferred on the *lutis* a sense of self-worth, which contributed to their ability to resist misgovernment.

Women also were part of the struggle against deprivation and arbitrary government. For example, they would participate in demonstrations in well-rehearsed scenes whenever the price of bread went too high, and the government administration seemed either to be conniving in keeping it up, or failing to control it. In the course of the century their role in political struggle became slowly more sophisticated, and the gradually enhanced role of women in *ta'ziyya* testifies to their activism in the struggle for justice against the intolerable hardships of arbitrary government. Women had a significant role to play in highlighting oppression and showing the courage to withstand it.

The very term *'adalatkhana*, used of the assembly of Fars in 1896, and later placed on the list of the movement that brought about the Constitutional Revolution in 1905–6, would have implied to many the implementation of fair practice, and more particularly, equalisation and balance. It also suggested greater social justice and a more equitable distribution of wealth. Now it would be the participants, not simply the government, that would weigh conflicting interests, develop policies to absorb change, decide how to encourage reciprocation, and thereby ensure stability and good order. Its judgement would have to be used to provide in financial terms an economic balance between the different components of society. The Constitutional Assembly in particular would ensure that disproportionate wealth did not fall into the hands of the few, and, where it existed, it should be redistributed. Even as early as 1891 at the time of the mutiny in Tehran, ideas were being mooted not simply on lack of pay but on the inequalities in salaries, particularly of the royal family, and at the cost of employing Europeans. Later in Isfahan in 1893, after the military found common cause with the populace over the high cost of living, an assembly of all classes decided the price of bread.

Into this whole system of negotiations the British and probably also the Russians were drawn, partly as foreigners with countervailing interests, but partly as elements integral to the process. Although the British brought might to their negotiations with Iranians, and became notably more aggressive as the country opened up in the 1890s, the facts do not sustain the view that they always got what they wanted. They may possibly have been more successful than local or other merchants in pressing the claims of British companies, but they were still sometimes obliged not infrequently, to settle for less than they had expected, or indeed for nothing at all.

Proposals for concessions were welcomed by Nasir al-Din Shah himself, even without much pressure from foreign powers. They had to be substantial, however, and bring in revenue, thus in his view helping to develop the country. Nevertheless, major concessions were significant in undermining the existing system. They threatened the established balance of resources, by virtue of the fact that the shah came to a remunerative agreement with a foreign concern which excluded the interests of his subjects, particularly the merchants. They led to an inability to bestow offices or manage the finances in a way that was flexible, whereby a balance could be maintained, and where all received the shares they would have expected. The absence of profitable trade for Iranian subjects was one of the factors producing the discontent which led to the Constitutional Revolution.

The rise in concessions, and the increasing involvement of foreign institutions interrupted the rise of an old group, that of the merchants. They had gradually become wealthier as the state remained poor, leaving them in a position to challenge it through their means and influence, as they became increasingly discontented. To the state's encouragement of foreign involvement, customs reforms were added in the late 1890s. This represented a further division of revenues as between the state and outside interests, all without the proceeds being accounted for once in the hands of the Iranian government. Urban society, wealthier and better organised than the tribal society on which the Shah still relied for his army, was able to mobilise to change the established order.

Protest in Isfahan, Shiraz and Bushire took different forms. Criticism of the state in Isfahan is notable for the use of religious language and terms, as also for the greater involvement of the 'ulama in representing popular discontent. Isfahan had wealthier institutions and endowments – a legacy of the Safavid period – and more recognition as a centre of learning. Shiraz, by contrast, with a populace that was more turbulent as a result of its stronger tribal element, depended less on verbal allusion to injustice, and more on outright combat with the state authorities. The challenge there for any governor was simply to keep order. In the early part of the nineteenth century, Bushire was not particularly distinctive as compared to

Shiraz and Isfahan. By the end of the century, however, prosperity, a big foreign trading community from many countries, and the presence of the British Residency do seem to have brought greater regularity and organisation into the state system, though complaints about the local authorities' mismanagement did not disappear. Change came in Iran from new ideas, and from the intelligentsia, including bureaucrats, who propagated them, as well as from financial indigence. It also came from the existing commercial and religious organisations striving to adapt, each in its own way to a new world. In that, Iran may be contrasted with Egypt, where the commercial sector had long been dominated by foreign interests, and the religious community was largely passive towards the government, and with the Ottoman Empire, where reform was brought about above all by its influential army.

The Constitutional Revolution came out of many factors, of which this book focuses on one, namely the way in which existing culture was bound up with negotiation and bargaining infused by Islamic concepts of justice and balance. The Revolution cannot be understood without reference as to how society as a whole was involved in this bargaining process and the way in which people of lower social levels were able to influence the political process. The emphasis of the study is, of course, on the urban areas in the south, the relationship of the government could or would have differed with tribes and villages, and with different parts of the country. In the urban areas there existed practices of consultation, organisation, representation of views, and a general mood of assertiveness when the population was discontented, all of which led to influence and involvement in politics.

In the past the tobacco movement has been perceived as suddenly appearing, with perhaps some warning in the crisis over the Reuter concession in 1872. Now it is clear that not only the Reuter and Tobacco Concessions, but also the Constitutional Revolution itself, emerged in part for a tradition of organised protest against the state, and of demands for justice and fair government. In addition to that, however, urban society began to change from the 1880s, so already, before the tobacco movement, many of its features were evident. The merchants were unhappy about the level of foreign involvement in trade and the privileges and advantages of foreign concerns. They noted as well how Western merchants benefited form the relative financial security and rationalised administration of their own countries. The 'ulama were disturbed and worried over the implications for Islam of the increase in the foreign presence and influence in Iran. The government, financially weak in the face both of foreign powers and its own subjects and tempted by new opportunities for funding, was caught between the pressure from its own subjects, and from foreign powers. If foreigners were organised so was Iranian society through its long established networks and mechanisms for protest, to which was added a readiness to engage with new technology, particularly in the form of unity of action and mobilisation through the telegraph.

The Tobacco Concession movement united local protest into country-wide opposition, and was a catalyst both in demonstrating the weakness of the state and its authority, and in demonstrating the means by which common goals and objectives could be brought together on the national level. It remained only for people to seize the opportunity that had opened up and to begin to formulate a vision for a new era. In that vision old values, ideas derived from adaptation to new circumstances, new solutions to political problems, and radical theories about the need to change the system of government, were both to fuse and to conflict. These processes were already evident in the 1890s with the more formalised methods of consultation drawing in a larger section of the community, and with the appearance of new language, speaking of reform and of the joint role of government and people, not state and subjects. The whole concept of consultation (*mashvarat*) had been applied as demonstrated in a variety of contexts and most levels of society in the nineteenth century, and was thus already deeply embedded in political practice. However, it came to the fore in the 1890s in a more formalised and organised way, with a movement towards institutionalisation of consultation in the processes of government, and above all in the demand for the *'adalatkhana* (house of justice). We may at last challenge Daulatabadi's always dubious claim that the request for a house of justice, (and the term he used was *divan-i 'adalat*) appeared on the list of demands of the 'ulama in 1905 because he put it there at an opportune movement, and that in this sense he played a momentous role in bringing about the Revolution.

By the 1890s urban Iranians were beginning to see that the existing consensus between shah and subject was breaking down. The shah was not behaving as an Islamic ruler should: he was not protecting Islam, and in particular he was coming to financial agreements with foreigners which profited himself and them, but excluded his subjects. On the other hand, the measures of reform he had brought in were not effective, particularly in introducing accountability into the finances. The part of foreigners in the existing balance was disturbed in another way. Britain and Russia, with an eye to impending war in Europe, came to an agreement in 1907 to settle their differences in Asia. As a result they were no longer part of the Iranian bargaining system, because they could no longer be played off against each other. Financial difficulty, much of it due to the encroachment of the world economy, combined with the effect of the political situation in Europe to take the destiny of Iran out of Iranian hands, and led to the occupation of the country by Britain and Russia in 1911. Finances, the very issue which had opened the way to new political development, also ended it.

Finally, one of the greatest challenges to the new Constitutional government was to absorb the Islamic balance and to develop it into a system of modern institutions and political relations. It was a challenge in which the Constitutional government failed, just as the Pahlavi regime that followed it failed. And solutions which came from without also failed, by generating more extremism. Why did the Constitutional regime itself fail to endure? Time did not allow the opportunity for compromise in the gradual adaptation of the nineteenth century practice of the shari'a to the needs of twentieth century society. Nor did it allow for the principles of the shari'a to be transferred into a modern legal system; for the means of social justice to be applied; for new institutions to provide the same security as the old organisations and networks, particularly the clan network; or for the new citizens to develop a sense of loyalty to the state, rather than to tribe and village; for the creation of a new and better means of establishing social justice and welfare in the form of modern institutions.

GLOSSARY

'adalat	justice
'adalatkhana	house of justice
'Atabat	the thresholds, refers to the Shi'i holy cities of Iraq, Kerbala, Najaf, Samarra and Kazimain
bast	sanctuary
bastinado	punishment by beating on the soles of the feet
bunakdar	wholesale dealer
darugha	magistrate, official responsible for policing
daulat	government, state
farman	royal rescript, command
farrash	servant
ghulam	male slave
haq	right
huquq	pl. of haq, rights
ihqaq-i huquq	confirmation of rights
imam jum'a	one appointed by the shah to lead the prayers at the main mosque of each town
jaur	injustice, oppression
kadkhuda	head of village or urban quarter
kalantar	mayor
kaniz	female slave
karguzar	foreign agent
kharaj	tax, land tax
khums	one fifth of a person's spare income levied as a canonical tax
luti	champion of the poor, popular entertainer, rough
madrasa	theological school
majlis	assembly, council, meeting
maliyat	tax, especially the land tax
malik al-tujjar	principal merchant
mashvarat	consultation
millat	originally the people or community, gradually came to mean the nation
mirza	title, usually of a member of the bureaucracy

mujtahid	a leading member of the Muslim clergy
pahlavan	hero, champion
panah	protector
pishkish	gift, often extracted as a kind of tax, or given as an inducement
qanun	law, normally used in the sense of modern law
rauzakhani	religious ceremony of commemoration
rifah	welfare
ru'aya	subjects
sarbaz	soldier
sarraf	changer of money and bills of exchange, banker
sayyid	one claiming descent from the Prophet
shari'a	the holy law of Islam
takiyya	building in which ta'ziyya plays are performed
tanbaku	tobacco, specially processed for the hookah
ta'ziyya	religious play, passion play, most usually depicting the martyrdom of Imam Husain
tullab	theological students
'ulama	the Muslim clergy
'urf	customary law or practice
vaqf	religious endowment
yavar	major
zakat	alms, canonical tax
zill allah	shadow of God, shah's title
zulm	oppression
zurkhana	lit. house of strength, traditional gymnasium

BIBLIOGRAPHY

Works in Persian

Abadian, H.,	'Junbish-i tanbaku: nigahi bih darun', *Tarikh-i mu'asir-i Iran*, 8, Autumn 1374, pp. 43–69.
Adamiyyat, F., and Natiq, H.,	*Afkar-i ijtima'i va siyasi va iqtisadi dar athar-i muntashir nashuda-yi daura-yi Qajar*, Tehran 1356.
Adamiyyat, M.H.R.,	*Danishmandan va sukhan sarayan-i Fars*, Tehran 1340.
Afshar Sistani, I.,	*Jazira-yi Kish va Darya-yi Pars*, Tehran 1370
Afshari, M.,	'Pahlavan', in *Danishnama-yi jahan-i Islam*, 5, Tehran 1379.
Afshari, M., and Madayini, M., eds,	*Haft Lashkar*, Tehran 1377.
Afshari, M., and Madayini, M., eds,	*Futuvvat va asnaf*, Tehran 1381.
Afzal al-Mulk, Mirza Ghulam Husain,	'Safarnama-yi Isfahan' in *Du safarnama-yi junub-i Iran*, ed. S.A. Al-i Davud, Tehran 1368.
'Ain al-Saltana,	*Ruznama-yi khatirat-i 'Ain al-Saltana*, eds, I. Afshar and M. Salur, Tehran 1374.
Al-i Ahmad, J.,	*Jazira-yi Kharg dar ijtima'-i Khalij-i Fars*, Tehran 1370.
Al-i Davud, S.A.,	*Namaha-yi Amir Kabir*, Tehran 1371.
Amin, A.,	'Iran dar sal-i 1311 hijri qamari', trans. M. Gharavi, *Majala-yi barisi-ha-yi tarikhi*, Year 9, No. 4, 1353, pp. 75–100.
Asif al-Daula, 'Abd al-Vahab,	*Asnad-i Mirza 'Abd al-Vahab Khan, Asif al-Daula guzida-yi asnad-i Khurasan*, eds, A.H. Nava'i, N. Kasra, Tehran 1377.
Bamdad, M.,	*Sharh-i hal-i rijal-i Iran*, Tehran 1347.

BIBLIOGRAPHY

Basir al-Mulk Shirazi, Mirza Tahir, — *Ruznama-yi khatirat-i Basir al-Mulk Shirazi*, eds. I. Afshar and M.R. Daryagasht, Tehran 1374.

Bastani Parizi, M.I., — *Tarikh-i Kerman*, Tehran 1361.

Bayani, Kh., — *Panjah sal tarikh-i Nasiri*, Tehran 1375.

Benjamin, S.G.W., — *Iran va Iranian*, trans. R. Rezazadeh-Malek, Tehran 1363.

Boroumand, S., — *Sar kunsulgari-yi Britannia dar Bushihr 1177–1332/1763–1914*, Tehran 1381.

Bulookbashi, A., and Shahidi, Y., — *Musiqi va sazha-yi musiqi-yi nizami-yi daura-yi Qajar*, Tehran 1381.

Bulookbashi, A. — *Qahvakhanaha-yi Iran*, Tehran 1375.

Dashti, R., — *Tarikh-i iqtisadi va ijtima'i-yi Bushihr*, Tehran 1380.

Daulatabadi, Y., — *Tarikh-i mu'asir ya hayat-i Yahya*, Tehran 1337.

Ettehadieh, M., — 'Naqsh-i zanan dar inqilab-i mashruta', *Tarikh-i mu'asir-i Iran*, 5 No. 18, 1380, pp. 157–169.

Ettehadieh, M., — *Inja Tehran ast*, Tehran 1377.

Ettehadieh, M., and Mir Muhammad Sadiq, S., eds, — *General Semino dar khidmat-i Iran 'asr-i Qajar va jang-i Harat 1236–1266q.*, Tehran 1375.

Farasati, R., — *Farmanha va raqamha-yi daura-yi Qajar*, Tehran, 1372.

Fasa'i, Hasan Husaini, — *Farsnama-yi Nasiri*, ed. M. Rastgar Fasa'i, Tehran 1368.

Flandin, E., — *Safarnama-yi Eugene Flandin bih Iran*, trans. H. Nur Sadiqi, Intisharat-i Ishraqi 2536.

Grummon, S.R., — *Chalish barayi qudrat va thirvat dar junub-i Iran az 1750–1850*, (The Rise and Fall of the Arab Shaikhdom of Bushire 1750–1850, Ph.D. John Hopkins University, 1985), trans. H. Zanganeh, Qum 1378.

Haqani, M., — 'Nahzat- i mashrutiyyat bih ravayat-i tasvir', *Tarikh-i mu'asir Iran*, 5, No.18, 1380, pp. 261–293.

Hidayat, Reza Quli Khan, — *Rauzat al-Safa*, ed. J. Kianfar, Tehran 1380.

Humayuni, S.,	*Shiraz khastgah-i ta'ziyya*, Shiraz 1377.
Humayuni, S.,	*Ta'ziyya dar Iran*, Shiraz 1380.
I'timad al-Saltana, Muhammad Hasan Khan,	*Al-ma'thir wa'l athar*, Tehran 1306.
I'timad-i Saltana, Muhammad Hasan Khan,	*Ruznama-yi khatirat-i I'timad al-Saltana*, ed. I. Afshar, Tehran 1377.
'Irfan, H.,	*Ta'ziyya dar ustan-i Bushihr*, Shiraz 1379.
Karamat, A.,	*Tarikh-i baft-i qadimi-yi Shiraz*, Tehran 1353.
Kasravi, A.,	*Tarikh-i mashruta-yi Iran*, Tehran 2536.
Khurmuji, M.J.,	*Haqa'iq-i akhbar-i Nasiri*, ed. S.H. Khadiv Jam, Tehran 1363.
Khurmuji, M.J.,	*Nuzhat al-akhbar, tarikh va jughrafiyya-yi Fars*, ed. S.A. Al-i Davud, Tehran 1380.
Kitabi, S.M.,	*Rijal-i Isfahan dar 'ilm va 'irfan va adab va hunar*, Isfahan 1375.
Madani Kashani, A.R.,	*Tarikh-i ashrar-i Kashan*, ed. H. Pur Madani, Tehran 1378.
Mahdavi, S.M.,	*Tarikh-i ijtima'i-yi Isfahan dar qarn-i akhar*, Qum 1367.
Mahmud, M.,	*Tarikh-i ravabit-i siyasi Iran va Inglis dar qarn-i nuzdahum-i miladi*, Tehran 1367.
Mir 'Azimi, N.,	*Isfahan zadgah-i jamal va kamal*, Isfahan 1379.
Mu'ayyir al-Mamalik, Dust 'Ali Khan,	*Rijal-i 'asr-i Nasiri*, Tehran 1361.
Muhammadi, A.,	*Shiraz*, Shiraz 1378.
Mustaufi, A.,	*Sharh-i zindigani-yi man ya tarikh-i ijtima'i-yi Iran*, Tehran 1324.
Mu'tazid, Kh., and Kasra, N.,	*Siyasat va haramsara (zan dar 'asr-i Qajar)*, Tehran 1379.
Nabavi, S.M.H.	*'Ulama va nivisandigan-i Bushihr*, translated extracts from Aga Buzurg-i Tehrani, ed. A. Mashayekhi, Bushire 1377.
Najafi, A.M.,	*Vaqayi'-i ilat-i Khamsa*, Tehran 1380.
Najafi, M.,	*Haj Aqa Nurullah Isfahani*, Tehran 1378.
Naraqi, H.,	*Tarikh-i ijtima'i-yi Kashan*, Tehran 1345.
Nazim al-Islam Kirmani, Mirza Muhammad,	*Tarikh-i bidari-yi Iranian*, Tehran 1357.

Nizam al-Saltana,	*Khatirat va asnad-i Husain Quli Khan Nizam al-Saltana Mafi*, eds M.Mafi, M. Ettehadieh, S. Sa'dvandiyan, H. Ram Pisha, Tehran 1361.
Nijhadirshadi, M.Z., ed.,	*Asnad-i Khalij- i Fars*, Idara-yi Intishar-i Asnad, 5, Tehran 1375.
Piemontese, A.M.	'Artish-i Iran dar salha-yi 1874–5 miladi az did-i General Enrico Andreini', *Tarikh-i mu'asir-i Iran*, 3, 1370, pp. 11–49.
Polak, J.E.,	*Safarnama-yi Polak*, (*Persien, das Land und Seine Bewohner*, Leipzig 1865), trans. K. Jahandari, Tehran 1361.
Qazvini, Muhammad Shafi',	*Qanun-i Qazvini*, ed. I. Afshar, Tehran 1370.
Rajabi, M.H.,	*Mashahir-i zanan-i Irani va Parsigu*, Tehran 1374.
Ravandi, M.,	*Tarikh-i ijtima'i-yi Iran*, Tehran 2nd ed. 2536.
Sa'adat, Shaikh Muhammad Husain,	*Tarikh-i Bushihr*, Tehran 1340.
Sadid al-Saltana, Muhammad 'Ali Khan,	*Safarnama-yi Sadid al-Saltana*, ed. A. Iqtidari, Tehran 1362.
Sadid al-Saltana, Muhammad 'Ali Khan,	*Bandar 'Abbas va Khalij-i Fars*, ed., A. Iqtidari, Tehran 1363.
Sadid al-Saltana, Muhammad 'Ali Khan,	*Piramun-i Khalij- i Fars*, ed., A. Iqtidari, Tehran 1371.
Safa'i, I., ed.,	*Asnad-i nau yafta*, Tehran 1349.
Safa'i, I., ed.,	*Asnad-i siyasi-yi dauran-yi Qajariya*, Tehran 2535.
Safa'i, I., ed.,	*Asnad-i barguzida az Sipah Salar, Zill al-Sultan, Dabir al-Mulk*, Tehran 1350.
Safa'i, I., ed.,	*Yik sad sanad-i tarikhi-yi dauran-i Qajariya*, Intisharat-i Babak, Tehran n.d., 2nd edition.
Sa'idi, G.H.,	*Ahl-i hava*, Tehran, 1345.
Sasani, Khan Malik,	*Siyasatgaran-i daura-yi Qajar*, Intisharat-i Babak, Tehran, 1338
Shafiqi, S.,	*Jughrafiyya-yi Isfahan*, Isfahan 1353.
Shahidi, E., and Bulookbashi, A.,	*Pajhuhishi dar ta'ziyya va ta'ziyya khani as aghaz ta payan-i daura-yi Qajar dar Tehran*, Tehran 1380.

Sipihr, Mirza Muhammad Taqi, Lisan al-Mulk, — *Nasikh al-tavarikh*, ed. J. Qa'im Maqami, Tehran 1337.

Sirjani, A.A.S., ed., — *Vaqayi'-i ittifaqiyya*, Tehran 1362.

Tabataba'i, M., — 'Nama'i az Haj Mulla Muhammad Sadiq Qumi bih Nasir al-Din Shah', *Vahid*, No.3, 1353, pp. 211–219.

Tafreshi, M.S., — *Nizam va nizamiyya dar daura-yi Qajar*, Tehran 1362.

Tahvildar, Mirza Husain Khan, — *Jughrafiyya-yi Isfahan*, ed. M. Sutuda, Tehran 1342.

Takmil Humayun, N., — *Tahavulat-i Qushun dar tarikh-i mu'asir-i Iran. Daura-yi Qajar*, I, Tehran 1376.

Tunakabuni, Mirza Muhammad, — *Qisas al-'ulama*, Intisharat-i 'ilmiyya-yi Islami, 1364.

Vadala, R., — *Khalij-i Fars dar 'asr-i isti'mar*, trans., S. Javadi, Paris 1920.

Ya Husaini, S.Q., — *Pishgaman-i mubariza ba Britannia dar junub-i Iran*, Bushire 1373.

Zill al-Sultan, Mas'ud Mirza, — *Khatirat-i Zill al-Sultan*, ed. H. Khadiv Jam, Intisharat-i Asatir, 1368.

Works in Languages Other than Persian

Abrahamian, E., — 'The Crowd in the Persian Revolution', *Iranian Studies*, 2, No. 4, 1969, pp. 128–50.

Afary, J., — *The Iranian Constitutional Revolution 1906–1911*, New York 1996.

Afshari, M. Reza, — 'The Historians of the Constitutional Revolution and the Making of the Iranian Popular Tradition', *International Journal of Middle Eastern Studies*, 25, No. 3, 1993, pp. 477–494.

Afshari, M. Reza, — 'The Pishvaran and Merchants in Precapitalist Iranian Society', *International Journal of Middle Eastern Studies*, 15, No.2, 1983, pp. 133–155.

Alcock, T., — *Travels in Russia, Persia, Turkey and Greece in 1828–9*, London 1831.

Algar, H., — *Mirza Malkum Khan*, California 1973.

Algar, H.,	*Religion and State in Iran 1785–1906*, Berkeley 1969.
Amanat, A.,	*Resurrection and Renewal*, London 1989.
Amanat, A.,	*The Pivot of the Universe*, London 1997.
Anderson, N.,	*Law Reform in the Muslim World*, 1976.
Ansari, S., and Martin, V., eds,	*Women, Religion and Culture in Iran*, London 2002.
Arjomand, S.A., ed,	*Authority and Political Culture in Shi'ism*, New York 1988.
Arjomand, S.A.,	*The Shadow of God and the Hidden Imam*, Chicago 1984.
Arnold, D.,	'Famine in Peasant Consciousness and Peasant Action', *Subaltern Studies III*, ed., R. Guha, Oxford 1984.
Ashraf, A.	'Bazar', *Encyclopaedia Iranica* VI, London and New York 1990, pp. 30–44.
Ashraf, A.,	'The Roots of Emerging Dual Class Relations in Nineteenth Century Iran', *Iranian Studies*, 14, Nos. 1–2, 1981, pp. 5–28.
Ashraf, A., and Hekmat, H.,	'Merchants and Artisans in the Developmental Processes of Nineteenth Century Iran', *The Islamic Middle East*, ed. A.L. Udovitch, Princeton 1981, pp. 725–750.
Atkin, M.,	*Russia and Iran 1780–1828*, Minneapolis 1980.
Avery, P.W., and Simmons, J.B.,	'Persia on a Cross of Silver 1880–1890', in E. Kedourie and S. Haim, eds, *Towards a Modern Iran*, London 1980
Baer, G.,	'The Administrative, Economic and Social Function of the Turkish Guilds', *International Journal of Middle Eastern Studies*, I, 1970, pp. 28–50.
Baer, G.,	'Popular Revolt in Ottoman Cairo', *Der Islam*, 54, 1977, pp. 213–242.
Baer, G.,	*Studies in the Social History of Egypt*, Chicago 1969.
Bakhash, S.,	'Center-Periphery Relations in Nineteenth Century Iran', *Iranian Studies*, 14, Nos. 1–2, 1981, pp. 29–51.
Bakhash, S.,	*Monarchy, Bureaucracy and Reform under the Qajars: 1858–1896*, London 1978.
Barazangi, N.H., Zaman, M.R. and Afzal, O., eds,	*Islamic Identity and the Struggle for Justice*, Florida 1996.

Barbir, K.K., *Ottoman Rule in Damascus 1708–1758*, Princeton 1980.
Bayat, M., *Iran's First Revolution*, Oxford 1991.
Bayat, M., *Mysticism and Dissent*, New York 1982.
Beachey, R.W., *The Slave Trade of East Africa*, London 1979.
Beck, L, *Nomad. A Year in the Life of a Qashqa'i Tribesman in Iran*, London 1991.
Beck, L. *The Qashqa'is of Iran*, New Haven 1986.
Beck, L., 'Tribes and the State in Nineteenth- and Twentieth-Century Iran', in Khoury, P.S. and Kostiner, J., *Tribes and State Formation in the Middle East*, Berkeley 1990.
Beck, L. and Keddie, N., *Women in the Muslim World*, Harvard 1978.
Benbassa, E and Rodrigue A., *Sephardi Jewry*, Berkeley 2000.
Binning, R.B., *A Journal of Two Years' Travel in Persia, Ceylon, etc.*, London 1857.
Bosworth, C.E. and Hillenbrand, C., eds, *Qajar Iran; Political Social and Cultural Changes, 1800–1925*, Edinburgh 1983.
Browne, E.G., *The Persian Revolution of 1905–9*, (1910), London 1966 edition.
Brugsch, H., *Reise der K. Preussischen Gesandtschaft nach Persien 1860–61*, Leipzig 1862.
Brunschvig, R., "'Abd', *Encyclopaedia of Islam*, 2nd Edition, Leiden 1960, pp. 24–40.
Brydges, H.J., *The Dynasty of the Qajars*, London 1833.
Buckingham, J., *Travels in Assyria, Media and Persia*, London 1829.
Burke, E., and Lapidus, I.M., eds, *Islam, Politics and Social Movements*, Berkeley 1988.
Burke, E., *Struggle and Survival in the Middle East*, London 1993.
Busse, H., *History of Persia under Qajar Rule* (trans. of H. Fasa'i, *Farsnama-yi Nasiri*), Columbus 1972.

Cahen, C., and Hanaway Jr, W.L., 'Ayyar', in E. Yarshater, ed., *Encyclopaedia Iranica*, London and New York, 1989, III, pp. 159–63.
Calmard, J., 'Le Mecenat des Representations de Ta'ziye', *Le Monde iranien et l-Islam*, 2, 1974, pp. 73–126 and 4, 1976, pp. 133–162.
Calmar, J., 'Le patronage de Ta'ziyeh: elements pour une etude globale', in P. Chelkowski, ed., *Ta'ziyeh Ritual and Drama in Iran*, New York 1974.

Calmard, J.,	'Les reformes militaires sous les Qajars (1795–1825)', in Y. Richard ed., *Entre l'Iran et l'Occident*, Paris 1989.
Calmard, J.,	*Le Culte de l'Imam Husayn*, Paris 1975.
Calmard, J.,	'Shi'i Rituals and Power II. The Consolidation of Safavid Shi'ism: Folklore and Popular Religion' in C. Melville, ed. *Safavid Persia*, London and New York, 1996.
Chelkowski, P., ed.,	*Ta'ziyeh: Ritual and Drama in Iran*, New York 1979.
Chelkowski, P.,	'Ta'ziyya', *Encyclopaedia of Islam*, 2nd edition, Leiden 2000, X, pp. 406–8.
Cottam, R.,	*Nationalism in Iran*, Pittsburgh 1964.
Coulson, N.,	*A History of Islamic Law*, Edinburgh 1974.
Cronin, S.,	'Conscription and Popular Resistance in Iran 1925–41', in E.J. Zurcher, ed., *Arming the State*, London 1999.
Cronin, S.,	*The Army and the Creation of the Pahlavi State in Iran 1910–1926*, London 1997.
Curzon, G.N.,	*Persia and the Persian Question*, London 1892.
Dabashi, H., ed. and trans.,	'Lives of Prominent Nineteenth-Century 'Ulama from Tunikabuni's Qisas al-'Ulama', in S.A. Arjomand, *Authority and Political Culture in Shi'ism*, New York 1988.
Davies, C.E.,	'Qajar Rule in Fars', *Iran*, 25, 1987, pp. 124–53.
Davies, C.E.,	*A History of the Province of Fars during the Later Nineteenth Century*, D.Phil., Oxford 1984.
Dieulafoy, J.,	*La Perse ouverte*, Versailles 1883.
Dieulafoy, J.,	*La Perse, la Chaldee et la Susiane*, Paris 1887.
Drouville, G.,	*Voyage en Perse*, Paris 1925 edition.
Dubow, S.,	*Racial Segregation and the Origins of Apartheid in South Africa, 1919–36*, Oxford 1989.
Eastwick, E. B.,	*Journal of a Diplomat's Three Years' Residence in Persia*, London 1964.
Enayat, A.,	'Amin al-Zarb I, Haj Muhammad Hasan', *Encyclopaedia Iranica* I, London 1985, pp. 951–3.

Enayat, A.,	'Amin al-Zarb II, Haj Muhammad Husain', *Encyclopaedia Iranica II*, London 1985, pp. 953–4.
Enayat, H.,	*Modern Islamic Political Thought*, London 1982.
Ettehadieh, M.,	'The Council for the Investigation of Grievances: a Case Study of Nineteenth Century Iranian Social History', *Iranian Studies*, 22, No. 1, 1989, pp. 51–61.
Ettehadieh M.,	*The Origins and Development of Political Parties in Persia*, Ph.D thesis, Edinburgh 1980.
Farmer, E., Hambly, G., Kopf, D., Marshall, B., and Taylor, R.,	*Comparative History of Civilisations*, Massachusetts 1977, I.
Fathi, A.,	'The Role of the Rebels in the Constitutional Movement in Iran', *International Journal of Middle Eastern Studies*, 10, 1979, No. 1, pp. 55–66.
Floor, W.M.,	'Bazar', *Encyclopaedia Iranica IV*, London and New York 1990, pp. 25–30.
Floor, W.M.	'The Office of Muhtasib in Iran', *Iranian Studies*, 18, No. 1, Winter 1985, pp. 53–74.
Floor, W.M.,	'The Creation of a Food Administration in Iran', *Iranian Studies*, 16, Nos. 3–4, 1983, pp. 199–227.
Floor, W.M.,	'The Guilds in Iran: an Overview from the Earliest Beginnings to 1972', ZDMG, CXXV, 1975, pp. 99–166.
Floor, W.M.,	'The Lutis – a Social Phenomenon in Qajar Persia', *Die Welt des Islams*, XIII, Nos. 1–2 1971, pp. 103–120.
Floor, W.M.,	'The Merchants (*tujjar*) in Qajar Iran', ZDMG, CXXVI, 1976, pp. 101–35.
Floyer, E.A.,	*Unexplored Baluchistan*, London 1882.
Foran, J.,	'The Concept of Dependent Development as a Key to the Political Economy of Qajar Iran (1800–1925)', *Iranian Studies*, 22, Nos 2–3, 1989–90, pp. 5–56.
Friedmann, W.,	*Law in a Changing Society*, Cambridge 1973.
Gardane, P.,	*Journal d'un voyage en la Turquie d'Asie et la Perse 1807–1808*, Paris 1809.
Garthwaite, G.,	*Khans and Shahs*, Cambridge 1983.

Gilbar, G.,   'The Big Merchants and the Iranian Constitutional Revolution of 1906', *Asian and African Studies*, II.3, 1977, pp. 275–303.

Gilbar, G.,   'The Persian Economy in the Mid-Nineteenth Century', *Die Welt des Islams*, XIX, 1–4, 1979, pp. 177–211.

Gilbar, G.,   'Trends in the Development of Prices in Late Qajar Iran 1870–1906', *Iranian Studies*, 16, Nos 3–4, 1983, pp. 177–98.

Gleave, R.M., ed.,   *Religion and Society in Qajar Iran*, London 2004, forthcoming.

Gobineau, A. de,   *Trois ans en Asie*, Paris 1856.

Gobineau, J.A. de,   *Depeches diplomatiques*, ed., A.D. Hytier, Paris 1932 edition.

Godineau, D.,   *The Women of Paris and the French Revolution*, trans, K. Streip, Berkeley 1988.

Gordon, M.,   *Slavery in the Arab World*, New York 1989.

Gurney, J.,   'A Qajar Household and Its Estates', *Iranian Studies*, 16, 1983, Nos. 3–4, pp. 137–176.

Hambly, G.,   'The Traditional Iranian City in the Qajar Period', *Cambridge History of Iran*, Cambridge 1991, VII, pp. 542–589.

Hay D., and Rogers, N.,   *Eighteenth Century English Society*, Oxford 1997.

Hedin S.,   *Zu Land nach Indien durch Persien, Seistan, Beluchistan*, Leipzig 1910.

Heude, W.,   *A Voyage up the Persian Gulf in 1817*, London 1819.

Hillenbrand, R.,   *Persian Painting*, London 2000.

Hitchcock, T., King, P., and Sharpe, P., eds,   *Chronicling Poverty. The Voices and Strategies of the English Poor 1640–1840*, Basingstoke, 1997.

Holt, P.M., ed.   *Political and Social Change in Modern Egypt*, London 1968.

Hourani, A., Khoury, P.S., and Wilson, M.C., eds,   *The Modern Middle East*, London 1993.

Houtum-Schindler, A.,   'Persia', in *Encyclopaedia Britannica*, London 1902.

Hughes, A.W.,   *The Country of Baloochistan*, London 1877.

Hughes-Buller, R.,   *Baluchistan Gazetteer Series, Vol. VII, Makran*, Bombay 1906.

Ibn Khaldun,	*An Introduction to History. The Muqaddimah*, trans. F. Rosenthal, London 1967.
Inalcik, H.,	*Essays in Ottoman History*, Istanbul 1998
Issawi, C.,	'Iranian Trade 1800–1914', *Iranian Studies*, 16, Nos. 3–4, 1983, pp. 229–241.
Issawi, C.,	*The Economic History of Iran 1800–1914*, Chicago 1971.
Jamalzadeh, M. A.,	*Isfahan is Half the World*, trans. W.L. Heskon, Princeton 1983.
Johnson, J.,	*A Journey from England to India through Persia, Georgia, Russia, Poland and Prussia 1817*, London 1818.
Jones, G.,	*Banking and Empire in Iran*, Cambridge 1986.
Kashani Sabet, F.,	*Frontier Fictions*, 1999.
Katouzian, H.,	*Iranian History and Politics*, London 2003.
Kazembeyki, M.A.,	*Society, Politics and Economics in Mazandaran, Iran, 1848–1914*, London 2002.
Kazemzadeh, F.,	*Britain and Russia in Persia, 1864–1914*, New Haven 1968.
Keddie, N.R.,	*Qajar Iran and the Rise of Reza Shah*, California 1999.
Keddie, N.R.,	*Religion and Rebellion in Iran*, London 1966.
Keddie, N.R.,	*Sayyid Jamal al-Din 'al-Afghani': a Political Biography*, Berkeley 1972.
Keep, J.,	*Soldiers of the Tsar*, Oxford 1985.
Kelly, J.B.,	*Britain and the Persian Gulf 1785–1880*, Oxford 1968.
Khadduri, M.,	*The Islamic Conception of Justice*, Baltimore 1984.
Khare, R.S.,	'Perspectives on Islamic Law, Justice and Society', in L. Rosen, *Justice in Islamic Culture and Law*, Oxford 1999.
Khoury, P.S. and Kostiner, J.,	*Tribes and State Formation in the Modern Middle East*, Berkeley 1990.
Kia, M.,	'Inside the Court of Naser od-Din Shah Qajar, 1881–1896', *Middle Eastern Studies*, 37, No.1, 2001, pp. 101–141.
Kia, M.,	'Pan-Islamism in Late Nineteenth Century Iran', *Middle Eastern Studies*, 32, No.1, 1996, pp. 30–52.

Kotzebue, M. von, *Narrative of a Journey into Persia*, London 1819.
Kreiser, K., 'Women in the Ottoman World: a Bibliographical Essay', *Islam and Christian-Muslim Relations*, 13, No.2, 2002, pp. 197–206.

Lambton, A.K.S., 'Isfahan', *Encyclopaedia of Islam*, 2nd edition, IV, Leiden 1978.
Lambton, A.K.S., *Islamic Society in Persia*, Oxford 1954.
Lambton, A.K.S., 'Justice in the Medieval Persian Theory of Kingship', *Studia Islamica*, 17, 1962, pp. 91–119.
Lambton, A.K.S., *Landlord and Peasant in Persia*, Oxford 1953.
Lambton, A.K.S. *Qajar Persia*, London 1987.
Lambton, A.K.S., *State and Government in Medieval Islam*, Oxford 1981.
Lapidus, I.M., *Muslim Cities in the Later Middle Ages*, Cambridge 1984.
Levy, D.G., Applewhite, H.B. and Johnson, M.D., *Women in Revolutionary Paris*, Illinois 1980.
Lewis B., *Race and Slavery in the Middle East*, Oxford 1990.
Linant de Bellefonds, Y., *Traite de droit musulman compare*, Paris 1960.

Macdonald Kinneir, J. *A Geographical Memoir of the Persian Empire*, London 1813.
Mahdavi, S., *For God, Mammon and Country: a Nineteenth Century Merchant*, Boulder 1998.
Mahdavi, S., 'Women, Shi'ism and Cuisine in Iran' in S. Ansari and V. Martin, eds, *Women, Religion and Culture in Iran*, London 2001, pp. 10–26.
Mahjub, M., 'The Effect of European Theatre and the Influence of Its Theatrical Methods upon Ta'ziyeh' in P. Chelkowski, ed., *Ta'ziyeh: Ritual and Drama in Iran*, New York 1979, pp. 138–143.
Malcolm, J., *The History of Persia*, London 1839.
Mallat, C., ed., *Islam and Public Law*, London 1993.
Marcus, A., *The Middle East on the Eve of Modernity*, New York 1989.
Marino, B., *Le Faubourg du Midan a Damas a l'epoque Ottomane*, Damascus 1997.

Martin, V.A.,	'Reform and Development in the Early Qajar Period', *Die Welt des Islams*, XXXVI, I, 1996, pp. 1–24.
Martin, V.A.,	*Creating an Islamic State*, London 2000.
Martin, V.A.,	*Islam and Modernism, the Iranian Revolution of 1906*, London 1989.
Martin, V.A.,	'The British in Bushire; Relations with State and Society at the Time of the First Herat War', forthcoming in *Anglo-Iranian Relations since 1800*, London 2005.
McDaniel, R.,	'Economic Change and Economic Resiliency in Nineteenth Century Persia', *Iranian Studies*, 4, 1971, pp. 36–40.
Meriwether, M.L., and Tucker, J.E., eds,	*Social History: Women and Gender in the Modern Middle East*, Westview 1999.
Migeod, H.G.,	*Die persische Gesellschaft unter Nasiru'd-Din Shah (1848–1906)*, Berlin 1990.
Mir Hosseini, Z.,	*Marriage on Trial. A Study of Islamic Family Law*, London 1993.
Mirza'i. B.A.	'The African Presence in Iran: Identity and Its Reconstruction in the 19th and 20th Centuries', *Outre-mers: Revue d'Histoire*, 2002, No. 2, pp. 229–246.
Morier, J,	*A Second Journey through Persia, Armenia and Asia Minor*, London 1818.
Moslem, M.,	'The Making of a Weak State', *CSD Perspectives*, Research Paper No. 6, University of Westminster 1995.
Mounsey, A.,	*Journey through the Caucasus and the Interior of Persia*, London 1872.
Nizam al-Mulk,	*The Book of Government or Rules for Kings*, trans. H. Darke, London 1978.
Nowshirvani, V.F.,	'The Beginnings of Commercialised Agriculture in Iran', *The Islamic Middle East*, ed. A.L. Udovitch, Princeton 1981, pp. 547–91.
Oberling, P.,	*The Qashqa'i Nomads of Fars*, The Hague 1974.
Ouseley, W.,	*Travels in Various Countries of the East, More Particularly Persia*, London 1823.

Parry, V.J., and Yapp, M.E., eds, *War, Technology and Society in the Middle East*, Oxford 1975.

Perry, J.P., 'Justice for the Underprivileged: the Ombudsman Tradition of Iran', *Journal of Near Eastern Studies*, 37, 1978, pp. 203–215.

Peterson, S.R., 'The Ta'ziyeh and Related Arts', in P.J. Chelkowski, ed., *Ta'ziyeh, Ritual and Drama in Iran*, New York 1979.

Philipp, T., 'Isfahan 1881–1891: a Close up View of Guilds and Production', *Iranian Studies*, 17, No. 4, 1984, pp. 391–411.

Planhol, X. de, 'Bushehr', *Encyclopaedia Iranica*, IV, London and New York 1990, pp. 570–1.

Porter R., *English Society in the Eighteenth Century*, London 1990.

Raymond, A., 'Quartiers et mouvements populaires en Caire au VIIIeme siecle', in P.M. Holt, ed., *Political and Social Change in Modern Egypt*, London 1968.

Raymond, A., 'Soldiers in Trade: the Case of Ottoman Cairo', *British Society for Middle Eastern Studies Bulletin*, 18, 1991, pp. 16–37.

Ricks, T.M., 'Slaves and Slave Traders in the Persian Gulf', in W.G. Clarence Smith, ed., *The Economics of the Indian Ocean Slave Trade in the Nineteenth Century*, London 1989.

Rosen, L., *The Anthropology of Islam. Law as Culture in an Islamic Society*, Cambridge 1989.

Rosen, L., *The Justice of Islam*, Oxford 2000.

Salo, T., ed., *Islamic Urbanism in Human History*, New York 1997.

Savory, R., *Iran under the Safavids*, Cambridge 1980.

Savory, R., *Studies in the Safavid History of Iran*, London 1987.

Scarce, J., *Women's Costumes in the Near and Middle East*, Edinburgh 1981.

Schacht, J., *An Introduction to Islamic Law*, Oxford 1964.

Schneider, I., 'Muhammad Baqir Shafti (1180–1260/ 1766–1844) und die Isfahaner Gerichtsbarkeit', *Der Islam*, 79, 2002, pp. 240–273.

Schneider, I., 'Religion and State Jurisdiction during Nasir al-Din Shah's Reign', in R.M. Gleave, ed., *Religion and Society in Qajar Iran*, London 2004 forthcoming.

Scott Waring, E., *A Tour to Sheeraz*, London 1807.

Segal, R., *Islam's Black Slaves*, New York 2001.

Seidman, A., Seidman, B., and Walde, T.W., *Making Development Work*, London 1999.

Seyf, A., 'International Trade and Surplus: Iran in the Nineteenth Century', *Middle Eastern Studies*, 13, No. 2, 1995, pp. 347–361.

Seyf, A., 'Iranian Textile Handicrafts in the Nineteenth Century: a Note', *Middle Eastern Studies*, 37, No.1, 2001, pp. 1–141.

Seyf, M., 'Obstacles to the Development of Capitalism in Late Nineteenth Century Iran', *Middle Eastern Studies*, 34, No. 3, 1998, pp. 54–82.

Sheikholeslami, A.R. *The Structure of Central Authority in Qajar Iran 1871–1896*, Atlanta 1997.

Sheikholeslami, A.R., 'The Patrimonial Structure of the Iranian Bureaucracy in the Late Nineteenth Century', XI, 1978, pp. 199–258.

Sheikholeslami, A.R., 'The Sale of Offices in Qajar Iran 1858–1896', *Iranian Studies*, 4, 1971, pp. 104–118.

Sheil, M., *Glimpses of Life and Manners in Persia*, London 1856.

Smirnov, A., 'Understanding Justice in the Islamic Context', *Philosophy East and West*, 46, No. 3, 1996, pp. 337–50.

Southgate, M., 'The Negative Image of Black Slaves in Some Medieval Iranian Writings', *Iranian Studies*, 17, No. 1, 1984 pp. 3–36.

Sparroy, W., *Persian Children of the Royal Family*, London 1902.

Sykes, P., *History of Persia*, London 1921.

Tancoigne, M., *A Narrative of a Journey into Persia and Residence in Tehran*, London 1820.

Tapper, R., *Frontier Nomads of Iran*, Cambridge 1997.

Tilly, C., *The Vendee*, Harvard 1976.

Toledano, E.R., *The Ottoman Slave Trade and Its Suppression, 1840–1890*, Princeton 1982.

Toledano, E.R.,	*State and Society in Mid-Nineteenth Century Egypt*, Princeton 1982.
Tousi, R.,	'The Persian Army', *Middle Eastern Studies*, 24, No. 2, 1988, pp. 206–229.
Tucker, J.E.,	*Women in Nineteenth-Century Egypt*, Cambridge 1985.
Usscher, J.,	*A Journey from London to Persepolis*, London 1865.
Von Thielmann, M.,	*Journey in the Caucasus, Persia and Turkey in Asia*, trans. C. Heneage, London 1875.
Wagner, M.,	*Travels in Persia, Georgia and Koordistan*, London 1856.
Watson, R.G.,	*A History of Persia*, London 1866.
Wills, C.J.,	*In the Land of the Lion and the Sun*, London 1883.
Wills, C.J.,	*Persia as It Is*, London 1886.
Yajnik, R.K.,	*The Indian Theatre*, London 1933.
Yapp, M.E.,	*Strategies of British India*, Oxford 1980.
Yapp, M.E.,	'The Modernisation of Middle Eastern Armies in the 19th Century: A Comparative View', in V.J. Parry and M.E. Yapp, eds, *War, Technology and Society in the Middle East*, Oxford 1975.
Zilfi, M.C., ed.,	*Women in the Ottoman Empire*, Leiden 1997.

INDEX

'Abbas Mirza 4, 25, 133, 134
'Abbas, Mirza, governor of
  Bushire 35, 36
'Abd 'Ali, Haji Shaikh, Imam Jum'a of
  Bushire 174, 176, 177
'Abd al-Muhammad, Aqa, merchant of
  Bushire 41
'Abd al-Muhammad, Haji, Malik al-
  Tujjar 32, 171
'Abd al-Muhammad, merchant of
  Bushire 38
'Abd al-Rasul al-Mazkur, Shaikh 31
Abdul Nabi, slave dealer 155
Abu Turab, Shaikh, *mujtahid* of Shiraz
  55, 58
Abu'l Husain, Mirza, vizier of Isfahan,
  descendant of the Safavids 76
Abu'l Qasim, Mirza, known as Fazil-i
  Qumi, *mujtahid* 105
Abyssinia 152
'adalat 21, 25, 73
'adalatkhana 66, 187, 190
'adl 8, 10
Afghani, Sayyid Jamal al-Din 26
Afghanistan 22, 34ff, 37, 38
Africans 152ff
Ahmad Khan, Mirza, principal
  administrator of Fars 55
Ahmad Khan, shah's emissary 56–7
Ahmad Mirza, descendant of the
  Safavids 76
'Ain al-Mulk, notable of Shiraz 123
Akbar Pahlavan, wrestler 157
Akhbarism 33, 45–6
Akhtar 7, 26, 60, 66, 90
'Ali, Mirza, merchant of Bushire 38
'Ali, singer and slave of Khesht 157,
  174
'Ali Akbar, Sayyid, *mujtahid* of Shiraz
  59ff, 62
Allah Verdi Khan, governor of
  Beshakerd 155

Almas (Diamond), black slave of the
  Imam Jum'a 157
America 150, 151, 159
Amin al-Sultan, 'Ali Asghar, chief
  minister of Iran 54, 60, 87, 172,
  175, 177
Amir Kabir, Mirza Taqi Khan 23–3, 25,
  53, 76, 135, 139, 160
Anbar, slave 155
Anglo-Iranian Slave Convention 1882
  163, 165
Aqa Beglerbegi, representiave in Shiraz
  council 64
Aqa Muhammad Qajar 22, 51, 105,
  110, 133
Aqa Najafi, Shaikh Muhammad Taqi,
  mujtahid of Isfahan 7, 74, 81ff,
  123, 185
Aqasi, Haj Mirza, Chief Minister 106,
  139, 160
Armenians 32, 38, 39, 43, 46, 59, 66,
  142, 168
Army 14, 23, 33–4, 38, 40–2, 60, 76,
  80ff, 84, 89, 91, 101, 110, 122,
  133ff
Army clothing 14, 34, 136, 147
Army pay 14, 33–4, 136ff, 145, 147
Artillery 136, 144
Asadullah, Aqa Sayyid, *mujtahid* of
  Isfahan 76, 184
Asadullah, Mirza, governor of
  Bushire 36–8
'Atabat 24, 60
'Azar al-Saltana, representative in
  Shiraz council 64

Babis 82, 91
Baghdad 91, 152
Baharlu 51, 62, 65, 143. 144
Bahrazain, black slave 151
Baluchistan 169
Bander Abbas 30, 43, 153, 174

INDEX

Baqir Fasarki, Mulla, *mujtahid* of Isfahan 88
Baqir Khan Tangestani, tribal leader 31, 37, 46
Bashir Khan, Haji, black slave of Bushire 3, 170ff
Basra 31, 38, 41, 60, 71, 163, 175
Bazaar 5, 15, 16ff, 33–5, 49, 53, 57, 60, 89, 102, 114, 139, 176, 180, 184
Bazaar-ulama alliance 18–19
Bibi 'Alam Khurasani, woman of learning 98
Bird, Mary, missionary 82
bombassis 152
Bombay 156, 164
Britain, British 1, 4–5, 14–15, 22–6, 30ff, 50, 59, 66, 73, 85, 87, 120, 127, 131, 136, 143, 154ff, 188, 190
Brussels Convention on Slaves 1892 161, 165
bunakdar 17
Bushire 5, 22, 26, 29ff, 53, 61, 115, 116, 137–43, 145–6, 153, 157, 161ff, 166, 170ff, 188

Caucasus 22, 152
Cavalry 133, 135, 136
Central government control 13ff, 41, 160
Chekazi, black slave 155
Coffee houses 83, 118, 131
Concubines 151
Constitutional Revolution 3–4, 49, 95, 108, 180, 185–7, 189
Consultation 21, 26, 39, 43, 66, 83, 86, 175, 190
Customs 30, 174, 188

Damuk tribe 32, 40
Darab 52
darugha 17, 39, 117, 121, 132
daulat 4
daulat va millat 87, 90
daulat va ru'aya 4, 87, 90
Dih-i Nau (village near Isfahan) 83

East India Company 30
Egypt 14, 25, 28, 95, 113, 116, 118, 145, 165, 189
Elias, British Residency *sarraf* 32, 34–5
Essai, British Residency *sarraf* 38
Eunuchs 152–3, 159

Famine 15, 23, 46, 54

Farhad Mirza, Mu'tamid al-Daula, governor of Fars 55, 186
farr-i izadi 8, 12
Fath 'Ali Shah 4, 22, 30, 51, 72, 105, 134, 147
Fiji 164
Flight from taxation 41, 63
Foreign Agent 38, 96, 140
France, French 6, 71, 96, 134, 164
futuvvat 113ff

Garusi regiment 140, 142, 186
Georgian slaves 121
Ghulam 'Ali, brother of Bashir 170, 175
Ghulam Husain Khan Sipahdar, governor of Isfahan 76
Ghulam Husain, Haj, *luti* of Isfahan 120–1, 186
Griboedov, Russian emissary 34
Guilds 17–18, 20–21, 75, 106

habashis 152, 156
Habl al-Matin 7, 27, 64, 90
Haidar Khan Zabit Tangestani, bailiff 140
Haidari and Ni'mati districts 50–1, 118–19, 123, 129
Halima, black slave 151
haq (pl. *huquq*) 9, 11, 80, 184
Hasan Al-i'Usfur, Shaikh, *qazi* of Bushire 33, 35, 36, 39, 40, 42, 45, 46, 116
Hasan Rashti, Sayyid, *mujtahid* of Bushire 173
Hashim, Haji, merchant of Shiraz 51
Herat 22, 29, 32, 34ff, 43, 55, 76, 116, 139, 160
hijab (Islamic dress) 96
Husain al-Mazkur, Shaikh 42
Husain Khan, chief of the Arab tribes 61
Husain Khan Galidar, widow of 99
Husain Khan, Mirza, Nizam al-Daula, governor of Fars 56
Husain Rashti, Haji Sayyid, *mujtahid* of Kerbala 176

Ibrahim Karbasi, Sayyid, *mujtahid* of Isfahan 103
Ibrahim, Haji Mirza, *mujtahid* of Shiraz 52, 55
'ibrat 13, 55
ihqaq-i huquq 21, 70, 184
Ilbegi of the Qashqa'i 16, 51, 56, 123

Ilkhani of the Qashqa'i, 16, 51, 57, 122–3
Iman Husain 6, 104–5, 112, 124
Imam Jum'a of Bushire 33, 37
Imam Jum'a of Isfahan 76–7, 78ff, 100, 118, 121, 123
Imperial Bank 24, 54, 63, 82, 87
India 22–3, 26, 30ff, 50, 167, 172, 174, 180
Infantry 133, 134
International economy 15, 23–4, 190
Isfahan 5, 24, 26, 55, 69, 74ff, 103, 109, 115–17, 119–21, 124, 143–5, 148, 188
islahat-i jadid 79
I'timad-i Daula, Haj Muhammad Ibrahim 51

Ja'far Siah Pahlavan, black wrestler 157
Jalal al-Daula, Sultan Hasan Mirza, governor of Fars and of Yazd 123, 152
Jamal Isfahani, Aqa Sayyid 129
javanmardi 113, 118
Jews 32, 34–6, 43, 46, 59, 62, 66, 70, 82, 91, 98, 104, 110, 120, 168
Jihad al-Akbar 89
Jiruft, black slave community 158
Joasemi Arabs 153
Justice 2, 8, 10, 12, 16, 20–21, 38, 50, 183, 187

kadkhuda 17, 30, 55, 119, 123
kalantar 17, 50ff, 144
Kangerun 153
kaniz 152
karguzar 38, 96, 140
Karim, Haji Mirza, *sarraf* of Shiraz 54
Karim Khan Zand 30, 48–9, 51, 74
Karun River 24, 48, 58–9, 66
Kashan 117, 120
Kazim, Haj, Malik al-Tujjar 172
Kazzaz regiment 62, 144
Kelat 160
Kerbalayee Ali Attar, slave dealer 155
Kerbalayee Taqi, slave dealer 155
Kerman 61, 120, 140
Kermanshah 139
Khalij regiment 62, 139, 144
Khamseh tribe 51–2, 62, 65–6, 68
Kharg Island 29ff, 36ff, 39ff, 153, 185
Khojah Mourad, merchant of Bushire 32

Kish Island 157
Kushak, village near Shiraz 106
Kuwait 41, 155

Labourers 137
Laristan, Khan of 40
Law 25, 77, 84–5, 97, 184
Law enforcement 17, 123, 132
Legitimacy 12–13, 19, 81, 148
Lingah 142, 153, 156, 160, 171
Locusts 15, 54, 144
Lutf 'Ali Khan Lari, garrison commander, Kharg Island 40
Lutf 'Ali Khan Zand 31, 51
lutis 6, 18, 52–3, 58, 76, 80, 101–103, 113ff, 187

madkhula 162
Mahbub, black slave 155
mahkama 38
Mahmud Khan, Mirza, Adjutant of the Ministry of Foreign Affairs 161
Mahmud Khan, Mirza, Slave Commissioner of Bushire 161
Majlis-i Istintaq 63
majlis 25, 66, 73, 86, 144, 174, 178
Malkum Khan, Mirza 23, 25, 60
Mariam, Mulla, slave trader 98, 162
Mashhadi Riza, singer of Shiraz 123
Mas'ud al-Daula, representative on Shiraz council 64
Ma'sum Juzani, Haj, teapot-mender and *luti* of Isfahan 119, 128–9
Mecca 161, 163
Merchants 4, 17–18, 21, 26, 30ff, 50, 53, 58, 60ff, 68, 70, 85, 87, 171–2, 188–9, 198
Mihdi Tajir, Aqa Sayyid, representative on Shiraz council 64
Military justice 138–9
millat 26, 87, 90
Mir Baqir, Aqa, merchant of Bushire 41
Missionaries 59, 66, 82, 92
mizan 8–9
Muhammad 'Abdullah, merchant of Yazd and *luti* leader 118
Muhammad 'Ali Bihbihani, Haj Sayyid, *mujtahid* of Bushire 172
Muhammad 'Ali, Haj, Malik al-Tujjar of Bushire 171
Muhammad Baqir Majlisi 10–11
Muhammad Baqir, Haji, Malik al-Tujjar 32, 38, 41–2

INDEX

Muhammad Baqir, Sayyid, merchant of Bushire 37
Muhammad Baqir, Sayyid, *mujtahid* of Isfahan 103, 121–2, 130, 186
Muhammad Baqir, Shaikh, *mujtahid* of Isfahan 80
Muhammad Hasan Shirazi, Haji Mirza, *mujtahid* of Samarra 60–1
Muhammad Hasan, Haji Mirza, *mujtahid* of Kerbala 178
Muhammad Isma'il, Haji, *sarraf* of Shiraz 59
Muhammad Khalil of Bushire 176–7
Muhammad Khan, *kalantar* of Tehran 101
Muhammad Mahdi, Haj, Malik al-Tujjar of Bushire, 171, 173, 174, 180
Muhammad Rahim, Aqa, British Residency Newswriter 172ff
Muhammad Shah 4, 22, 34, 37, 55, 106, 116, 120, 121, 138, 139
Muhamad Taqi Fasa'i, Haji Mirza, representative on Shiraz council 64
Mu'in al-Tujjar, Haji Aqa Muhammad 24, 26, 64, 66, 174, 176–7, 179, 180, 182, 185
mujtahid 4, 18–20, 33, 55, 76, 81, 84, 97, 100, 102–3, 120–1, 173, 178, 185
Mulla Rafi', Haj, chief *mujtahid* of Rasht 129
Muravarid (the Pearl), Jewish trader 98
Muscat 31, 32, 33, 165
Mushir al-Mulk, Mirza Abu'l Hasan Khan 50, 52–3, 70
Mushir al-Mulk, Mirza Muhammad 'Ali 70
Music 59, 63, 70, 72, 82, 103, 114, 157
Mustaufi al-Mamalik, Mirza Yusif, minister 77ff
Mutiny 138ff, 187
Muzaffar al-Din Shah 25, 88

Na'ib al-Sadr, brother of Imam Jum'a of Isfahan 78
Nasir al-Din Shah 4, 11, 22, 25, 62, 68, 80, 83, 84, 87, 88, 106, 140, 160, 174
Nasir al-Mazkur, Shaikh, 31ff, 185
Nationalism 15, 85, 135, 158
Nayib Mihrab, *luti* of Isfahan 117
Nazim al-Daula, and Shiraz council 63
Neyriz 63, 108, 185
nizam 114

Nizam-i Jadid 134
Nizam al-Saltana, Husain Quli Khan, 62–3, 163, 177
Nurullah, governor of Shiraz 55
Nurullah, Haj Aqa, brother of Aqa Najafi of Isfahan 88–9

Opium 171
Oppression 9, 26, 56, 119, 124, 184
Ottoman Empire, Ottoman 14, 22, 25, 29, 35, 37, 46, 79, 86, 87, 137–8, 151–3, 158, 165, 189

Pan-Islamism 26
Pawnbroker, woman 125
Persian Gulf 22, 23, 30ff, 48, 153ff, 171, 180
Physicians 125
pishkish 21, 52, 54
Post Office 23, 102
Power 13ff
Prostitutes 97–8, 109, 132

Qaimas Khan, black hero 157
Qamar al-Saltana, wife of Sipah Salar 106
Qanun 25, 60, 66, 90
qanun-i 'adil 77, 184
Qashqa'i tribe 16, 48, 51, 56–7, 65, 122, 123
Qavam al-Mulk family, *kalantars* of Shiraz 48ff, 51ff
Qavam al-Mulk, 'Ali Akbar 52, 53ff, 68–9, 148, 186-7
Qavam al-Mulk, 'Ali Muhammad 52, 68, 73
Qavam al-Mulk, Muhammad Riza 53, 59, 61ff, 70–2, 103, 143, 172, 186
Quarter leader 17
Qum 55, 65
Qumsha 142
Qutb 12, 135

Rahim, Mulla, villager of Siwund 56
Rahman bin Jabir, pirate and slave owner 157
rauza khani (religious ceremony) 124
Religious endowments 69
Reuter Concession 23
rifah 64
rishsifidan 18
Riza Dallal, Aqa, slave dealer 155
Riza Khan, chief of the Arab tribes 61, 63, 98

Riza Qasi, Haji, *luti* of Shiraz 117
Robbery 54, 103, 114ff
ru'aya 80, 84
Rukn al-Daula, Muhammad Taqi, governor of Shiraz 61, 63–4, 72, 186
Rukn al-Mulk, Mirza Sulaiman Khan, deputy governor of Isfahan 88–9
Russia, Russians 1, 4, 14, 22–3, 30, 34, 61, 75, 97, 120, 133, 135–6, 142, 152, 188, 190

Sa'd al Mulk, Muhammad Hasan Khan, governor of Shiraz and of Bushire 101, 174ff, 178
Sa'adat School Bushire 172
Sa'id al-Saltana, Amir Tuman, head of Shiraz Council 64
Sacotra woman, slave 156
Safavids 10, 74, 76–7, 104, 114, 133
Saham al-Mulk, governor of the Barharlu, 62, 98
salah-i millat va daulat 88
Salman, Shaikh, nephew of *qazi* of Bushire 34, 36, 39, 42, 46
Sanctuary, *bast* 153, 172, 185
sarbaz, soldiery 39, 40, 55, 59, 60, 119
sarhang 134
sarraf 24, 32, 34–5, 54, 63, 87–8
sartip 134
Sartip Muhammad 'Ali, female relatives of 99
shabih khani (playing a part, acting) 105
Shaikh of Charrack 136
Shari'a 8–9, 11–13, 18, 21, 36, 49, 84, 88, 97, 139, 160, 173, 175, 177, 179, 184, 191
Shiraz 5, 24, 26, 33, 41–2, 48ff, 103, 111, 115–20, 122–3, 125, 130, 137, 139, 141–4, 146, 159, 188
Shu'a' al-Saltana, governor of Shiraz 153
sidis 152
sigha 162
sina zani 20, 98, 123, 131
Sipah Salar, Mirza Husain Khan 23, 140–1
Slaves 6–7, 35, 98, 121, 150ff, 172ff
Soldiers 6, 134ff, 185
Suez Canal 23, 48
Sulaiman, Agha, chief eunuch of Zill al-Sultan 152
Sultan Haji Sanda's slave, riot leader 157

Tabriz 15, 22, 75, 112, 134
takiyya 104

Takiyya-yi Daulat 106
taqviyyat-i millat 88
Taxation 14, 16, 21, 24, 26, 30, 32ff, 50, 53ff, 76, 137, 139, 156, 180
ta'ziyya 6, 20, 104ff, 187
Tehran 7, 15, 34, 42, 48, 52, 60–1, 66–7, 73, 75–6, 80, 83, 100, 112, 118, 136, 139, 141, 144, 173, 174, 176–8
Telegraph 23, 58, 66, 77ff, 103, 172, 189
Tobacco Concession, 1890-1 4, 23, 26, 59ff, 81–2, 84, 86, 143, 148, 189, 190
Trade 23–5, 30ff, 58ff, 75, 81, 85
Tribes 16, 50–1, 61, 116, 134–5, 137, 143–4, 147, 118
tullab 61, 71, 87
Turkomanchai, Treaty of 1828 22
Twelver Shi'ism 6, 10, 18

'Ulama 4–5, 11, 17–21, 23, 34, 42, 50, 54, 56, 59ff, 62–4, 77, 78ff, 84, 89, 100, 112, 114–15, 121, 123, 139, 148, 163, 168, 173, 176, 180, 189
'Umar kushi 98
umur-i mubah 151
'urf 12–13, 84, 89, 174, 179, 183

vaqf 69

Weavers, women 98
Wine, drink 35–6, 42, 46, 49, 82, 84, 119–20, 130, 132, 142
Women 5–6, 66, 82, 86, 91, 95ff, 121–2, 124–5, 142, 152ff, 167, 170ff, 187

Yadullah Zurab, *luti* of Isfahan 118, 124
yavar (major) at Bushire 41, 142
Yazd 120, 123

Zahra, slave 156
Zain al-'Abidin Mazandarani, Shaikh, *mujtahid* of Kerbala 175–8
zakat 8, 19
Zaman, Haji, *darugha* of Shiraz 122
zangis 152, 156
Zanzibar 153
Zill Allah 8, 12, 119, 135
Zill al-Sultan, Mas'ud Mirza 7, 11, 70, 74, 77ff, 102, 144, 152, 186
zulm 9, 184
zurkhana 117, 119, 129, 131

www.ingramcontent.com/pod-product-compliance
Lightning Source LLC
Chambersburg PA
CBHW061442300426
44114CB00014B/1804